STOWE LEGENDS

OF THE

ROXBURGH ERA

STOWE LEGENDS
OF THE
ROXBURGH ERA

Anthony Meredith

Troubador Publishing Ltd
Unit E2 Airfield Business Park
Harrison Road, Market Harborough
Leicestershire LE16 7UL
Tel: 0116 279 2299
Email: books@troubador.co.uk
Web: www.troubador.co.uk/matador

ISBN 978 1 80514 188 4

British Library Cataloguing in Publication Data.
A catalogue record for this book is available from the British Library.

Printed and bound in Great Britain by 4edge Limited
Typeset in 12pt Minion Pro by Troubador Publishing Ltd, Leicester, UK

Matador is an imprint of Troubador Publishing Ltd

CONTENTS

Preface   xi

1   The Revd. Ernest Earle   1
The gentlemanly founder of Bruce & Chatham
Stowe 1923-34

2   Ivor Cross   11
The Roxburgh protégé who ran Temple & Chatham
Stowe 1923-43

3   Philip Browne   33
The first Head of Music, an elusive figure
Stowe 1923-28

4   Herbert Neville   44
The first Head of Art, whose wife became a legend too
Stowe 1923-34

5   Ian Clarke   56
Founder of Grenville & Walpole, forester & rugby Blue
Stowe 1923-39

6   The Revd. Edward Habershon   67
     The first Chaplain, creator of 'the Habitation'
     Stowe 1923-31

7   Major Richard Haworth   79
     A gentlemanly soldier who founded Chandos & the O.T.C.
     Stowe 1923-47

8   Martin MacLaughlin   93
     The first Head of History, a giddy star performer
     Stowe 1924-32

9   The Revd. Humphrey Playford   104
     Bruce Housemaster for twenty-five years
     Stowe 1925-58

10   Charles Spencer   121
     The first Head of English, dynamic & fragile
     Stowe 1926-32

11   Leslie Huggins   132
     Head of Music, Huntsman & Tingewick Legend
     Stowe 1929-52

12   T. H. White   149
     Novelist whose time at Stowe proved his major inspiration
     Stowe 1932-36, Stowe Ridings 1936-39

13   George Gilling-Lax   180
     A Grenville Housemaster of outstanding quality
     Stowe 1932-41

14   Robin and Doreen Watt   191
     The couple who inspired the new Art School
     Stowe 1934-48

Contents

15   James Todd   203
Mathematician, Winemaker & Headmaster-in-waiting
Stowe 1934-48

16   Ewald Zettl   212
Much-loved Modern Linguist & husband of Liz
Stowe 1935-66

17   Peter Wiener   223
The controversial founder of Side 9
Stowe 1944-48

18   G. Wilson Knight   235
The Shakespearean scholar moved by the Genius Loci
Stowe 1941-46

Bibliography   247
Index   250

PREFACE

When Noel Annan's *Roxburgh of Stowe* was first published nearly sixty years ago, he summed up in his Preface the three things he was aiming to do: to set Roxburgh against the Public Schools of his times; to analyse the educational changes Roxburgh wanted to effect; and to portray his great teaching skills. In no way, Annan declared, was the book to be a history of the school's first quarter of a century, for that would have meant including too many other things, like 'writing more about the members of the teaching staff'.

Stowe Legends, to a certain extent, addresses that particular omission. Some forty to fifty legendary masters of the Roxburgh era were researched and in line for possible inclusion. A monster volume, however, would have resulted. Some much-needed culling and cutting saw the Legends eventually reduced to the eighteen chapters here presented. There is, of course, a further legend who features in every chapter, John Fergusson Roxburgh, the common denominator in all the lives.

In his introduction to the second edition of *Roxburgh of Stowe* (specially brought out by the school governors for the fiftieth anniversary of 1973), Anthony Quinton wrote warmly of 'J.F.'s achievement'. It was, he declared, very much 'a triumph of personality', and that personality had been 'brought vividly to life before the reader'. I hope the same may occur in *Stowe Legends*. Certainly, the school's centenary year is a fitting time for us to be re-exploring the Roxburgh era, re-meeting the great man as he presides adroitly over the young school, and learning about some of those who worked under him. The Roxburgh era still has relevance today, for, as J.F. himself wrote in his introduction to *The Treasury of Knowledge*, 'Everything has its roots in the past. No new departures are absolutely new... Man hangs by his history as a spider by the lengthening thread.'

* * *

Not all the school files of early masters survive, but many do, and, thanks to the kindness of the Old Stoic Office, they proved a highly useful first port-of-call for research. The support of the OSS office has been much appreciated all along, and so, too, has been that of Chris Atkinson, surely a modern Stowe legend.

Help has come on a wide variety of fronts. I hope I have not forgotten too many kind people when I thank Karin Aikman, Alexandra Aslett, Dr Charlotte Berry, Michael Bevington, Gina Birdsall, Jane Bradford, Anne Braid, James Butterworth, Wendy Butler, Claire Butlin, Stephen Chambers, Charles Clare, Max Clark, George and Sally Clarke, Fiona Colbert, Gary Collins, Mary Connor, Judith Curthoys, Canon Greville Cross, Hannah Dale, Robin Darwall-Smith, Katy de la Riviere, Tom Davies, Kevin Farmer, Suzanne Foster, John Fredericks, Elizabeth Garver, Dr Helen Geissinger, John Gore, Francesca Halfacree, Dr Bethany Hamblen, Helen Harrington, Jacqueline Haun, Lois and Anthony Houghton-Brown, Danny Howell, Dr and Mrs Duncan Hyslop, Paul Jordan, Dr Charles Knighton, John Layton, Gráinne Lenehan, Catherine Lewis (the Stowe School archivist), Philip Mather, Charles and Gillian Macdonald, Douglas Marcuse, Bernie Marsden (*Tingewick My Village*), Joseph Massey, Peter Monteith, Sasha Moss, Jackie Nash, Michael Neville, Ian Neville, Jos Nyreen, Rowena Pratt, Roger and Elizabeth Rawcliffe, Andrew and Juliet Rudolf, Emily Rycroft, Anna Semler (Old Stoic Society Director), Catherine Smith, Jonathan Smith, Michael Stansfield, Biddy Stephan, Stewart Tiley, the Revd. Christopher Turner, Hannah-Louise Vine, Dr Eric Webb, Claire Welford-Elkin, Caroline Whitlock, Robert Winckworth, Mandy Wise, Sheelagh Wurr and, last but not least, dear Elizabeth 'Liz' Zettl.

Most grateful thanks, too, to the ever-willing archivists of Balliol College, Oxford; Bilton Grange School; Cambridge University Library; Charterhouse School; Cheltenham College; Christ Church College, Oxford; Clare College, Cambridge; Clifton College; Cumbria Archive Library; Eastbourne College; the Gallipoli Association; Harrow School; Harry Ransom Center, University of Texas, Austin; Keighley Library; Lancashire Fusiliers Museum, Bury; Brotherton Library, University of Leeds; Keble College, Oxford; Kendal Library; King's College, Cambridge; Lawrenceville School, New Jersey; Magdalen College, Oxford; Marlborough College; Milton Keynes Library; New College, Oxford; Newcastle-under-Lime School; Rugby School; St Aldhelm's Church, Bishopstrow; St John's College, Cambridge; St Paul's School; Sedbergh School; Slade School of Fine Art; Tingewick Historical Society; Trinity College, Cambridge; UCL Special Collections; University of Victoria, Canada; Wheaton College, Massachusetts; and Winchester College.

I am extremely grateful, too, to Troubador, for all their splendid help with the book. Particular thanks to Beth Archer and Hannah Dakin.

Tony Meredith
Akeley
11 May 2023

1

THE REVD. ERNEST EARLE

The gentlemanly founder of Bruce & Chatham
Stowe 1923-34

Ernest Earle, an amiable and civilised master with 'nervous brown eyes and floppy grey hair', was J.F. Roxburgh's unofficial deputy when the school opened. At nearly fifty, he was the oldest of the nine members of Common Room of May 1923, most of whom were in their twenties. There is a photograph of him sitting in the South Front portico on J.F.'s right, the day before term began. The first five prefects stand dutifully behind. The only other housemaster that summer, Ivor Cross, sits on Roxburgh's left. In their tweed jackets and plus fours, both Earle and Roxburgh look archetypal country gentlemen, and the similarity of dress reflected one of outlook. Not only did Earle identify closely with Roxburgh's desire for the school to be more civilised and gentlemanly than the current norm, free from as many rules and regulations as possible, with each individual allowed sufficient recreational time to develop intellectual and cultural pursuits, but he himself had also pursued similar liberal ideals for several years in the Prep School world.

⋈ ⋈ ⋈

His father, the Revd. Walter Earle, had founded two Prep Schools, Yarlet Hall in Staffordshire and Bilton Grange, just outside Rugby. Ernest Henry Earle was born at Yarlet in March 1874. He subsequently flourished at both schools, winning a scholarship to Marlborough, where he duly became Head Boy. A scholarship to New College, Oxford, followed, though his four years as a classics undergraduate ended disappointingly with a Third, the result, perhaps, of too active an interest in country pursuits. He was also a good games player and a member of Vincent's.

After teaching at Wellington College for a year, he suddenly left to study for the church. However, when in holy orders, instead of seeking a curacy he returned to Bilton Grange to teach under his father, and, on the latter's retirement in 1902, became Bilton's second headmaster. He was just twenty-eight.

The young clergyman's enlightened headship lasted nearly twenty years, and he became a much-loved character. He used the school's attractive setting to awaken an appreciation of all things beautiful, ever exhorting his pupils 'to love the highest when we see it'. In the classroom he took the top classics set, treating the pursuit of knowledge 'as an exciting sport in which boys could have fun in joining'. He founded the school magazine, enthused about sport, coached performances of potted Shakespeare and encouraged music, but he never let his many school duties interfere with his major passion. He regularly hunted twice a week. Fishing was another keen interest, his holidays often being spent with friends in a wide selection of fishing inns from the Cotswolds to County Kerry. As a term-time treat, he would take parties of pupils to fish Lord Sherborne's stretch of the Windrush.

The First World War affected him deeply. He took a deep interest in all the leavers. (He would give each one a Greek New Testament, inscribed in Latin: 'A gift from E.H.E., once a master, always a friend'.) Perhaps the wartime losses of many former pupils played a part in a mid-life crisis. At all events, in 1921, when a former Marlborough contemporary who had become Bishop of North Queensland needed a Bush Missioner for one of his sprawling domains, Ernest Earle impetuously left Bilton and answered his call.

He was soon based fifty miles south-west of Cairns at the small rural town of Atherton, coping as best he could with sweltering heat and devastating rain. His new 'parish' was virtually the size of England. The five scattered churches and endless small townships, cattle stations and farms, to which he ministered each week, necessitated hundreds of miles on horseback, often through deserted bush. Alone in his tiny house in Atherton on weekends, he would have plentiful cockroaches and other weird creatures for company. The cockroaches, he reported, were 'of a literary turn', devouring his books.

Eventually disaster struck. Bucked off by a recalcitrant bronco, he seriously aggravated an old injury and could no longer ride. He reported to Bilton Grange:

Few roads are possible for driving; my legs won't carry me far in this climate; the railways are designed for the convenience of (1) milk-cans, (2) tree-trunks, (3) bullocks (the line being subject to being washed away at intervals). I have now acquired a reputation as a pedestrian.

The adventure had gone on long enough. By the Christmas of 1922, after a year and a half abroad, he was back in England, where, fortuitously, there was a public school about to open. Stowe looked distinctly more promising than the Australian bush. Country pursuits would abound, and it was not far from Bilton, which had become a private company with himself as one of its directors. He was happy to learn from J.F. that, until a chaplain was in due course appointed, he would also be responsible for the school's religious life.

* * *

11 May 1923 came swiftly round, with J.F. greeting the first Stoics on the North Front steps. All those wearing red-banded boaters shook hands with him before scurrying onwards into the mansion to meet Ivor Cross in Temple. All those with green-banded headgear headed off to Bruce, to be welcomed by Ernest Earle. There were to be ninety-nine pupils altogether including five older prefects. Two days later, one of the ninety-nine would write a first letter home:

Mr Earle is my Housemaster and luckily my form master too. He is so nice and so jolly... I am as happy as a king.

Ernest Earle's calm and mature approach as stand-in chaplain was very much what Roxburgh needed as he began the delicate job of countering the demands of the Revd. Percy Warrington, the evangelical governor whose manic crusade against high-church schools had played a big part in the founding of Stowe. For the school's first term Earle took services in the mansion, in the lovely old Cedar Chapel that was to survive another six years. 'The Chapel is very nice,' wrote a Bruce new boy, 'a quite small panelled room, which has always been a Chapel, the Commandments above the altar. We each have a chair and three books – hymns, prayer and Bible. There is a lovely piano and no organ.'

The two boarding houses occupied the western side of the mansion. Two further Houses, Grenville and Chandos, would be on the east side in the second term. But it was a very piecemeal arrangement. 'The geography of all the four founder Houses,' commented George Clarke, 'was like the holdings of a mediaeval farmer, split up into strips of territory all over the place. The only piece of obvious logic was that all the dormitories were on the first floor.' It was, early on, an administrative and disciplinary nightmare.

Initially there were few seniors, so little call for studies. Both houserooms were accordingly crowded. For the first term Bruce used the Garter Room, and, afterwards, the Music Room. As Temple had been given the western staircase, Bruce had to make do with the spiral stairs, coming out by the Servery. Ernest Earle's study was in no-man's land, between the North Hall and the Temple stairs.

The hurriedly modernised mansion left much to be desired in that first year, with miles of obtrusive piping and wiring, and the all-pervasive smell of the hasty new plumbing. Ernest Earle, however, was very content. Soon after his arrival he wrote to a former pupil:

> *The work suits me very well; it is a beautiful place and over £100,000 has already been spent on turning it into an up-to-date Public School. The fact that there are more than 1,000 boys entered to come to the school is an assurance of its future success, and shows that it is supplying a want.*

He was in his element, too, in that virtually the entire student body had come straight from Prep Schools. One of the 1923 intake, Dudley Steynor, was later to write of his first term:

> *I was placed in Remove B. David Niven was one of us. He had a gift for amusing everyone with his quick sketches of events going on outside the classroom windows. Our Form Master was the Rev. Ernest Earle, a delightful man. He had a great sense of humour, had no difficulty in keeping strict discipline and, as a result was a good teacher. He must have been, for I obtained a Credit in Latin in my final Certificate. And Niven, for all his cunning, was nicely brought down to earth when Mr Earle was asking each of us what subjects we wished to take in the final Certificate: 'Niven, may I suggest you take Drawing?'*

By 1925 Ernest Earle had been given the nickname 'Pop', by which he was universally known. And he had a new challenge facing him. Stowe's first Speech Day, that July, was to be Pop's last as housemaster of Bruce. A new house was in the process of being built, and Pop had been invited to run it. As a building standing on its own, Chatham promised an easier brief for the housemaster. J.F. was sure that Pop would soon put his gentlemanly stamp on it, even if there had been the occasional disciplinary problem in Bruce.

That first Speech Day, J.F. let it be known that Chatham's imminent opening marked the end of Stowe's immediate development. School numbers had been brought up to 420. There, for the present, it was intended to stop. A fund for a chapel had been begun, but, overall, the policy would now be one of consolidation.

When Chatham opened in the autumn of 1925, twenty-two boys moved over to it from Bruce (several of whom, like Granville Carr, had come from Bilton Grange) to join forty-six new arrivals (wearing purple labels for identification). Building works were as yet incomplete. Scaffolding proliferated. Pop cheerfully wrote about 'a kind of builders' morass' that was to surround the House for many months. The noise of builders was constant.

Sixty years later, when reminiscences were invited for a *Chatham Register*, memories of its early days soon surfaced. 'It was full of naked concrete and so it remained for our time there'. Such negativities, however, were balanced by Pop's friendliness – 'On half holidays he would hack round the park with us' – and gentle avuncularity: 'A kindly old man addicted to horse riding and an unsafe driver of an old car;' 'a gentle man, who had time for the students in Chatham – this was not always the case in other Houses.' One Old Stoic remembered a rare flash of anger: 'I started the House Library and wrote round to all the parents asking for donations or books. Pop was initially furious, but mollified as cash and books started to arrive.'

There were memories, too, of a housekeeper and valet ('A couple by the name of Penn, who lived in and looked after Pop'), as well as two of his cars and their number plates ('PP2416: a Wolseley tourer and WL 5449: a Morris Oxford saloon'). Then there was Latin in the Lower Remove:

> One day early on Pop called out to Gavin Maxwell to stop talking. Gavin replied, with cheeky assurance, that he wasn't talking. Pop fixed him with an amused frown. 'If I say you're talking,' he replied, 'then you are talking, whether you are talking or not.' There was no further trouble, for we were all very fond of Pop...

Pop's Chatham was high-spirited. After lunch each day, he would dole out Lines, which had to be copied out on special paper and presented to the master who had set them. Pop kept a stock of Lines in his study, situated in isolation between doors to the houseroom and the private side. The House, however, was riddled with experts at forging his signature and almost everyone filched handy supplies of virgin 'Lines' from his desk. Pop accordingly always delighted in how brilliantly Chatham was behaving and how few Lines he had to give out most terms. 'I can do Pop's signature even today!' confessed one elderly Old Stoic. Other pranks included his car. One typical day, finding that it would not start, poor Pop summoned help from a Buckingham garage. A mechanic duly arrived and found there was absolutely nothing wrong. Just before the mechanic's arrival, however, the Chatham prankster had changed over the leads on the plugs to correct the 'fault'. There were several variations on this theme.

It was sensible not to keep Pop's car off the road too long, for it was a key component in the way he embellished his charges' spare time. Granville Carr, for example, noted many occasions when former members of Bilton Grange (all in Chatham) were taken up to their old school for functions. Such trips might well end in Buckingham at the Grenville Tea Rooms in West Street. Similarly, as a keen member of the Buckingham Lawn Tennis Club, Pop would often take three members of Chatham over there to play doubles with him.

Granville Carr's diaries recorded his Housemaster's regular involvement at card sessions that took place in his study: 'Pop and Ellis beat Boyd-Carpenter and me at bridge. We had grapefruit and biscuits.' 'Pop and I beat Pick and Ellis at bridge.' 'Pop and I beat Ellis and Boyd-Carpenter at bridge.' 'Boyd-Carpenter and I played Pop and Ellis, each winning 1 rubber. They won on points. Cakes and cocoa.' Pop could not abide to sit idly by as dummy, so used to walk around the table to give his bridge partner hints on the playing of the hand.

Few memories of Pop did not include the magnificent Sunday morning breakfast parties that everyone would enjoy once or twice a term. 'Superb, old-fashioned breakfasts, and cultural occasions as well.' 'The highlight of each term was to be invited to have breakfast with Pop Earle. If you had a Birthday, you could be extra lucky and have two invitations.' Granville Carr's diary would even itemize the delights: 'Breakfast with Pop. We had egg, sausage, toast and coffee.'

On Sunday evenings a large number of juniors would gather in his study while he read aloud in expert style. Granville Carr included several mentions of these much-enjoyed events. On one occasion 'after supper, Pop read us two very weird and exciting stories...'

Pop's dry sense of humour came to the fore in the naming of the infamous outdoor lavatories that, as the future Lord Taylor remembered, he called 'Wilkie's' because, like the radical eighteenth-century politician John Wilkes, they had been 'thrown out of the House'. It was Pop Earle, too, who in December 1928 inspired the more rebellious of the seniors to publish a satirical magazine, *The Epicurean*, its title (a parody of *The Stoic*) invoking a more liberal school of ancient Greek philosophy. With Pop's own humorous contributions raising its standards, it came out each term for several years until pressure from the more reactionary housemasters eventually resulted in a ban.

Pop's sense of humour regularly featured in the Chatham House Log. 'A tame deer was presented as a mascot for the House by Sir Hereward Wake,' he wrote in Autumn 1925, 'and called Miss Wake. A suggestion that the House motto be "We keep awake" was rejected.'

* * *

Unfortunately, Chatham became steadily more unruly, and, in 1931, Ivor Cross took over from Pop. He stayed on at Stowe, however, for three final years, until his sixtieth birthday, enjoying his new ability to help more in Chapel and local churches. In October 1931, for example, he celebrated Harvest Thanksgiving in Buckingham:

In an impressive address, based on a singularly appropriate quotation from the words of the prophet Habakkuk, the Rev. E.H. Earle alluded to the present national difficulties[1] and the effect of the weather upon the crops. Thanksgiving, said the preacher, was a very hard practice to learn when things were going wrong. Personally, he was not pessimistic about the world's future. He believed that the world would come through its present difficulties in some way ennobled and purged, and that it was working out, in the providence of God, a far better future. It would be shown, in spite of all that was often said to the contrary, that the world was far better than it used to be.

They could not ignore the fact that they were vastly superior to their cave-dwelling ancestors. They had, each of them, a great deal to be thankful for, not least of all for the fact that they were born in a civilised country and under a

---

1   1931 was the central year of the Great Depression.

British Government and not perhaps under Soviet rule; that they had been born in a land in which they had the privileges of the Christian Faith. The Jews were thankful people. The Psalms overflowed with the spirit of the old prophet who said that, in spite of all his troubles, he was going to thank God. Thanksgiving was the duty that the creature owed to the creator.

* * *

Pop had served Stowe in his unique gentlemanly way for eleven years, when he left, in the Easter of 1934, to become a country vicar. He moved to the Wiltshire Rectory of Bishopstrow, just outside Warminster and thirty miles from Sherborne. It was a village he knew well. He had stayed there at Eastleigh Court with a cousin, John Greville Earle, and got on well with the patron of the church, the local squire, Grenville Newton Temple of Bishopstrow House. The squire, as his names suggest, was a descendant of the Temples of Stowe.

St Aldhelm's is a beautiful fourteenth-century church. There was still much doffing of hats there on Sundays, when the squire arrived. His wife went in first and sat in the front pew. The squire stood outside, greeting everyone. 'He used to wear a tall hat,' remembered one of the parishioners, 'and he would be the last one to walk into church. He walked in as if he owned it. He had a good rapport with the Vicar, Mr Earle.'

Pop had found himself again in a lovely setting. His eighteenth-century rectory stood in large grounds beside St Aldhelm's and an idyllic cricket ground. A former Bilton Grange pupil later recorded:

As a gentleman he liked simple and natural people of all ages and as an aristocrat, with aristocratic standards, he appreciated especially rugosities of character in country folk... His parsonage and garden lay girdled by green hills and bright streams, where he rode his horse and fished most skilfully for the Wylye trout and drove his car, less skilfully, and cultivated his garden, and earned the respect and affection of his flock. He lived quietly but sociably as something of a squarson and got on splendidly with his patron, his squire, and his parishioners. (W.S. Blacklaw, More Than A School To Us)

The benefice only gave him £200 a year, but Pop's private means were considerable. One villager affectionately recalled:

Mr Earle had a manservant and a housekeeper who were husband and wife and they had the top floor of the Rectory. The day I was confirmed, there were so many people in the church they couldn't get all inside… They had to relay the service to the others outside. Afterwards we had a beautiful tea on the lawns of the rectory. It was a real feast… Mr Earle had a lot of money. He spent quite a bit on the church. His rectory garden, by which he set much store, was open at all times to the children of the village.

Pop ensured there were regular charabanc trips to Weymouth where tea and cakes abounded. He took on a nearby parish, Norton Bavant, when it was in danger of closure, with no alteration in salary, and also funded big events for the county set, centred on the Wylye Valley Hunt.

Revelling in this late-life flourish, Pop would regularly invite old friends to Bishopstrow. There were some big gatherings of the Earles, too. In 1938 he and his brother, the Reverend Granville Earle, officiated at St Aldhelm's at the marriages of two nieces. One of the ushers on the second occasion was Ion Earle, who had spent four years in Chatham with his uncle Ernest.[2] Arrangements had been made for a further family wedding at St Aldhelm's in September 1939, when Pop would officiate at his brother Granville's late marriage, only for the outbreak of war to necessitate a change of plan.

Pop's warmness of heart was in its element in Wiltshire. On one occasion, a homeless young couple, whom he had just married, ended up for a while in the rectory:

We had nowhere to live. I knew the housemaid at Bishopstrow Rectory, Winnie Bartlett, a friend of mine. She said, 'Come and live at the Rectory.' So we did. The rector, the Reverend Earle, didn't object. He was quite happy. We shared his kitchen.

Wartime memories of Pop also abounded. 'I was 19 when the Revd. Earle married us in 1941. He didn't charge us. He married us for nothing as a wedding present.' Just as Pop had read to the boys of Chatham on Sunday evenings, so he would spend his wartime Wednesday afternoons reading soothingly as a large gathering knitted socks for the troops.

---

2   Ion was the son of Pop's brother, Stephen. He had just graduated at Oxford. In 1996 Ion, aged 80, was to graduate again, at the same Oxford ceremony as his grand-daughter.

* * *

Pop was over seventy when the war ended. Retirement beckoned. Eventually, in late October 1947 he moved to the Milford House Hotel at Milford-on-Sea, where he was close to a sister and niece. In a two-day auction, he had sold up most of the personal belongings that had filled his capacious rectory. The hotel dated back to Georgian times and stood in fine grounds, looking out towards the Solent. But he was to be there only very briefly, for on 10 November 1947, on returning from a cycling trip to nearby Keyhaven, he misjudged things as he turned into the hotel, hit a kerb and fell heavily off his bike. He was taken to Milford-on-Sea War Memorial Hospital, his injuries including a neck fracture. Nine days later, after slowly lapsing into unconsciousness, he died. He was seventy-three.

He had kept in touch with J.F. and maintained a deep interest in both Stowe and Bilton. The funeral, however, was confined to a few family members, for, thoughtful to the last, Pop had asked that news of his death should not be widely promulgated until after his funeral. It was a long journey down to the south coast, and he was not one to put others to inconvenience. He was buried in the churchyard of All Saints Church.

There were some touching tributes. Roxburgh, only two years from retirement himself, wrote movingly: 'We shall not forget him as long as we live… Stowe has lost not only one of its creators but one of its most faithful and devoted friends. Peace be to his soul!'

2

IVOR CROSS

The Roxburgh protégé who ran Temple & Chatham
Stowe 1923-43

The two housemasters of May 1923 were notably dissimilar. Ivor Cross, at twenty-five, was almost half the age of Ernest Earle. He had, however, double the enthusiasm for good discipline. Grateful to have been invited to participate so fully in the school's creation, Ivor would devote himself to it with relentless energy. For half of his twenty years of housemastering, he would be J.F.'s unofficial senior master, serving with devotion 'the greatest man I was ever to know'. But for all the shared excitement and ambition, the relationship between the two would not always move smoothly forwards. Indeed, it would at times be intriguingly problematic, though the whole-hearted Ivor could never quite understand why.

* * *

They had first met at Lancing back in 1911. At twenty-three, John Fergusson Roxburgh had just joined the staff, an Old Carthusian with a first-class Cambridge degree in classics and a *Licence-ès-Lettres* in classical literature from the Sorbonne. Ivor Malcolm Cross, by contrast, was a thirteen-year-old scholar from a small Prep School in Bexhill, impressed by the new French teacher's arrestingly stylish presence, his melodious voice and seemingly inexhaustible supply of well-tailored suits. His colourful cap and gown from the Sorbonne lit up the Lancing corridors. In a world that had little time for thirteen-year-olds, the smiling J.F. was a sympathetic exception. He had time for everyone. Ivor was soon viewing him with devotion.

Back in 1897 Ivor had been born into a family coming unhappily apart. His father, an architect with a roving eye, was often a mysterious absentee. Ivor accordingly was sent away to Prep School when just three. After his parents' divorce, he spent the holidays with his mother, living in genteel poverty in a small first-floor London flat close to Hammersmith Bridge.

He had determinedly made a success at Prep School, both academically and as a diminutive goalkeeper and wicket-keeper. At Lancing, too, lucky to have J.F. as his form-master early on, he had prospered in work, sports, the choir and Officers' Training Corps. He ended up as a Prefect, before leaving in 1917 for the First World War.

He was sent to France as a nineteen-year-old Second Lieutenant in the Royal Artillery and soon active on the Western Front with huge 60-pounder guns, pulled by teams of horses. His daughter Karin remembers:

He loved the great carthorses. He had trained in the RA's cavalry school and was a most accomplished rider. He once told me about how he had to ride bareback over the course of jumps sitting on his horse with his arms folded – they had to learn to stay on, no matter what.

He spent the winter of 1917-18 fighting around Nieuport in Belgium and then near Ypres, forward of Vimy Ridge. The 60-pounders were deafening, and by the end of the war Ivor was suffering from impaired hearing. In later years he would rarely speak of his experiences, but he did once describe it to Karin as 'organised murder':

My mother told me that he had some very narrow escapes, having to cut the traces of the horses from the guns, mount quickly, and gallop away as the Germans overran their position. He was once in a forward observation post which had a direct hit from a shell...

In 1918, a serious leg injury required an operation back home. By chance Roxburgh was also on leave from the Western Front. 'Met dear old J.F. at Les Lauriers,' Ivor wrote in his diary. They managed to meet up once more at the chic French restaurant in Piccadilly before war ended. In April 1918 he wrote: 'Roxburgh unexpectedly called and we had dinner together at his Club[3], followed by a good talk about the things that matter'. Ivor's son, Canon Greville Cross, believes this talk about 'the things that matter' was of great significance to his father:

> *The idealism forged in war, tempered by the loss of comrades and friends, settled at the very core of his being. It is all too common for the idealism of youth to become compromised by the realities of life. But for Father, essentially a very sensitive person, such compromise was never possible without breaking faith with his fallen comrades and the entire loss of his own integrity.*

Ivor rejoined the 135th Heavy Battery that summer at Amiens, as part of the Fourth Army. He was devastated to learn that his former unit had been annihilated in the great German offensive that March. Greville Cross recalls:

> *I don't think my father ever recovered from the First World War. Nowadays it would be termed Post Traumatic Stress, but his generation simply had to get on with life as best they could. I doubt if he ever really came to terms with the immense sense of loss.*

He struggled on through the final horrors. In his diary were carefully copied extracts from Whitman's *Leaves of Grass* and other uplifting poetry and prose to help steady his morale. In due course the Artillery moved through France and Belgium in the final push. 'Sunday 13 October,' he noted in his diary. 'Time to write at last and time to get clean. What a life this is, awful in the wet.' A month later, when he was able to write, '11 November: Peace from 11a.m. Armistice signed', he joyfully underlined 'Peace' three times.

In 1919 J.F. duly returned to Lancing as a Housemaster, while, thanks to a Service Grant, Ivor took up a Choral Exhibition at Gonville and Caius College and acquired a degree in History after two years. A job at Eastbourne College ensued, though, as his daughter Karin writes, teaching was not his ambition:

> *He had a very artistic side, loved painting and drawing and wanted more than anything to go into the family firm and become an architect, but the firm was*

---

3   The Athenaeum

pretty well bankrupt by that time. His elder brother Kenneth was working hard to turn it around and there just was not the money or the work for another partner.

* * *

J.F.'s appointment at Stowe was a late one, only made in December 1922. He was soon in touch with Ivor, sounding him out. The acceptance was immediate. By February 1923 J.F. was writing:

All is going well and I hope you will have a nice little House with about 40 waiting for you in May. It would probably be just as well (as you say) to be in England a week or so before the term begins. (May 11). The geography of the place needs a lot of learning.

Ivor's letters were full of enthusiasm for his work at Eastbourne, not least in his out-of-class endeavours. He was active in the Corps ('we have a Field Day on Tuesday with Lancing'); produced a play ('there's nothing like this sort of thing for getting to know the lads and I'm enjoying it ever so much'); taught English as well as History ('somehow or other by the end of term I have to get to Tennyson and co.'); and, though devoted to soccer, was proving enthusiastic at the alternative ('I launched out into rugger yesterday and had a splendid game!'). By March J.F. had decided that Ivor should take on Temple House. 'It is awfully decent of you to think of giving me a House,' replied Ivor, 'and you know that all of me will go into it'. When Ivor mentioned the possibility of spending some of the summer together in Bruges, J.F. readily agreed to a week in Belgium in April: 'Only, if we go together, we must make it an absolute rule that we do not talk Stowe.'

Ivor was to bring to Stowe clear-cut values. As one of his pupils was later to write, they were 'Kipling-esque in content, deeply Christian and strongly propounding self-discipline'. His great cri-de-coeur would be 'There's no such thing as "teach" – School is about learning to learn – a lifelong process.'

* * *

The Stoic affords early glimpses of Ivor: playing for The Masters against The School both at cricket (opening the innings and keeping wicket) and golf (on a hastily improvised course); impressing with a baritone voice of great quality at concerts and displaying his knowledge of painting and drawing, at the Art Club. In the summer holidays of 1924, he wrote to J.F.:

> *I'm trying not to think of Stowe for a fortnight, but I'd like to bear testimony to the superlative way in which you conduct it. Honestly there is no other word and I mean it entirely.*

In December 1924, when the Debating Society began its existence, Ivor acted as Vice-President under fellow historian Martin MacLaughlin. In the club's first debate, as a staunch Liberal, he proposed (and lost) a motion expressing anxiety at a Conservative election victory. A year later Ivor became Vice-President of The Twelve Club, an elite gathering of sixth-form intellectuals (with Boyd-Carpenter as its first secretary and J.F. its President). Ivor led off with papers on 'Hamlet in Modern Clothes' and 'Liberalism'.

He acquired a car in 1924, many years before the establishment of driving tests. 'My dear Ivor,' wrote J.F. 'I'm glad you got to Kettering without hitting anything. It was certainly rather clever of you after two days' practice.' In the summer of 1925, Ivor wrote Roxburgh an eight-sided letter on the teaching of history in the lower school and possibilities of making Civics a Stowe speciality. J.F., holidaying in Scotland, was full of enthusiasm for Civics – 'As you know, I did a bit towards the end with the Sixth at Lancing'. He had good news about the public exams:

> *The Certificate results are thoroughly good, and I am most grateful to you once more for your splendid work. We got twenty certificates and may feel very well pleased with ourselves, I think.*

In the summer of 1926 Ivor led a Stowe history party to Normandy.

Ivor particularly enjoyed editing of *The Stoic*. The cover that his architect brother designed for him was to be retained for several decades. Inside, there continued to be more glimpses of him: singing in the Gym and Marble Hall as well as the newly-built Chapel, where, in a performance of *The Messiah*, 'Mr Cross's rendition of "The People that Walked in Darkness" was impressive'; lecturing on architecture with any number of lantern slides; and attending the recently-begun Old Stoic dinners at Cambridge in the company of J.F.

By the end of the Twenties, however, there was no longer the same total accord between the two. Ivor expected rather more from J.F. in the matter of good discipline. 'I think my father believed that boys should be taught to do what was right, because it was right,' comments Karin, 'whereas it seems that J.F. liked to be popular with the boys and to feel that they were doing what was right because J.F. would approve.' An incident from J.F.'s early Lancing days is interesting in this regard:

> *A boy returning with a cricket-bag stuffed with bottles of beer and cider for an end-of-term party had the misfortune to be offered a lift by J.F. who heaved the bag into the car. He said nothing as the bottles clinked but, when he dropped him, handed him a packet of fifty cigarettes and said, 'Perhaps these will come in useful'. (Roxburgh of Stowe)*

In Ivor's view Stowe was becoming over-indulgent. Several of the Houses certainly saw far less of their housemasters than Temple. Cobham, for example, were regularly en fête after 10.00 pm each night, when 'Cheerful Charlie' Acland departed to bed on the dot. Demanding the most of himself at all times and frequently overtired, Ivor could sometimes struggle to keep a balanced outlook. When faced with a sudden frustration or a seeming disloyalty, he could give way explosively to mounting irritation.

In 1930, for example, some Temple parents with strong connections with J.F. had complained of what they felt was Ivor's total lack of sympathy in a set-to with their son. Ivor wrote hotly to J.F., demanding a letter supporting all he had said and done, stating his refusal to be ashamed of his own temperament, and perplexedly querying why J.F. should consider him 'too conscientious and devoted' to his work. The only alternative to such a letter of support, he wrote, was that the boy should be removed to another House.

J.F. ignored these requests, offering instead some fatherly advice. It was Ivor's 'first business' to put right what was clearly 'the culmination of a long history of mutual irritation'. Immediate oil was needed for troubled waters. 'The attitude that peace is only to be obtained by the other fellow's submission is always a hopeless one'.

Ivor's preparedness to speak his mind at all times and his unwillingness to concede ground when he believed important moral issues were at stake would make for further stormy moments. Only two months later, he was offering J.F. his immediate resignation after being made to feel that the way he was running his House was not 'in the spirit of Stowe'. An olive branch was quickly offered and gratefully clutched:

> *I have felt that you saw in myself – and therefore in my 'show' – something not quite true to the spirit of Stowe, and you must pardon me (as a balmy egoist, if you like, or as a keen schoolmaster, as I hope) for thinking at times that the spirit of Stowe was no longer true. And that has been what has been the matter with me. But gone is all that. And if I take your kind letter as an invitation to stay on at Stowe, then I accept it – and with alacrity.*

There was further gratitude shortly afterwards, when J.F. asked Ivor to take over Chatham and sort out its current discipline problems.

The move, however, nearly didn't happen. Ivor was appalled to learn that Eddie Capel Cure, a liberal modern linguist who had recently been Chatham's Underhousemaster, was to be given Temple. Some subconscious jealousy may have added fire to the flames. Capel had been Head of J.F.'s House at post-war Lancing and very much had J.F.'s ear at Stowe. So Ivor penned a five-page letter of protest: He could not face working in Chatham if Temple were being run 'by somebody out of sympathy with the point of view upon which the House has been built'. Temple would not be Temple, and 'it ought to go on being Temple, just as Chatham ought not to go on being Chatham'. He felt that 'both houses had stood for things, and that Temple has proved to be right'.

J.F.'s response was firmly calm:

> *My dear Ivor.*
>
> *I am offering Temple to Capel. He has not yet accepted but I expect he will. I am truly sorry to be going against your wishes for I realise that no-one has more right to be heard on a question affecting Temple than the man who has just made it what it is … Personally, I do not doubt that you will see Capel rising to the height of his big position and making a contribution of his own to the many-coloured web of Stowe as well as to the distinguished history of Temple…*

Ivor backed down, but was soon approaching J.F. with an idea, hatched by his architect brother, to disguise Chatham's stark red brick. J.F.'s forthright response brooked no further correspondence:

The only architectural scheme in existence which concerns Chatham is that at some remote day when money is plentiful the house shall be rebuilt on a site proposed fifty yards to the West of its present position on an alignment with the other buildings. No doubt when rebuilt the house would not be coloured so harsh a red. All this however belongs to the distant future.

* * *

Ivor brought the recalcitrant House to heel within a couple of terms, but the effort involved hardly made him popular. Old Stoics contributing to the *Chatham House Register* of 1985 largely painted him in dark colours: 'He was a rotund, red-faced figure, with narrow, deep-set eyes which hardly ever looked at you directly, but, when they did, bored gimlet-like right through you'. 'An old-fashioned disciplinarian, not an instinctive communicator'.

A minority took a more balanced view: 'He was a rather formidable man and, of course, very strict, but he showed me great patience and understanding. I remember him with gratitude and affection.' 'Within his particular limits, he had the interests of his boys very much at heart and I always got on well with him.' 'He was just unworldly! He once drove a new car without using top gear!' Several made special mention of the annual Chatham sing-song ('beer or cider provided in moderation') when 'Ivor's rich tones' would lead the final deafening chorus of 'For tonight we'll merry merry be'.

Ivor's anxieties about the Common Room's liberals were multiplied in 1934, when Bill McElwee arrived, the inspirational new History Tutor and Ivor's Head of Department. It was not long before he was outraged by the smoking, drinking and gossip that the historians were said to be regularly enjoying in the McElwees' bohemian home in Dadford. Accordingly, activities that he had once enjoyed, like debating and drama, now had to be vigorously opposed, tainted as they had become in his eyes by McElwee. There would be no House plays in Chatham during Ivor's twelve years in charge.

For Stoics, the feud was a delightful entertainment. One of Bill McElwee's Chatham historians later wrote of his Tutor and Housemaster openly disagreeing about absolutely everything. 'I cannot explain the speed at which the enmity between Ivor Cross and Bill developed. Bill had, after all, only been at Stowe for two terms when I came, but already he and Patience stood, in Ivor's eyes, for subversion and disloyalty'. It made his own relationship with Ivor very tense, until, 'by my final year, he forgave me my sundry disloyalties and peccadilloes, gave me a birthday present (*Art* by Clive Bell, that I still have) and made me a monitor.' Several scurrilous ditties about Ivor, that might well have had their beginnings at Vancouver Lodge, were circulating around at this time and long remembered:

> *I have made my house so clean*
> *That there's nothing to be seen*
> *But me and my ideas*
> *And my big stick*
> *And my dog Mick*
> *And Dan, who cleans The Rears.*[4]

* * *

Current affairs were always his passion. In December 1933, a branch of the League of Nations Union had been founded at Stowe with Ivor as President. In the Library, at the initial meeting, he talked about the Aims of the League and its value as a factor in world politics. The branch flourished under his leadership, with strong support from J.F. Membership rose to over three hundred. Meetings with important visiting speakers were held in the Gym. The alarming political situation of the 1930s even transcended that bitterest of Common Room rivalries, with Ivor and Bill McElwee regularly appearing on the same platform as President and Vice-President.

The move to Chatham had not improved the relationship with J.F., who, early on, had upset Ivor with an abrupt intervention:

> *I have assumed your approval for allowing Hesketh-Prichard*[5] *to spend Saturday night with Lady Helen Cassel. There is to be a coming-of-age party for Lord Verulam's eldest son at the family place, Gorhambury.*

---

4   'The Rears' were the quite appalling lavatories on the outside of the building, at the back, eventually bulldozed and replaced by a ground-floor extension in 1980.
5   Alfgar Hesketh-Prichard was the son of a famous explorer, big-game hunter and cricketer and would himself win a posthumous MC as a heroic secret agent. His mother served for thirty years as a close courtier of Queen Mary, which probably accounted for the royal visit of 1927.

H-P will come back on Sunday evening.

Ivor, like many of the housemaster barons of the period, felt J.F. sometimes interfered too much in his preserve. The 'sanctity of prep' proved another bone of contention. When the popular Head of Science, Hugh Heckstall-Smith, seemed to be stepping out of line, Ivor dropped J.F. a note:

> *HWH-S has been asking boys to his room to listen to his gramophone during prep time. I had an application from Hesketh-P and Buxton, and turned it down at once in each case. I think it is a case of a note from you, perhaps in the name of the Housemasters in general, as I am quite sure they all feel the same about it. I myself feel that he has no business to do it.*

Heckstall-Smith was the kind of imaginative eccentric that J.F. tended to encourage, and Ivor received an unexpected rebuff:

> *H-S's Musical Evenings are really of value educationally – in my opinion. He plays only classical music and makes the thing a real lesson in musical appreciation… I think the boys who go gain rather than lose.*

Though it might at this juncture have been in his own best interests to accept this ruling, Ivor bravely let his understandable dismay show:

> *My point was, mainly, sanctity of prep. It is extremely hard to teach it. If H-S's musical evenings are of educational value, there are other times on Sundays and half holidays. I am definitely against boys going in Prep-time – and felt almost sure that you would support me.*

In the summer of 1933 Ivor had a serious falling-out with a Chatham sixth-former, Jeremy Hutchinson, later Lord Hutchinson and a leading barrister. (John Mortimer would base the character of *Rumpole of the Bailey* on him.) Hutchinson's distinguished parents, moreover, moved in circles that included Virginia Woolf, T.S. Eliot and Aldous Huxley.

The alarmed J.F. was soon ringing Ivor up to tell him he must make an apologetic peace straight away. Undaunted, Ivor responded with some criticisms of his own:

I do not think that the 'right or wrong' factor is put at its proper value in the School – I mean among the boys. But I feel that all the other good things that they learn here – in the name of 'liberty' in a progressive school – are of secondary importance to this, and that, in the long run, the School will be judged by the opinion that people have as to its moral worth…

At the start of the following holidays, perhaps realising that he had overstepped the mark, Ivor wrote to J.F., suggesting they take a short break together. J.F. replied:

I am afraid that our jaunt with cars and cameras will hardly be able to come off this time. On the 18th I must clear out from here to give the servants a holiday and I promised my mother to go to her first. After that I shall try to slip abroad for a spell and then it will be time to come back here. But the idea was a good one and I was grateful for it. Perhaps we shall be able to go through with it another time. Meanwhile I regarded your suggestion as a most welcome olive branch.

* * *

In the Christmas holidays of 1934-35 came a crucial turning-point in Ivor's life when, at thirty-seven, he met the twenty-one-year-old Barbara Kennard Davis at a ski resort on the continent. Barbara, daughter of the Headmaster of Magdalen College School, was a highly intelligent and sports-minded young lady, currently studying for a history degree at Oxford. The pair clearly had much in common and a whirlwind romance followed. Indeed, Ivor came back from the holiday, engaged to be married.

J.F., of course, was the first to be informed, and Ivor was overwhelmed by his response:

What a letter – and who else in the world could have written it! I can only say, with sincerity, that I feel unworthy of the feeling it expresses.

The marriage went ahead in September, Barbara having acquired her degree that summer. She was to make an immediate and lasting hit with J.F. Later, when writing a testimonial on Ivor's behalf, he nursed no reservations:

I find Mrs Cross a charming person. Although clever, she is very natural and simple (having been a Hockey Blue among other things) and I find that the boys' mothers talk to her with great freedom and seem to appreciate the welcome she gives them. She is, of course, very young, and she is also very good-looking, though in an entirely unadorned, fresh, athletic sort of way.

Back from honeymoon, they stayed for a while at the White Hart, while Fielding Dodd, the School's architect, effected changes to Chatham's private side, but soon Ivor was leading Barbara triumphantly into Chatham. 'We have the use of a few rooms and are getting straight by degrees,' he wrote to J.F. 'Dodd looked in today and took me round the new houses[6].' Ivor had a fresh sparkle about him. When one of his latest Chatham fallouts happened to be with Leonard Cheshire, he accepted Roxburgh's advice with cheerful acquiescence.

Barbara's presence helped civilise Chatham. She also worked hard on easing Ivor's relationship with J.F. In 1937, after a particularly helpful chat with him, she wrote by way of follow-up:

I told Ivor of your appreciation of his qualities as a Housemaster and his remark was, 'Well, that does restore one's self-respect'. I feel convinced that this is the key to the whole situation, and that as long as he remains assured of your confidence in him, trivial events will not cause him to explode. I also handed on your criticisms, but there is certainly no 'grimness' in the atmosphere today!

By now, however, there was too great a divergence of ideals for there to be any complete rapprochement. Ivor seemed unable to accept how much the relationship had developed since 1923, continuing to hope to be the persuasive voice in the inner counsels of the school that he had once been.

What counts is the life of the spirit. I should like to be able to talk to you, at times, absolutely without reserve, feeling that I have your confidence and that therefore there is nothing between us.

It was wishful thinking. Ivor, however, doggedly continued to fight for his beliefs.

---

6   The Field Houses, now part of West House.

If J.F. proved elusive, he inexorably pursued him, feeling the rightness of his cause forbade caution:

The best service that can be rendered to the boys as individuals is to improve their moral and self-disciplinary standards... I write to ask whether we might discuss between now and the end of term the substance of my letter to you at the beginning of this term... It has been something of a disappointment to me that you have not referred to it since...

When J.F. countered this by expressing disappointment that he had had to advise Ivor's Head of House to leave early, to avoid the imminent clash between a young prefect of liberal ideas and a Housemaster, rooted in tradition, Ivor fought back strongly. The failure of this particular relationship should be balanced with his success in teaching a spirit of obligation and duty to the House as a whole. A nine-page letter of criticisms and suggestions followed. He agreed it was a good thing the housemasters were humane and liberal in their outlook, 'but as schoolmasters I believe we have to learn that school life for the boy is, fundamentally, a moral enterprise, requiring our judgement as well as our friendship'.

Both men, deep down, yearned for the old rapport. And there were still times when the past closeness returned. There was deep sympathy from J.F. when Ivor and Barbara had the tragedy of losing their first child after only a few days of life. And there was a memorable occasion, shortly before the outbreak of war, in the summer of 1939, when Roxburgh drove Ivor and Barbara out to Great Brickhill, where, twelve years earlier, he had purchased land on which he proposed to build a house for his retirement.[7] There they rejoiced in the beauty of the views and pored over Fielding Dodd's drawings that, alas, were never to reach fruition.

Ivor had for several years been putting in applications for Headships for major schools and was still doing so. In time, understandably, the nature of the CV he was receiving from J.F. became something of a concern to him and he raised the issue. Were all his Stowe initiatives, like the introduction of Civics into the school

---

7   Fielding Dodd's 'proposed layout' of 1937 shows a large mansion in ample grounds approached by a lengthy winding drive. Dodd drew three additional buildings: two small cottages, acting as entrance lodges, and, behind them, another sizeable house. In 1939 J.F. leased a cottage in Brickhill to act as his base for imminent work on the buildings and grounds. War, however, was to prevent this. J.F.'s post-war compromise (1947) was to sell much of the land and just have a small building, 'Garden Cottage', built on the Dodd site.

curriculum, being included? Likewise all the camps he had supervised in South Wales in the school holidays, when Chatham boys went digging for the unemployed? Then what about his support for games, and the winning of the Laurus Cup by both Temple and Chatham?

It was of little use. Though J.F. was, on the one hand, writing of Ivor as 'a pillar of this place since we started', 'a man of high ideals', 'an exceptionally straight and strong man, and a very capable one too', he was, on the other, making non-committal comments that needed little reading between the lines:

If he is interviewed by the governors, they will be able to judge for themselves whether he has the adaptability which a change to a headmastership would require him to display.

* * *

The headmastership never materialised. But soon after the onset of the Second World War, J.F.'s intermittent health problems allowed Ivor to deputise for him, a task he clearly relished. One letter to the incapacitated J.F. was a litany of success: good discussions with Patrick Hunter; friendly skating with Capel; a much appreciated 'piano show'; and a 'Reading Over' with the School in the Marble Hall that could not have gone better …

No sooner was J.F. back in action than Ivor, yearning for approbation, was apprising him of current Stowe shortcomings. Inspired by a fine Roxburgh sermon in July 1940, he wrote:

You and I ought to see more of each other, both on personal and on professional grounds. If my point of view has any value – and I have always appreciated the point you made last night about being honest with oneself – then it is wrong that I should be made to feel a political outsider, because I was one of the early critics of Chamberlainism…

1942 was a harrowing year for both of them, as regular news came through of the death in action of many Old Stoics. Life in wartime Chatham remained far from easy. Barbara now had two very small children to look after, domestic help was unavailable and petrol rationing exacerbated problems. An application for a tiny supplementary allowance (one and a half gallons a month) kept being turned down. They regularly ran out of basic items like potatoes and paraffin.

With all the tragedies, disappointments and privations, Ivor's nerves were on edge. A complaint by Patrick Hunter that he had missed a lesson caused a massive explosion, and Ivor's frustrated career ambitions led to the wild idea of turning Chatham into a feeder Prep School.

The tensions with J.F. came to a head in late October 1942. Well-intentioned as ever, Ivor criticised Stowe's lack of spiritual leadership:

> *I heard last night Smuts' moving and, I thought, profoundly encouraging address. I believe that in its poise, sense of proportion and statement of war-aims it has meaning for us here and ought to strike some chord in response. Does it?*
>
> *It is because I don't feel that it does that I write to you on the subject. I am oppressed by the negative spirit – the soullessness – that seems to be developing here. The sheep are hungry to be fed. The question is whether they are being fed.*

Heated words followed. Chatham was the only house, Ivor declared, where boys were encouraged in spirituality and attended voluntary chapel in worthy numbers. J.F. himself should give a stronger message from the pulpit. Without his clear lead 'the things of the spirit will not gain dominion over the developing minds of those in our care'.

His hurt over J.F.'s lack of approval also surfaced:

> *Last term, at your request, I preached in Chapel. I took a good deal of trouble to say what I meant and what I said was not out of accord with what has been said since by the accredited leaders of our country. I'm not making stupid comparisons, but I talked of 'crusades' (so did Smuts) and of making ourselves 'worthy of victory' (so does Billy Temple). Yet you said not one word to me in acknowledgement… Why should my effort in Chapel be politely ignored because in it I insisted that it was a spiritual conflict…?*

Like an uncoiling spring, Ivor's crusade gathered pace:

> *I believe that we are not serving the country by putting on one side, for the*

duration, our high calling as schoolmasters. That is Nazification as I see it...
There cannot surely be one ethical code for peace-time and another for war-
time... The purport of this letter is to beg you to help us to be more true to
ourselves, our system and our ideals...

Roxburgh, understandably, snapped. His usual ability to avoid confrontation, despite provocation, deserted him. Ivor, he responded, had gone too far. There were now differences between them too great for there to be any point in their continuing to work together.

For some time Ivor had been airing the possibility of starting his own small tutorial, a place where he could put his beliefs into practice without their constantly being undermined. He accordingly told J.F. that he would leave a term hence, in the Easter of 1943. It would be a fitting moment: the twentieth anniversary of Stowe's first term.

A couple of months after the row, he bought the premises he needed. It was an impulsive choice – no time for second thoughts – for he and Barbara had suddenly found, and completely fallen in love with, a large private house in a remote and beautiful part of Wales. There the dreams of headship could at last be fulfilled.

Ivor never nursed his grievances for long. In January 1943, as he began his final term in Chatham, he was writing to J.F. of the future as if the past had held no disappointments:

...We have already got one boy through Truman's, age 11 and backward. I hear
this morning that Stewart of Akeley wants to place a backward boy for C.E. with
a Tutor and I hope to go over and see him on Sunday...

I, too, shall have my feelings about parting company with you, and they will
be much the same as yours. However, it won't be a complete severance, I hope,
even professionally...

For all the excitement of the new venture, departure after twenty years could not have been easy. Not only would they have to uproot their family (currently of two young daughters) but they would lose the immediacy of important friendships. There was Edward Dewing, for example, a devoted Stowe scientist for thirty years, to one of whose sons Ivor was godfather; Muriel Johnston, Barbara's closest friend, Walpole's popular and long-serving matron, known as 'Miss J', famous for her nightly

Ovaltine parties; and the highly gifted classicist/historian, George Greville Gilling-Lax, very soon to perish in the War.

Ivor's departure was given appropriate prominence in *The Stoic*. Indeed, instead of the usual editorial in April 1943, J.F. wrote him a warm valedictory tribute. There, too late, was real approval:

His contribution to the making of Stowe has been weighty, individual and enduring. He has provided an element without which the School would not have been what it is – an element of strength, of high purpose, of idealism both civic and Christian and of a devotion to duty which demanded the most from himself and our best from us all...

* * *

The new home proved an inspirational choice. Lapley Grange was an Edwardian villa, not far from the village of Eglwys-fach, a dozen miles outside of Aberystwyth. Its many rooms and eighteen acres offered great potential; its oak panelling, a scholarly atmosphere; its architectural foibles, a touch of class. It stood out boldly on the hillside, its broad front terrace commanding extensive views across the Dovey estuary to the Merionethshire mountains.

Lapley Grange was to be a school for boys struggling to pass Common Entrance. Ivor started with just three pupils and initially aimed at only twelve. Full of confidence, however, he boldly commemorated the school's foundation in Latin on a large wooden plaque in the hall:

1943

SUPRA PETRAM

FUNDATA DOMUS

'A house founded on a rock' referred both to the Bible and the dynamiting of the hillside in 1904 to facilitate the house's creation.

It was not many weeks before J.F. was hearing about the enterprise:

We started term on May 6, having got into the house on April 6. A scramble...
Barbara teaches Maths and everyone how to run things. I do Latin, French,

English etc. We don't provide science... I can't imagine what good Faerie made me walk up this colossal drive and buy this colossal house (especially as I hadn't any means). The hall, by the way, is like a Dutch interior (see Vermeer's 'Lady at the Harpsichord'). The rooms are vast and the walls are thick...

Market gardening is going to be our second line of defence. We have a huge, walled-in and well-stocked kitchen garden in an awful muddle, and a noble conservatory for tomatoes. We all work on the kitchen garden when we can, and we rope in the boys...

Somehow the gallant Barbara held everything together. In addition to bringing up her own family of four – for in Wales the two daughters were to be joined by a girl and boy – she operated as matron and headmaster' secretary. Some days, too, she would be the cook or floor cleaner.

In peacetime came deserved prosperity. By 1947 there were twenty-one pupils and a teaching staff of six. By the 1950s the school's optimum number was thirty; by the 1960s, thirty-five. Latterly, C.S. Lewis's stepson joined Lapley as a pupil and really flourished there.

'Lapley was a happy place,' remembers Greville Cross, 'and that was largely down to my mother and her great sense of fun. She worked very hard, but was also involved in the local community both in Church and Parish councils.' Both she and Ivor were able to indulge their love of cricket, Ivor only retiring from the game when in his mid-fifties.

The challenging Lapley enterprise brought Ivor precious self-fulfilment. His daughter Karin recalls:

He cared deeply about everyone's well-being and happiness. He was strict and had a very firm and clear sense of what was right and an absolute commitment to it. He wasn't always serious, of course. I remember him sometimes reading P.G. Wodehouse to us tremendously entertainingly. We all fell about.

When we first moved to Lapley, father had a very nice horse called Miranda[8] which he loved and we always had one or two ponies to ride. He would go out with me sometimes and he rode in the cavalry position with long stirrups and legs forward and straight while he sat well back in the saddle.

He managed to produce a pretty reasonable choir, on whose training

8   Miranda had been stabled with Mary Connor's father at Stowe. She remembers a great friendship between her father and Ivor.

and rehearsal he worked very hard. There were some lovely Christmas Carol Services. We sometimes sang carols or hymns together as a family, taking the different parts.

In 1954 Karin received a letter from J.F., her godfather, full of his usual interest in her welfare. He died shortly afterwards. Ivor was to make the long journey back from Wales to be present for J.F's funeral in the Chapel. It took place on 11 May…

* * *

From 1954 the poet R.S. Thomas arrived as the vicar of the Eglwys-fach church, where the school worshipped every Sunday. Ivor and many fellow parishioners were appalled as a radical redecoration ensued. Everything wooden was painted matt black. The walls were stripped of their memorials and painted white. Karin remembers:

My father did not like the alterations to the church at all. He felt it was a calvinistic, joyless approach to worship. Father loved church music of the joyous kind and hated the Eglwys-fach 'dirges', too. To him religion should express joy and light…

We knew R.S. Thomas very well. He taught Divinity at Lapley for a time and often had lunch with us… My father and R.S. were very different people, like chalk and cheese, and I don't think they were the greatest of friends, though they were always perfectly polite to each other, in my presence at least! There may well have been some differences of opinion over the choir and how the school services were organized. They were both strong characters in their very different ways.

Greville, however, sees it as an essentially positive relationship:

It is true that R.S. hated the English upper crust in Eglwys-fach, but we were never a part of that set… R.S. was closely involved in the school and readily participated in cricket and other non-teaching events. I remember on one occasion Father falling and breaking a leg as we descended the hill behind the house. R.S. happened along and half-carried father back home. Remote yet kind, he was a mass of contradictions.

* * *

In 1962, when sixty-five, Ivor at last retired, installing a resident headmaster at Lapley and moving with the family to a nearby house, Hafod-y-Garth. There in a garden studio, there was further fulfilment as he indulged a long-thwarted passion for painting.

Lapley Grange sent several pupils to Stowe, but Ivor himself rarely visited. In 1963, however, on the School's fortieth anniversary, he attended the Commemoration Dinner. It was the time of Donald Crichton-Miller's imminent departure and left him concerned about the future of the School. He returned, perhaps still in some anxiety, to a Stowe dinner the following summer, where he met Crichton-Miller's successor, Bob Drayson. He wrote afterwards:

> … I hope you will allow me to tell you how good it was to see Stowe herself again! I sensed a change in the atmosphere of the school which took me back I don't know how many years… In your hands Stowe has at long last the chance to measure up to her educational opportunities, which are unique, and to bear witness that unity in the Spirit is the mark of a City of God.

There would be no future visits, though Stowe interest was undimmed.

Ivor, like J.F. before him, had worn himself out by his mid-sixties. In April 1966, clearly not well, he turned out at R.S. Thomas's little black and white church one final time for a very special occasion, his daughter Karin's wedding:

> I remember father singing, right beside me, with his lovely baritone voice filling the church. He died a week later, and I sometimes think he bravely kept going just to see me safely married.

Barbara recalled:

> He did not fear death. In the event, he went to sleep after a very happy evening and did not wake up again. To me it seemed quite clear that he was breaking out of a body which had become a burden to him.

Richard Fairley, a Lapley and Stowe pupil, who had kept in close touch, was living nearby at the time:

> *On his last evening, I happened to spend a quiet hour with him in his study at Hafod-y-garth. As ever, he stressed clearly his considerable concern at the challenges to his code of values, fearful lest those in control throughout society should lose sight of them…*

R.S. Thomas took the funeral service at Eglwys-fach. There was also a memorial service with the church packed with present and former pupils. 'With the help of God', wrote Barbara afterwards, 'Ivor at Lapley made his boys turn themselves into something bigger and better than they had imagined they could be…'

Barbara wrote warmly to Bob Drayson:

> *Ivor was greatly relieved, after his meeting with you, that you would understand on what inspiration Stowe was really based from its early days…*

Gently, she mentioned Ivor's reservations about the portrait of Roxburgh in Noel Annan's biography:

> *While he appreciated much of it, he did not feel that it really gave the essence of the man he had known and loved. I know that Ivor, who could not compromise with what he thought wrong or second-rate and who would always tell J.F. where he disagreed with him, would want you to know his opinion that behind the 'persona' which appears in the book was a great, good and spiritually-minded man…*

Ivor's hero-worship had remained to the end:

> *J.F. was often in Ivor's thoughts. On one occasion he told me that he had seen him in a dream and they were again, as in the early days, as one, 'in complete accord and understanding, with everything put right between them'. He talked of death several times, and of his absolute certainty that this would happen.*

* * *

Lapley Grange carried on for a while. It was sold by Barbara in the early 1970s. Barbara herself died in 1992 aged 79, to be buried with Ivor in Eglwys-fach. Today, converted into flats, Lapley has a new name, Plas Einion, but Ivor's Latin inscription miraculously survives in good condition in the hall.

At Lancing College, there is now an Ivor Cross memorial window in the Chapel Crypt. It features both the crests of Lancing and Stowe. Meanwhile, far away on the Welsh coast, Eglwys-fach Church is still decorated in R.S. Thomas' black and white that had caused Ivor so much dismay. Outside, in the churchyard, nestling quietly between the mountains and estuary, Ivor and Barbara's gravestone stands under a charming line of trees. She had carefully chosen for him a short but highly appropriate Latin epitaph: *Certavi et vici*. 'I fought the fight and came out on top.'

3

PHILIP BROWNE

The first Head of Music, an elusive figure
Stowe, 1923-28

Philip Austin Browne was only twenty-five when he arrived in May 1923 as Director of Music. It was a shrewd appointment, for Browne could teach classics equally well, and, as a burly young man over six feet tall, offered all-round sporting expertise, not least as a cricketer. Indeed, Philip Browne did most things with easy aplomb. Whether he was debating the latest political crisis at the Athenaeum, overseeing Latin Prose scholarship papers or playing the drums, piano and organ, he at all times exuded confident, Wykhamist *savoir faire*.

He was, however, a complicated individual, with distinct chameleon tendencies. Many different Philip Browne personae wander into focus. There was, for example, Browne the Wit, the only master who could never be outshone by J.F. in verbal exchanges, a very different figure from Browne the Social Reformer, ever full of plans for helping the humblest members of society, or Browne the Beatrix Potter Devotee, devotedly cherishing his childhood's collection of books. Philip Browne seems to have been an intriguing man for all seasons.

* * *

Born in 1898, the son of a well-to-do London barrister, he entered Winchester College in 1911, ending up as a prefect and winning a place in classics at Magdalen

College, Oxford. He was following his brother, who, five years earlier, had graduated there in Maths, en route to becoming became a Winchester housemaster and notable rowing coach.

The First World War stopped Philip going up to Oxford. Instead, in 1916, he found himself for a few short months in an Officer Cadet Battalion, a new creation by the British Army, which had only just realised that the commissioning of Public School leavers without proper training was leading to mass slaughter. In a letter from a Newmarket camp, Philip explained his current situation to Sir Herbert Warren, Magdalen's President, whom he seemed to know already:

The work is quite hard – harder than at most Cadet Battalions, so I gather. But most of the men are very decent. Of course, the change of life from Winchester with its wonderful romance and associations is violent and for the time almost overpowering, but it is healthy and very good for one! While I was away with my father last month in Devon and Cornwall I read Virgil's II and IV Aeneid with very great pleasure. I hadn't read much Virgil before, except the Georgics, which I read last term at Winchester. I also began, just before coming up here, that extremely beautiful old play, the Supplices. I was sorry to have to leave it, but there is not too much time for reading here…

In January 1917, when barely nineteen, Browne was commissioned into the Black Watch (the 1st Battalion of the Royal Highlanders) and as Lieutenant Browne saw active service on the Western Front. He was hospitalised at one stage, but, unlike several close Winchester friends, saw the war through. In the autumn of 1919 he finally took up his place in Oxford, and there his music blossomed alongside his classical studies. He was a regular participant in concerts and music clubs.

Accordingly, after graduating in classics, he stayed on an extra year to complete a B.Mus., encouraged to do so by the distinguished organist and choirmaster Haldane Campbell Stewart. The cantata which he wrote for this degree – *A Passer-By* (to words by poet laureate Robert Bridges) – still survives in the Bodleian Library. In 1922, at twenty-four, he enrolled at the Royal College of Music, but gave this up to come to Stowe, on the proviso he could also commute to Oxford to pursue a D.Mus. at Magdalen.

* * *

For a few weeks there was more commuting, Philip being temporarily housed in Brookfield (now part of the Royal Latin School) with one or two other masters, driving to Stowe for breakfast at high speed in an old Buick and returning to Buckingham, at equally high speed, late at night. He was allocated a small, damp study under the west colonnade.

Music was woefully under-resourced in 1923. Philip wrote that its development was 'principally a matter of pious hope'. There would be an inevitable period of marking time:

> *The facilities for the performance of instrumental music are as yet quite unavoidably limited: there is no organ; there are seven pianos, only four of which are ordinarily available for practice; and if there were more it is difficult to suggest where they could at the moment be placed... At present only three boys learn the violin...*

Singing, too, had its problems.

> *The voices of over half the school are now in the uncomfortable stage of breaking, so that any singing they indulge in is not only painful but even deleterious.*

He was undaunted, however, by the challenge, looking forward to the time when tunes from Bach's B Minor Mass would oust from Stowe current popular hits like 'Yes! We have No Bananas!' He made a start with a brass band, raised under the auspices of the O.T.C. (forerunner of the C.C.F.). 'There is something about a trombone,' he wrote, 'which appeals to a boy who might view with indifference the prospect of singing the alto part in the chorus of Stanford's *Revenge*.'

From the second term onwards he acquired an accomplished helper, the outstanding organist Sydney Watson, later to run the music at Radley, Winchester and Eton. Early Philip Browne innovations were a Gilbert and Sullivan Club and informal Sunday evening recitals, often given by his friends and visiting celebrities. Philip himself regularly performed, one early concert including piano versions of Rimsky-Korsakov's *Capriccio Espagnol* and Dvořák's 'New World' Symphony. Two of the earliest Stoic pianists, Patrick Savill and Dudley Steynor[9], helped advertise the

---

9   Dudley Steynor, at the age of 87, made two delightful CDs of his favourite piano music. Patrick Savill is commemorated with a bust at the Royal Academy of Music, where he was a long-serving Professor.

new school by playing Schumann duets at a Public Schools concert in London. It took time to create a school orchestra, but there were early concerts from visitors like the Oxford Symphony Orchestra (with Philip Browne on the timpani), conducted by a lifelong friend, his Winchester and Magdalen College contemporary, Guy Warrack.[10]

* * *

Philip's musical activities outside Stowe were considerable There was already a flourishing Buckingham Music Society, and so it was a receptive group which he addressed in September 1923 at the Old Latin School, urging the start of a competitive Buckingham Music Festival, involving outlying villages. The first one, in March 1924, proved a huge success with many hundreds attending.

With the school numbers remaining modest in the first years, Philip was able to head off to Oxford for work on his D.Mus. without too much trouble. In the course of these studies, he wrote a sonata for violin and piano and a viola concerto, both of which, like his cantata, still survive in the Bodleian, though seemingly untouched.

By 1926 Browne was known around the school as 'Pa', the somewhat inappropriate nickname stemming from his initials. That year he introduced the first House Music Competition, offering two sections, vocal (unison and two-part) and instrumental. For the unison song there was a stipulation of a minimum of thirty-five voices and the caveat 'Mere loudness will avail nothing'. An instrumental concert of three items was also to be offered, with a minimum of three participants. The first adjudicator was Guy Warrack; the second, Adrian Boult.

Creation of a school orchestra was a necessarily slow process. Occasional practices took place in unsatisfactory venues like small classrooms and the Marble Hall (noisily sandwiched between two houserooms). The more players there were, the less satisfactory the spaces into which they were crammed; the less players, the less able they were to cope with worthwhile works. It was three years before Pa Browne's orchestra boasted a clarinet or French horn. In 1927 he was advertising for a viola and double-bass prior to the orchestra and choral society combining in two spirited concerts, featuring Coleridge-Taylor's *Hiawatha's Wedding Feast* and Stanford's *Revenge*. Improvement was steady. In 1928 *The Stoic* stated:

---

10   A highly distinguished musician, Guy Warrack conducted the BBC Scottish Symphony Orchestra many
     years. His son was the music critic John Warrack.

The orchestra showed a distinct advance on last year, especially in the wind department. Mr Watson's 'Miniature', much the hardest of the four pieces, was creditably played and vociferously encored. The March from Scipio was also encored and provided the biggest noise of the evening, though it could have done with a few trumpets and trombones to add brilliance and heaviness.

Pa Browne himself accompanied three other masters (Ian Clarke, Ivor Cross and Sydney Watson) in the singing of two part-songs.

The early Common Room contained any number of enthusiastic singers, Pa encouraging many of them to perform with him locally in their spare time. By 1924, for example, he and five others (Cross, Haworth, Neville, Clarke and Granger) were putting on an evening entertainment at Tingewick. Ivor Cross was the chief soloist, impressing as ever with Stanford's sea songs ('Drake's Drum' always drawing huge applause) and Schumann's 'Two Grenadiers'. Any number of different part-songs were offered, from quintets like Purcell's 'Sound the Trumpet' to a charming trio from *Iolanthe*. Pa's several piano solos ranged between Percy Grainger's 'Shepherd's Hey' and Paradies' Toccata in A. ('Mr Browne quite charmed his hearers with his excellent playing.') Pa would likewise often slip away to give organ recitals.

* * *

Central to his job were the religious services. For the first term Pa had worked with Ernest Earle in establishing the school's routine, playing an upright Brinsmead piano in the gallery (the first third of the Aurelian Room) of the lovely Cedar Chapel. By the second term, when he started working with the chaplain Edward Habershon, numbers had risen to around 190, so the services during the week were held in the Music Room. Here the Brinsmead proved inadequate, sounding to Pa 'like a band of mandolins and combs, giving more pain than pleasure even to the most devoted'. For the longer Sunday services, Stowe Church was used in two sittings. A year later, they moved into the new gym (a wooden building, meant to be only temporary, but surviving until 1978). There the unsatisfactory Brinsmead was replaced by a second-hand Buhl and, eventually, a Bechstein Concert Grand. When the gym was being used for exams, Pa was kept very busy with a whole series of staggered services in the Cedar Chapel (not converted to secular use until 1929).

* * *

Pa coached cricket and played it whenever he could. In 1923 he naturally featured in The Masters' team versus The School. Opening the innings with Ivor Cross, he top-scored with a modest 17. By 1924, however, Pa was a central figure as the Stowe Masters played against several local villages as well as the Christ Church Warrigals, the Trinity Triflers and Buckingham. In 1925 Pa was playing for Whittlebury against the lst XI, he and Cross this time putting on 50 for the lst wicket, though *The Stoic* dismissed this effort as 'a stodgy start'. He also turned out against the school that year for Viscount Curzon's Lords and Commons XI. Every year, right up to the Second World War, he would make his way to Oxford for the cricket at the Balliol College Teachers' Courses. 'He was quite a useful batsman,' remembered one colleague, 'and usually made 50.'

Pa was a keen golfer, too, often representing The Masters. In 1924 there were four holes between the South Front, the Rotondo and the Octagon and another five on the Hawkwell field. *The Stoic* reported that 'the greens at the first, third and fourth holes have been made up, while other greens are beginning to respond to assiduous rolling'.

* * *

As a classicist Pa was outstanding, though his teaching was necessarily limited. When two young members of the department (Timberlake and Simmonds) edited for publication an ancient Greek satyr play, Euripides' *The Cyclops*, they naturally turned to Pa to give it scholarly scrutiny. A talk he gave in 1927 to the Classical Society, deferentially reviewed in *The Stoic*, showed his immense expertise in Latin verse composition.

But above all, he was a scholarly all-rounder, someone 'for whom there were few things in heaven and earth that did not come within the range of his inquiring and amused scrutiny'. Mathematical and philosophical problems entertained him. He was also a top bridge player, and, in the evenings would welcome enthusiastic Stoics. When Granville Carr, as a new boy, sought him out about joining the Choral Society, he was in for a surprise. 'Went to Dr Browne's room after dinner,' he wrote in his diary. 'He showed us some bridge problems. We then had voice trials...'

* * *

Pa seemed so at ease with everything that it was surely a surprise when, in December 1928 after five and half years at Stowe, he left to become a school inspector. So, too, did another of the Common Room's original team of nine, the first Head of English, Francis Arnold, great-grandson of the famous Rugby headmaster. Both would from time to time revisit Stowe together, so they would seem to have left amicably, though *The Stoic*'s farewell to the pair lacked detailed endorsement:

> *The school will be permanently the poorer for the loss of Mr Arnold and Dr Browne. They had become part of the place, which they had done so much to form, and when they have left us we shall realise the spirit of 1923 can never be quite recaptured without their presence.*

The comment suggests that the school had changed in atmosphere by 1928, and perhaps the lost 'spirit of 1923' partly accounted for the thirty-year-old Pa's decision to be a schoolmaster no longer. One can only guess at what that 'spirit' was. An atmosphere of debonair make-do, where routine was embellished by style and wit? The primacy of the entertaining and the unusual over the predictable and the mundane?

Pa's dislike of compulsory religious services, not least those held in a gloomy gym, may also have played a part in the decision never to work again as a Head of Music. Added to this, of course, was the presence of a manically evangelical governor, the Revd. Percy Warrington, no doubt upset that the music was in the untrustworthy hands of a Wykhamist with high church sympathies, justifying a close watching brief.

Pa's last contribution to *The Stoic*, a highly bizarre one, offers a clue in this direction. Pa, it seems, had been asked for an overview of the hymns and psalms during his time – requested, perhaps, to impress the watchful Percy Warrington. It was not the kind of thing to delight someone who preferred the pleasures of life to its dull minutiae, and, in a piece surely loaded with irony, Pa supplies hugely detailed facts and figures, plucked, one suspects, out of thin air, yet presented with earnestness. His opening sets the tone:

> *The first chapel service was held on Saturday May 12th, 1923, at 6.30 pm. The first hymn sung by the school was no. 481, 'Through the night of doubt and sorrow' which has since been sung 28 times, up to the time of going to press...*

Pa then lists the eleven most frequently played hymns. 'Abide with Me', 'Praise, My Soul' and 'Soldiers of Christ, Arise' share top place 'with 31 performances apiece'. There follows a long list of the hymns sung 'with perceptibly greater heartiness than the rest', his own setting of 'Christian, Dost Thou See Them' notably high up. He similarly details the psalms, from the most popular (no. 90) downwards. Information follows on the various kinds of hymn books used, the Church Hymnal having been supplemented 'by a collection known as *Cantata Stoica*, the first of which, 'City of God', was sung on the evening of 8 May, 1927'.

Somehow, in his five and a half years Pa never got round to forming a Chapel Choir, and this, it seems, had been a disappointment to some crusty members of Common Room, for the article's final paragraph, surely written with a smile, offers the vexed topic a cheerfully specious apologia:

The main answer as to why there is no chapel choir is that, wherever one exists, so too does a natural tendency for the congregation to listen to it rather than sing itself and that a deterioration in the congregational singing would be catastrophic. Reasonably good church choirs are to be found in most of our towns; a good volume of congregational singing, however, is rare, even today, in the south of England. Surely it is better to play cricket oneself, however incompetently, though it be on the Bourbon field, than spend one's afternoons watching Hendren and Hearne, or even Barratt and Constantine, batting...[11]

Whatever the cause of his departure, Stowe had lost a superb musician. A contemporary at Oxford, Thomas Armstrong (later to become the distinguished President of the Royal Academy of Music) would later write of him:

Philip Browne was a most unusual and gifted man. His intellect in all respects was powerful and incisive; his talent for music was near-genius. He could play at sight almost any pianoforte piece ever written; he was a splendid accompanist, and could give on the pianoforte a wonderful impression of a full score. He was one of the best amateur percussion players of his day; and his own compositions showed a genuine creative impulse with great sense of beauty... He was wonderful with young people and had a tender insight into their difficulties

---

11   Four great cricketers of the day, Fred Barratt and Learie Constantine being known for their hitting.

and problems… This sympathy made him a fine teacher, particularly of problem pupils.

In music Browne could have reached an eminence in any one of several fields if it had been in his character to become a specialist, but the strict concentration of his interests into one channel would have been a denial of his nature…

* * *

Pa returned for a while to the family home in Richmond. It was a good base from which to start inspecting Surrey secondary schools. He was back helping run the three-day Buckingham Music Festival in March 1929, dazzling everyone with two Brahms intermezzos and some of MacDowell's Sea Pieces. 'The delicacy and sureness of his performance,' commented the *Buckingham Advertiser*, 'is always a delight to hear.'

In 1930, on his father's death, Pa and his mother moved down to Cornwall, buying the eighteenth-century Old Mansion House on the quayside in Truro. There he was to spend the majority of his fifteen years as a school inspector, touring the county happily, encouraging hard-pressed teaching staff and exhorting young people to love, and make, music. He had a favourite Latin tag for what education was all about: *Scientiam vitae dulcedinis carpebant.* Teachers were to 'garner a knowledge of the sweet taste of life'. Headmasters in Cornwall would later write emotionally of the deep affection in which he was held all over the county.

The job allowed him time for his own musical pursuits and a busy social life. He was soon a great friend of the Bishop and regularly playing the organ in Truro Cathedral. He wrote a small book about Brahms' symphonies, published by the OUP (1933), and a charming work for piano and clarinet, 'A Truro Maggot'. Written in Truro, it was based on an eighteenth-century air, 'The Earl of Salisbury's Maggot,' a 'maggot' in those days meaning a whim. The leading clarinettist of the day, Jack Thurston, enjoyed great success with his recording of it. A number of Pa's songs were also published – notably 'Rags and Bones' (1930) and 'The Lamb' (1941). Several modern choral recordings have featured other music he wrote in Truro.

When war came, Pa at once volunteered for the Home Guard, serving as a Company Commander until 1944. His mother had died by then. So, too, his brother at Winchester. A promotion in the Inspectorate took him briefly north, his departure from Truro being marked by a 'Dr Browne Fund' set up for the relief of needy teachers and their dependants.

In 1946 came Pa's final move, a return to London as the Chief Inspector of Secondary Education for the Ministry, work for which he was awarded the CBE. For much of this time he had a flat in Blomfield Court in Little Venice. He continued to write music, reflecting the pastoral manner of Finzi.[12]

He was still coming back to Buckingham after the war, to help the town's Music Festival, and in 1950 was a guest of honour at the 21st event. He was present, too, at J.F.'s funeral on 11 May 1954. There in Chapel he would have used the latest edition of *Cantata Stoica*, the book of hymns which he and J.F. had first concocted in 1927. It would have amused rather than irritated him, that *Cantata Stoica* was regularly to be attributed to his successor.

* * *

Pa was to die on 4 March 1961, aged 62, after only two years of retirement. He had been living at 12 Redcliffe Square, Kensington, and was in the middle of a book on Anthony Trollope. He had attended a Stowe Speech Day in 1958 with Francis Arnold, thirty years on from their joint decision to go into the Inspectorate.

There was a large gathering of friends at his funeral service at Golder's Green Crematorium, taken by Canon Adam Fox, a Fellow of Pa's old Oxford college, Magdalen. The organ was played by Sir Thomas Armstrong and the former Stowe music master, Sydney Watson. Guy Warrack was there, both as friend and chairman of the Sherlock Holmes Society, another of Pa's later interests. There were many representatives of the Inspectorate as well as the English Bridge Union, and British Bridge League. Representing Stowe was Patrick Hunter, whose friendship with Pa dated all the way back to their shared schooldays at Winchester.

A few of his many eccentricities were affectionately listed at the time of his death: a habit of playing patience between courses at restaurants; a passionate love of both soup and rice pudding that could lead at lunchtime, if rice pudding happened to be off the menu, to his starting and finishing with soup; his handing out of rolls from a paper bag to his guests at the Athenaeum because he disliked the club bread; the preference for books over pyjamas, if going on holiday and

---

12 His published works included 'The Snowy Breasted Pearl', an old Irish tune, arranged for viola and piano (1947); Bourrée (from J.S. Bach's Violoncello suite no. 4) for viola and piano (1953); 'David of the White Rock', arranged for viola and piano (1953); and a (Stainer & Browne) choral arrangement of 'Love Divine' (1956).

pressed for suitcase space; and a lifelong dislike of going to bed before one in the morning…

Philip Austin 'Pa' Browne remains an elusive figure, aptly symbolised, perhaps, by that concerto in Oxford that might tell us more about him, if only it were performed. In the meantime, we can at least salute a cultured and discriminating musician, who spent his days encouraging others to 'garner a knowledge of the sweet taste of life'.

4

HERBERT NEVILLE

The first Head of Art, whose wife became a legend too
Stowe, 1923-34

Herbert 'Bertie' Waterford Neville was a successful and much-liked Head of Art, whose eleven Stowe years were to be the highlight of his professional life. He was a quiet and modest character, unphased by the school's rough and ready nature in the 1920s, including the lack of any purpose-built art facilities. Like Pop Earle, he was forty-nine when he joined the other newcomers on 11 May 1923.

His sunny and unruffled personality probably owed much to his early life in a Northumberland rectory. He was born in 1873, the son of Hastings Neville, the Rector of St Michael's in the village of Ford, a few miles from Berwick-on-Tweed. He was educated locally and at home by his parents, who enthusiastically encouraged his artistic talent.

Bertie's unusual middle name, Waterford, stemmed from his illustrious godmother, the local lady of the manor, Louisa Beresford, the Marchioness of Waterford. The Marchioness was a highly talented Pre-Raphaelite water-colourist who had modelled for Millais and enjoyed a long friendship with Ruskin. As a boy, Bertie grew up beside the sweeping, life-size Biblical scenes she had painted in the local school hall.

In 1893, aged twenty, he left Northumberland for Hertfordshire and a startling new experience, studying at the art school founded at Bushey by the distinguished and forward-thinking painter Sir Hubert von Herkomer. It was based in 'Lululaund', a four-storey castle Herkomer had just built in Romanesque Revival style, the name celebrating his late wife, Lulu, the interior decorated with his own elaborate wood carvings. The whole of the castle's interior could be most dramatically illuminated, for Herkomer was also a leading expert on theatre lighting, using new-fangled electricity.

A formidable figure who did not brook poor work or laziness, Herkomer was full of new ideas. There was to be no dull learning by rote, no continual copying of classical masters and no boring examinations. The liberation of the imagination was all-important. Under Herkomer's influence Bertie emerged as a confident portrait and landscape painter, well-rounded culturally and alive to the latest ideas in the arts.

* * *

After a year's study in fin-de-siècle Paris frequented by Toulouse-Lautrec, Degas and Renoir, Bertie's early years as an artist were somewhat anticlimactic. He was set up in studios in Newcastle, supplementing the irregular sale of his work from occasional exhibitions by teaching, sometimes as art tutor in grand country houses, sometimes in small private schools. By 1904, when just into his thirties, he was back home, painting the attractive landscapes around Ford and occasionally exhibiting work at the Royal Academy. From 1911 he was based at Grassington, near Skipton in the north Yorkshire dales, again augmenting the sale of his water colours with work as a tutor to the landed gentry. One of his closest Yorkshire friends was the successful novelist Halliwell Sutcliffe.

Though thirty-eight at the outbreak of the First World War, Bertie tried to enlist in Kitchener's army. Twice rejected because of his age, he eventually talked his way into the Army Service Corps, serving as a staff sergeant with the New Forest Volunteer Force, as it operated the transport systems delivering ammunition, food and equipment to the troops on the front line in France. He was also attached for a time to the 55th Remount Squadron, training horses for the Western Front.

Settling on the Hampshire coast after the war, he resumed the double life of artist and art tutor. 'Herbert W. Neville gives instruction in DRAWING and PAINTING,' ran an advertisement in the *Western Gazette* in 1921. 'For particulars, apply Tile Cottage, Lymington'. There he might well have stayed for the rest of his life, for he was already in his late forties, when, in early 1923, while running a painting holiday course at Rye, he fell in love with one of his students. The lively Marjorie Stewart

Gardner, the daughter of a retired doctor, was a highly talented artist. Among the many interests they shared was one for cars. Marjorie had learnt to drive at an early age, her father being one of Bournemouth's pioneer motorists. During the First World War, as a Sergeant Major in the Women's Army Corps, she had driven ambulances and ridden motor bikes. Despite immediate mutual affection, however, there was no question of marriage, for Bertie's income was too irregular to secure Marjorie. Fortunately, a new public school needed an art master. Inspired by Marjorie, he interviewed well, and in May 1923 set out in an old car, determined to prove that he could hold down a steady job and support her.

* * *

The photograph of Roxburgh and his nine masters that May shows Bertie as an avuncular, bespectacled figure with a bushy moustache and grey flecks in his centrally-parted hair. He and the Bursar, the only two not wearing gowns, flank the back row, standing a little detached from the others, as if in deference to those with academic qualifications. Thanks to the progressive Herkomer, Bertie was lacking in these. In the masters' lists his name would only be followed by the initials NSA, albeit, in its own way, an impressive endorsement. Encouraged by his friend Algernon Talmadge, who for a time ran an art school at St Ives, Bertie had spent periods down in Cornwall during his peripatetic years, eventually becoming a member of the Newlyn Society of Artists.

After a necessarily chaotic beginning, Bertie was soon teaching in a basic classroom, called, rather grandly, 'the Drawing School'. There he initiated an Arts Club as an extra-curricular activity (with Ivor Cross as his Vice-President). Participants paid a sizeable sum, half-a-crown per term, helping secure a steady supply of *The Studio* magazine.[13] 'Wood carving tools can be borrowed,' wrote Bertie, introducing his new club in *The Stoic*, 'and modelling paste and tools, drawing boards, easels and water colour boxes.' It would soon be possible to take up sketching, colour-block printing and oil painting. Indeed, the Club would do what it could to help members to take up any branch of art they wished.

Immediately popular, Bertie was soon organising regular Arts Club trips outside

---

13　An influential magazine of fine and applied art, which had championed the Arts and Crafts and Art Nouveau movements and was doing the same for modernism in the 1920s and 1930s.

the grounds, Oxford being an early choice. In the write-up of one such trip, he was gently urging on his young artists a discriminating eye:

> *I believe it was Ruskin who said that the High in Oxford was the most beautiful street in Europe. Whether we agree with this or not, it is interesting to discover under what aspect it looks its best and from what place in the street you get the finest view. For my part, I think that looking down towards Carfax from a little distance below Magdalen is the view, and the time should be just after sunset, when the towers begin to look dark against the sky...*

The next issue, he was writing in similar vein after a sketching trip to the splendid church at Hillesden:

> *A fine afternoon in winter is not the worst of time to choose for seeing a lonely church among wide, bare fields. Interesting as the building is, with many beautiful details, its position is solitary, and both it and the surrounding traces of the once great house of the Dentons[14] are better seen by the dim light of the rising moon than in the full sunlight of a summer's day.*

* * *

Bertie's other official job was to re-stock and run the old library. To do so he had largely to rely on donations, but his *Stoic* reports were quietly optimistic:

> *The library has suffered dispersal twice in its history, and for a third time the shelves are now gradually being filled. They are capable of holding 20,000 volumes, and we hope once more to form a library of books which shall be worthy of the noble room that will contain them ... As a building, the library is one of the finest of its kind in England. The modern furniture harmonises well; it is handsome – indeed, luxurious.*

Several parents in 1923 were particularly generous. The father of the future speed record-holder at Brooklands, Oliver Bertram, had filled whole shelves with 'a beautifully

---

14   The house of Alexander Denton, a Royalist, had featured significantly in the English Civil War.

bound collection of old books, many of them rare and valuable'. The School's governors had donated two hundred books, augmented by the Revd. Percy Warrington's five volumes of 'The Book of Nature Study'. Roxburgh's many donations included 'two very rare pamphlets of the Eighteenth Century on the Gardens of Stowe and Stowe House' (probably Seeley's guides), a set of the Aldine edition of English poets, Addison's complete works and two volumes on the Antiquities of Buckinghamshire. The Vicar of Stowe Church, the long-serving Revd. Clements, contributed in similar vein. Bertie, as the enthusiastic recipient of much heavy learning, responded gratefully, while not disguising his hope that some lighter reading might also be donated.

After only two terms, he was able to state rhapsodically:

The Library no longer wears the rather bleak, wintry aspect of emptiness; the brown, bare shelves are gradually becoming coloured with the blossoms of literature. Tints of many shades, green, grey and blue, of sunset and orange – gleams of scarlet and gold – are bursting out along the shelves.

There was also the news that Kipling had become the Library's most popular author: 'It was said recently that he had moulded the thought of a generation. He is certainly moulding the thoughts of a second, if that be so.' By December 1924 Bertie was writing that almost all of the closed bookcases were full, but elsewhere there was still plenty of room.

His report that year illustrated his strong antiquarian interests. He had found 'amongst the old parchments' in the library 'two manuscript volumes'. One was a Household Book, beginning in 1674, carefully listing all the housekeeping bills. He clearly found it fascinating:

We regret to see that vast numbers of larks were consumed. There is a very full list of wines: claret, sherry, white wine, champagne, port, Rhenish and sack. The wines are entered as coming from the cellars and butteries of Stowe, so possibly the book has come from some other house of the Temples.

… In this somewhat severe volume only two names appear; even the housekeeper (or butler) has only signed it by initials; above them we find 'Finis Huius Libri – 1679' Imagine a twentieth-century housekeeper's book ending with a remark in Latin! One name is that of one Thos. Hall and the other is of 'Bridget ye cooke'…

* * *

By this time Bertie had at last managed to convince Marjorie's family of his dependability and they had married at Lymington on 10 April 1924, when Bertie was fifty and Marjorie thirty-four. It was the first Stowe Common Room marriage. A colleague duly noted the event in *The Stoic* with cheerful male chauvinism:

> *He had the warmest good wishes of the school on the day when he took this bold step, and since we have come to know Mrs Neville he has had our congratulations too.*

There was, of course, no married accommodation at all on the campus, so the couple ended up near the Corinthian Arch, in the New Inn. 'New' was hardly apt. It had been built in the late eighteenth-century to accommodate visitors to the Landscape Gardens and had not been lived in for sixty years. There, however, they spent ten very happy years. Their two sons, Michael and Martin, were both to be born at the New Inn, the Godfathers including J.F., the writer Halliwell Sutcliffe and artist Harry Fidler (a former Herkomer student with strong Newlyn connections).

In the New Inn the Nevilles happily found themselves reliving the Victorian age. Martin recalled:

> *There were no modernisations whatsoever. Marjorie had to pull water by hand from a cast iron pump in the yard and would polish the broad oak floors of her drawing room with halved coconut shells. The kitchen initially was a corrugated iron lean-to…*

Early on, Bertie's financial anxieties led to their travelling everywhere by donkey and cart. The return journey to Buckingham accordingly took for ever. Marjorie, who had expensive tastes and was not best pleased, soon ensured less work for the donkey by the acquisition of the first of a number of cars.

Marjorie impressed with her confident, no-nonsense approach to the male chauvinist bastion. Aided by her new best friend, Fanny Parish, the legendary, long-serving matron of Grafton, she set about tidying up the old inn to give it a new lease of life as the School's second tuck shop. Having cleaned the place up, the pair created a charming teahouse, largely for Stoics when games were over. It was soon dubbed 'the Nevillery' and became a much-valued port of call. Marjorie and Fanny's own delightful concoctions – wonderful fudges and exotic coconut ices to the fore – became the talk of the school.

* * *

By 1925 Bertie and his students were giving their modest 'Drawing School' premises a boost, removing the partitions, scrubbing everything scrub-able, colour-washing the walls, staining the beams and whitewashing the ceiling. It was soon abuzz with 'modelling, taking casts, water-colour sketching, wood-carving and pen-and-ink work'. Not long afterwards Bertie was allocated as his 'Art Room' the large central classroom on the first floor of today's Adam Block, approached by a staircase from Stone Yard. He celebrated by putting an extra-large painting of his own on the ceiling, and, in 1930, his student committee provided an even more modern ambience, decorating the room in cream and red.

Parallel to his Art Club was the Arts Club over which he presided for a time as President. Many lectures, usually illustrated by lantern slides, were given by colleagues. Ivor Cross held forth on Architecture; Patrick Hunter on Greek Sculpture; Martin MacLaughlin on Pompeii; Charles Spencer on Italian Painting; John Saunders on the History of English Folk Dancing; Anthony Ireland (Baron von Simunich) on William Blake; and left-wing historian George Rudé on his recent visit to Russia. Bertie's own lecture on 'Some Modern Movements in Art' was reviewed in *The Stoic* by the Club secretary (and future poet and writer) James Reeves:

> *He touched on Velasquez and El Greco and took us through the French classical and romantic movement. Constable, Crome, Turner and Cotman were given as examples of modern English painters, while the Pre-Raphaelites and the Dutch School were also described. The President concluded a very interesting paper with some illuminating remarks on the more recent movements – Cubism, Dadaism, Vorticism and Post-Impressionism.*

In 1931 Bertie spoke on a lifelong love, the Pre-Raphaelites. His own enthusiasms, however, were catholic. When giving a talk on 'The Study of Pictures', he appealed to members to broaden their tastes – 'An Artist's faith should include Cubism and other heresies' – and exhorted them not to give themselves away to particular schools. 'Always approach Art in the spirit of the *student* rather than the *critic*,' he urged.

* * *

Bertie continued arranging Art Club trips outside Stowe. An expedition to Oxford in 1925 was particularly interesting in that it was a joint venture with the Photographic Club, run by the delightfully eccentric Edward Whitaker. Bertie drove several Stoics to Oxford in a Crossley, loaned to him by Roxburgh. The rest of the 'imposing cavalcade' consisted of 'a large charabanc, Ivor Cross's car and Edward Whitaker's motorbike and side-car'. Bertie enthusiastically led a small party around New College and the Ashmolean, though a comment in *The Stoic* suggests something of a party atmosphere:

> *If the Muse of Art had for a while to bow to the subtle sirens in the teashops, and if the call of the river proved too clear to be denied even by the most inveterate artists, well, perhaps we can put it down to the heat.*

Bertie pressed on. In the summer of 1928 there was an ambitious Arts Club expedition to Stratford-upon-Avon, Warwick Castle and Kenilworth Castle. Transport was largely supplied by members of the Common Room, leaving only a few of the less fortunate to travel 'in the Finmere bus'. In March 1929 no less than fifty Stoics were taken to the Royal Academy's exhibition of Dutch Art.

Summer visits to the Royal Academy became annual treats. In 1931 there was one exhibit of considerable Stowe significance, a first sighting of Walpole House. Fielding Dodd's drawings of the proposed building excited 'much interest and a good deal of admiration'. In his review of the 1932 Summer Exhibition, Bertie found Walter Sickert's 'Raising of Lazarus' curiously arresting – 'very fine in colour, and, had it been finished, it might have been a masterpiece! But the artist never does finish a picture!' He also liked Lutyens's designs for Liverpool Cathedral and Lancelot Glasson's 'The Young Rower', a painting of a rowing girl in shorts.

* * *

It only took a couple of years before the school magazine started including illustrations of Stoics' art work, the very first being a lovely pen and ink drawing of the South Front portico, steps, and balustrade by James Reeves in December 1925. The following issue featured a charming lino-cut of a ploughman by Reeves and two further lino-cuts by the future architect Andrew Carden.

By the end of the decade *The Stoic* was being impressively visually embellished. In July 1928 a special supplement featured Laurence Whistler's superb scale drawing of the South Front (and also a one-page Doric Arch); in 1929 came his Palladian Bridge; in 1930 the Temple of Venus. Another Grenvillian, the future modernist architect James Melvin, inspired by Whistler, produced fine scale drawings of the Rotondo, the Boycott Pavilion, the Corinthian Arch and the Museum.

The annual exhibitions on Speech Days were, of course, important occasions for Bertie, and he was lucky that, through Laurence Whistler, he twice enlisted his elder brother Rex to come and adjudicate. The young Rex Whistler, who was deeply influenced by the beauty of the Stowe grounds, 'spent the whole afternoon in the Art Room' in 1928. Among the prizes he awarded was one to his sixteen-year-old brother. (Laurence's last year at Stowe was marked by the precocious publication of his first book, *Children of Hertha and Other Poems*, with four attractive cartouches by Rex as well as a glorious title page.) In 1930 Rex was back again. 'Mr Whistler,' noted *The Stoic*, 'considered the standard of work high, but remarked on the fewness of entries in the Arts Club section.' James Melvin's overview similarly had reservations:

Tea was served in the Upper Arts Room, where the exhibition was showing. The room had been decorated with plants and flowers and for once had shod its unkempt 'arty' appearance. As in all Private Views, the pictures had less importance than the tea, and the conversation was more about the sports, the crowds and the latest fashions than about the pictures.

* * *

Bertie himself was a prolific artist all his life. Several of his competent line drawings adorned *The Stoic* in the early 1930s. He was probably at his happiest, however, painting landscapes in water colour. He and Marjorie were for ever motoring around the country in the school holidays, sketchbooks and easels to hand. Bertie's paintings not only featured at the Royal Academy and Paris Salon but the Royal Institute of Painters in Water Colours and in many provincial galleries.

When in the Summer of 1928 Bertie had a water colour of Richmond Castle hung in the Paris Salon, the official art exhibition of the Académie des Beaux-Arts, *The Stoic* proudly reprinted the summary of his skills as *un paysagiste* (a landscape artist) supplied by Edward Hart Dyke, a Stowe modern linguist, for the programme:

Fidéle à la nature et fidéle aux examples de ses maîtres (Cézanne, Courbet et Constable), il est demeuré le paysagiste, finement observateur et finement ému, qui cherche à s'exprimer soi-même dans le cadre des harmonies naturelles.

Subsequent paintings of his displayed in Paris included two studies of Corfe Castle; Dorset's 'Eggerdon Down'; and 'A Norfolk Landscape'.

* * *

His retirement, at sixty, was prefaced and seriously marred by ill-health. It seems he had a bad fall when skating on one of the lakes, resulting in the need for a wheelchair. Further complications set in. *The Stoic* writes of an 'illness overtaking' him, some form of serious wasting disease, appearing first in his legs. When he left Stowe, very quietly, in the summer of 1934, he was still in a wheelchair.

His departure had been prefaced that May by a poignant four-day sale of the many paintings that had accumulated at the New Inn. Held at the Masonic Hall in Buckingham's Hunter Street, it made for a massive exhibition of places Bertie had loved and haunted: the harbours of Poole and Lymington, villages and farms in Somerset, the Cotswolds, the Fens, the Welsh mountains, Ludlow and Wharfedale. There were many local paintings, too.

At Stowe Bertie had established his subject with charm and efficiency, contriving to make the Old Art Room the centre of the School's artistic existence 'Many Stoics,' stressed one valediction, 'owe to Herbert Neville a new interest and a new sense of values, and some owe to him a new course of life.' This achievement was all the greater in that it had been made without a purpose-built Art School.

Ironically, he had spent the last two years advising on the very building that his successors, Robin and Doreen Watt, would use so effectively. The eleven-year endeavours of Bertie Neville would start fading almost as soon as that admirable pair entered the new building in the Spring of 1935.

By this time the Neville family had moved down to Milford-on-Sea, four miles from Lymington. Their new home, Bray Cottage in West Road, was a bungalow looking out on the Solent. A number of marine artists lived nearby and for a while Bertie tried to paint. Edward Habershon, Stowe's first chaplain, visited him a year after the move, reporting afterwards to J.F.:

We saw the Nevilles the other day. They have a delightful bungalow, just the very thing for them. Bertie looked well and is completely fit above the knees. He is trying all sorts of treatment and is himself confident that he will be well in a year or less, but his wife says he is incurable.

Bertie battled on with his infirmities, but was to die in the Milford Cottage Hospital a year later, on 25 August 1936, of pneumonia, brought about by general 'muscular atrophy'. He was sixty-two. He and Marjorie had been a popular couple, and the Parish Church, where Ernest Earle was to be buried eleven years later, was full for the funeral. Ivor Cross, always a strong supporter of the Arts Club, was among the mourners, representing J.F. The service ended with comments specially written by Marjorie. She concluded:

He was the bravest of the brave. Day by day he was always the same, cheerful, happy and very grateful. He never let any of us feel he was an invalid. The quick end was a Victor's Crown. He never knew what a terrible ordeal awaited him, had he lived longer... Sweet slumbers, Herbert, and a happy waking!

J.F.'s obituary in *The Stoic* likewise made much of the patience and humour that had never deserted him: 'He retained to the end the qualities which made him so beloved at Stowe.'

* * *

Marjorie stayed on in Bray Cottage, ensuring a good education and start in life for Michael and Martin, only seven and twelve at the time of their father's death. Later on, in 1946, she moved to Corfe Castle. On her death – at nearly ninety – she was buried next to Bertie, back in Milford-on-Sea. She had lived long enough to see her multi-talented granddaughter, Sophie Neville, star in the 1974 film of *Swallows and Amazons*.

In auction rooms, from time to time, Bertie's paintings still come up for sale, attracting modest prices. He received a mention, too, in 2010, when the Art School was impressively redeveloped and refurbished. In 2013 came a splendidly enduring tribute. The National Trust, on opening their new visitor centre at the New Inn, saluted both Bertie and Marjorie by naming their smart cafeteria 'The Nevillery'.

5

IAN CLARKE

Founder of Grenville & Walpole, forester & rugby Blue
Stowe 1923-39

There is a small stone memorial near the entrance to the Bourbon. It stands at the top of the line of trees flanking the approach, and though it has been there for over eighty years, its inscription still reads clearly:

> This avenue of Red Cedars
> was planted in 1940 to the memory of
> I.A. Clarke (1890-1939), Housemaster,
> who loved Stowe and cared
> especially for its trees

Ian Clarke had perhaps been Roxburgh's most inspired acquisition back in May 1923. For a school responsible for historic gardens and parkland. the presence of a trained and experienced forester was a huge asset. He was also a devoted sportsman, a former Oxford rugby Blue, who would coach the 1st XV many years and be in charge of all school games. The whole Bourbon sports ground would be planned and created by him, including the planting and after-care of the 'Jubilee' and 'Coronation' shelter belts of trees. Shortly before his premature death, he would be planning an avenue of red cedars running down to the ha-ha, little thinking that they would be planted in his memory.

He possessed staunch dependability as well as 'the fine appearance and the dignity which claim leadership as their due'. It made him an obvious choice, in September 1923, to become Grenville's first Housemaster. Eleven years later, he would be similarly entrusted with the start of the newly-built Walpole. He was a man of much self-belief, not lightly to be crossed, a stern Scotsman, brought up in a devout family committed to muscular Christianity. Like his fellow housemasters of 1923, Ivor Cross and Richard Haworth, he was also a product of the First World War trenches, possessing a consequent missionary zeal. Without his 'stubborn common sense and unchangeability', Stowe in its earliest years might even have lost its way.

* * *

Ian Anderson Clarke was born and brought up in Aberdeen. His middle name honoured his aristocratic mother who came from the distinguished Anderson family. His father, an Aberdeen headmaster, was, at the time of his son's birth in 1890, shortly to become a Lecturer in Education at Aberdeen University. It was a family of high achievers. One of Ian's sisters, for example, was to take a First at Cambridge and become a Headmistress.

Ian was educated at Aberdeen Grammar School and Aberdeen University, emerging with a Bsc in Agriculture, but sport was always his forte. In 1912 he won the Scottish (120 Yards) Hurdles. Two years followed at Christ Church, Oxford, where he studied for a Diploma in Forestry, achieved a half-blue in athletics and, in December 1913, became a rugby blue. As a member of the Oxford scrum, he played his Varsity Match at the Queen's Club before 15,000 people.

The Great War interrupted his studies. For the past four years, in his university vacations he had served in the local territorials as a private in the Aberdeen Highlanders. Accordingly, in September 1914 he was gazetted Lieutenant in the 4th Battalion of the Gordon Highlanders. In February 1915, aged twenty-four, he crossed to France, joining the 3rd Division of the Eighth Brigade. By March he was in the front-line trenches, fighting at Bellewaarde and Hooge, where, that June, he was wounded for the first time. By October Captain Clarke was back in the trenches again, only to be wounded a second time. He returned to the Western Front in 1916, serving in a Machine Gun Corps with the 51st Highland Division in the four bloodiest months on the Somme, participating in attacks on High Wood, Thiepval and Beaumont Hamel. In 1917, Major Clarke and his machine gunners fought in the offensives at Arras, Ypres (the battles of Pilckem Ridge and the Menin Road Ridge) and Cambrai, Ian's exploits ending with severe wounds, the worst yet received, that enforced long hospitalisation. In January 1918 he insisted on being allowed to return to France, only this time, to his frustration, he was employed as an instructor behind the front lines. J.F. was later to meet some of the men who had served under Ian in the First World War. They spoke in awe of his bravery and pre-eminence as a leader.

With the advent of peace he returned to Oxford to complete his Forestry Diploma. Although his wounds would prevent him from playing rugby ever again, he helped coach the university and the college teams. In 1920 he started work as a District Officer of the Forestry Commission in north-east Scotland.

* * *

At thirty-two, Ian was one of the older of J.F.'s nine original masters. He had no teaching experience, of course, but in 1923 that would seem almost to have been a recommendation. J.F.'s confidence in him was shown in his role as the escort of the large party of pupils coming up from London on 11 May. The *Buckingham Advertiser* reported:

> *Quite a number of persons assembled on the front of the passenger station at Buckingham on Friday to witness the arrival of the boys for Stowe School. Mr I.A. Clarke, one of the Masters, had proceeded by train earlier in the day to Euston and accompanied the boys, who were accommodated with special carriages on the 4.15 train from Euston, and which were slipped at Bletchley and attached to the ordinary train for the Banbury branch and arrived at Buckingham shortly after six o'clock.*
>
> *Some of the boys, who numbered about ninety, carried cricket bats. Two large lorries were filled with bicycles and luggage. The boys entered two charabancs which had been specially engaged from Oxford by the White Hart Hotel, and the latter were also running for the first time their own motor bus.*
>
> *As they passed the celebrated Stowe Avenue, they saw it to the best possible effect, the trees being clothed in their spring and varied-hued foliage. The Union Jack floated from the top of the Corinthian Arch...*

Ian Clarke's busy first day was not yet over. He had a certain amount of umpiring to do:

Cricket was enjoyed on the vastly-improved level situated on the north front of the School, but the game was interrupted by a hail-storm.

Ian's favourite exhortation of 'Be thorough!' was soon echoing round the classrooms. From the first he had 'an undisputed sway' over his forms, but it was leavened by 'a dry sense of humour'. By his thoroughness and enthusiasm he was to help many generations of Stoics understand the intricacies of Latin. He also taught Forestry classes for the first twelve years. As form master he began with the most junior groups of all, but soon became a fixture with Middle Five C. Roxburgh was later to write:

To be taught by I.A.C. was a bracing experience and sometimes a diverting one. It was an uncommonly useful one too. For his lucidity and persistence often got knowledge into heads which had previously been impervious to it, and he expected a standard of care and effort to which some members of his Form had never risen before.

In the school's second term 'Be thorough!'[15] was also echoing round Grenville House, which, to Ian's great delight, immediately became pre-eminent on the games field. Impressively, it was to win the rugby cup for seven consecutive years. But there was a cultural emphasis in Ian's Grenville, too, with Laurence Whistler amongst its early intake.

Ian's reassuring air of supreme confidence was sometimes to the amusement of his more relaxed colleagues. 'He was a very Scots housemaster,' thought the wry Hugh Heckstall-Smith, 'A good fellow, but sadly affected by the Scottish conviction that he had been born knowing everything worth knowing.' Heckstall-Smith also noted that he 'tended to assume that any good cricketer or three-quarter must necessarily be a complex of all the virtues,' quoting a conversation over dinner in the masters' mess soon after the all-round athlete and future star golfer P.B. 'Laddie' Lucas first arrived in Grenville. Lucas, remarked one diner in quiet irony, was clearly destined to be a future Head of Grenville, 'Don't be so sure,' remarked another. 'He'll have to improve his inside passes!' Ian Clarke flushed, noted Heckstall, but refused to be drawn.

---

15   Indeed, it became its motto.

Ian may have irritated the more progressive members of the common room, but he had several staunch supporters. He was delighted to have a study in the mansion that was adjacent to that of Chandos' Major Haworth. The two could not have run their Houses more differently, yet, from the first were the closest of friends. Their brisk walks together through the grounds on Sunday afternoons were to be a regular Stowe feature of the Twenties and Thirties. The pair often enjoyed evening get-togethers, too, the alcohol supplied by 'Whisky' Clarke and the cigars by 'The Murch', even though he didn't smoke.

Another regular Stowe feature was the sight of Ian refereeing school rugby matches, clad in his dark blue Oxford blazer. As a coach, he was a hard taskmaster. In the autumn of 1923, when four matches were played successfully against local Prep Schools, Ian was far from satisfied. The 'all too-common present tendency to throw out clasping hands at a man's neck' strained his patience. 'Tackle low!' thundered as fiercely on the games field as 'Be thorough!' in the classrooms. Ian deplored the high 'scragging', everywhere in evidence. 'Quite apart from anything else, it is sheer joy and one of the most glorious sensations of Rugby to feel your opponent crash down as your hands close round his knees.'

In 1924 Ian was again deploring faults which, if not eradicated, would grow 'like pernicious weeds'. 'Low, clean tackling' was still the need. So, too, 'going down on the ball'. As school numbers had grown (to well over three hundred by December 1924), so had the 'pernicious weeds'. The 1st XV improved slowly, Ian lamenting in 1925 that 'some of the team are still inclined to scrag a man's ears'. In 1926 he had further disappointment. 'There is no-one in the school who can run really fast.'

His messianic zeal, however, paid off. The steady increase in school numbers and senior pupils helped too. December 1927 was memorable for the first occasion on which Stowe met another Public School on equal terms. Not only that, Stowe, captained by the future England scrum-half Bernard Gadney, beat Radley 16-0.

By the summer of 1930 the creation of the Bourbon Field had begun. *The Stoic* commented on the 'excellent start' to 'levelling work by voluntary labour', though the school's satirical magazine, *The Epicurean* (encouraged by the Common Room's liberal faction) was to publish a parody of 'The Walrus and the Carpenter', querying how 'voluntary' some of that labour had actually been:

The J.F. and the I.A.C.
Were walking hand in hand;

They wept like anything to see
Such lots of unused land.
'If this were only Bourbonised,'
They said, 'It would be grand.'

'If seven fools with seven tools
Scraped at it every day,
Do you suppose,' the J.F. said,
'They'd scrape it all away?'
'I doubt it,' said the I.A.C.,
'But still, they'd need no pay…'

The parody continues with the senior Stoics opting out of the project, and Ian Clarke having to commandeer some junior 'volunteers':

'The time has come,' the J.F. said,
'To dig a little ground,
With picks and spades and aching backs
In perspiration drowned,
And when the sun is broiling hot
To wheel the trucks around.'

'But wait a bit,' a young child cried,
'We cannot do that yet.
For most of us are out of breath
And some of us are fat.'
'Ye're slacking!' said the I.A.C.
and cuffed the little brat.

'It seems a shame,' the J.F. said,
'To play them such a trick.
To keep them in this broiling sun
With shovel, spade and pick!'
The I.A.C. said nothing but
'Don't wheel those trucks so quick!'

'Weel, children,' said the I.A.C.,
'Ye've had a lot of fun.
Shall we be running home again?'
But answer came there none;
And this was scarcely odd because
Not one was left to run.

* * *

It was as a forester that Ian's value was probably greatest. In 1922 the Stowe Landscape Gardens were ready to be obliterated, either farmed or built upon. After being saved by the school and steadily researched by Stowe historians, their importance was more and more respected, but it was to be nearly seventy years before the might of the National Trust would ensure their long-term future with ongoing professional restoration. In 1923, however, there at least was Ian Clarke, with his expert forestry skills, able to be an active point of reference for the first tentative steps in the landscape gardens' necessarily slow amelioration.

He began determinedly, with a detailed article on 'The Trees of Stowe' in the very first *Stoic*, in which the challenge of the current neglect came through strongly. Of the cedars, for example, he wrote:

There are many magnificent specimens… Unfortunately, many of these trees have suffered from neglect. Some have died and still stand naked and gaunt; storms have taken toll of others and have broken down great limbs, which urgently call for the skilled surgeon's axe and the healing balm of the tar-barrel.

He described lyrically the great variety of species to be found. Of the beech trees, for example, he rhapsodized:

Just now, when they are in full summer dress, their chief glory lies in the beauty of their rounded form and in the toss of their sprays when the wind blows, but each season will show us something in its own way as good; autumn will show us the changing colour of the leaf, sometimes brown, sometimes flaming copper; winter the whole of the smooth grey bole and the marvellous tracery of the twigs; spring the delicate green of the opening leaves.

In another early article in *The Stoic*, Ian was well before his time in attacking the world's sorry history of deforestation.

The trees meant everything to Ian. In addition to his timetabled forestry lessons he somehow managed to get his Latin sets out into the grounds, gathering up seed. Their efforts one term were said to have enabled the Forestry Commission to plant 50,000 extra trees. Forestry duly became one of Stowe's most active extracurricular pursuits. Early issues of *The Stoic* chronicled all manner of positive work: along Stowe Avenue, near the Oxford Lodge, in the Chatham Field, around the Octagon, near the waterworks, near Concord and Victory… Detailed eighteenth-century knowledge may have been lacking, but at least youthful vitality re-awakened the long-slumbering grounds.

The practical work was supported with the regular showing of Forestry Commission films and invitations to visiting lecturers. There were talks in 1927 by Sir John Stirling-Maxwell (the Chairman of the Forestry Commission), William Bean (Curator of Kew Gardens) and Frederick Balfour (on whose historic Dawyck gardens in the Upper Tweed Valley Ian himself had worked). Most years there was similar stimulation.

* * *

Ian remained a staunch Scotsman all his life. Most holidays he would return to the parental home in Aberdeen, where a strong social life included shooting, fishing and many a round over the Balgownie links, home of the Royal Golf Club of Aberdeen. In the Easter holidays of 1934 he was up there as usual when, to the surprise of many, his engagement was announced to Margaret Elphinston Adam Smith, daughter of the Very Rev. Sir George Adam Smith, the long-serving Principal of Aberdeen University. At twenty-four, she was twenty years Ian's junior.

He had, in all probability, gone up to Scotland that vacation with the prospect of a proposal very much in mind. For J.F. had offered him the chance that summer to move from Grenville (after eleven years) and open Walpole, Fielding Dodd's admirable new creation, which would include accommodation for housemaster, wife and family.

They were married in August. It was very much an Aberdeen University wedding, the service (taken by Margaret's father) held in its Chapel (King's College), and the reception at Elphinstone Hall. There were 400 guests, with more than a sprinkling of the Scottish aristocracy. Among the telegrams of congratulation were ones from the Archbishop of Canterbury and novelist John Buchan.

* * *

After the muddled geography of Grenville, the physical precision of Walpole would have been a delight to Ian's orderly mind. He threw himself at once into all his usual pursuits. A Walpole Glee Club soon emerged. Walpole House concerts, too.

He continued to lead extracurricular activities reflecting his forestry skills. At Housemasters' meetings, with strong support from Haworth and Cross, he would seize upon any lament about those 'loafing around' at weekends, and put it to the gardens' advantage. In the summer of 1937, for example, a party of would-be loafers was repairing the ha-ha under Ian's eagle eye 'between the bicycle sheds and the school'.

Hitler, of course, loomed large. As one of J.F.'s inner circle, Ian was there beside Capel Cure, Hunter and Haworth, when J.F. cracked a bottle of celebratory champagne after Chamberlain announced his Munich agreement. 1939 had its auspicious side, too. Shortly after the beginning of the summer term the Clarkes' second child, Janet, was born, a sister for Alasdair, three years her senior.

War, however, was clearly imminent. The Inspection of the O.T.C. by General Wavell was a very big event that summer. Major Ian Clarke had been an integral part of the O.T.C. since Major Howarth had first inaugurated it. Both would have been delighted at Wavell's very favourable report. The courses that Ian was running with Robin Watt, inculcating the wide range of field tactics possible in operational situations, was singled out for praise.

By the time term ended, however, Ian was far from well, his great joy in the birth of his daughter somewhat tempered by the onset of a mystery illness. Margaret's parents, on her father's retirement from Aberdeen University, had resettled in a large house in Balerno, a village on the outskirts of Edinburgh. Accordingly, the family headed there in the holidays in the hope of his speedy recuperation.

Tragically, he was found to be suffering from a rare and incurable disease of the marrow. He died in an Edinburgh hospital on 30 September 1939 at the age of forty-nine. War had just been declared. Term had just restarted. Walpole was temporarily under the control of a hastily appointed stand-in.

* * *

J.F. was among the mourners when the funeral took place at the little parish church of Currie, an adjacent village to Balerno, looking out to the Pentland Hills. 'After the service,' noted a newspaper, 'a small company drove to Sweethillocks, Balerno, the home of Mrs Ian Clarke's parents, to see her two children.'

A School Chapel memorial service was swiftly held, at which Major Haworth read the lesson. The next issue of *The Stoic*, too, omitted its usual Editorial. In its place, uniquely, the magazine began with a six-page tribute, four pages of which were written by J.F. himself. 'Ian will never be forgotten,' he declared. 'Stowe can never be the same for me, or for any of those who were with him in Grenville in the early days of the School.' Hard though J.F. would have tried to control his emotions, they clearly showed in the heartfelt essay. Even the chinks in Ian's armour as a housemaster were suddenly not chinks at all:

> *He was not a Housemaster of quite the accepted type. Even to his Prefects and Monitors he seemed a little remote. Yet he knew far more about the individual members of his House than most of them ever suspected, and had far more sympathy with them, both in their successes and their difficulties, than he ever allowed them to see.*

Perhaps it was J.F.'s inner shyness, matching Ian's, that, in addition to the shared Scottish ancestry, made for the particularly strong relationship:

> *Of Ian Clarke as a friend it is hard to speak. His energy, his dry but gay humour, his unchangeableness, his stubborn common sense, and his fine clear brain, added to the warmth and depth of his kindness, which he tried so unsuccessfully to conceal, made him the best man to be with on every kind of occasion. Those who have played games with him or shot with him know that there was no-one like him out-of-doors, as all his friends know that there was no-one like him as a counsellor in adversity or a companion in prosperity.*

* * *

The same *Stoic* also included details of the scarlet oaks to embellish the short new road leading from the Ha-Ha bridge at the end of the Grecian Valley to the Bourbon:

The oaks when larger will give a fine display of colour in the autumn. Future generations will be able to thin them out when they grow too large for their present spacing. But that will not be, at the earliest, until the great-great grandsons of present Stoics arrive at Stowe.

* * *

Ten years later, the trees were all well-established when Ian's son, Alasdair John 'Sandy' Clarke, who had been entered for Stowe on birth, arrived in Alasdair Macdonald's Chatham. He would enjoy five highly successful years, and, in the fullness of time, become Chairman of the Old Stoic Society.

6

THE REVD. EDWARD HABERSHON

The first Chaplain, creator of 'the Habitation'
Stowe 1923-31

Stowe's first Chaplain, the Revd. Edward Francis Habershon, was born in 1886. His early life was spent among the green fields of Surrey's Charlwood Park, his father being a gentleman of means thanks to a well-established family architectural business. Christian service was also a strong family tradition. Several of Edward's ancestors had been missionaries, and his Aunt Ada was a notable hymn writer. She had been involved with the evangelists Moody and Sankey and many famous gospel singers. When, in 1905, Charles Alexander had asked her for some songs for a big missionary venture, Aunt Ada had supplied him with 200.

The eldest of four children, Edward Habershon flourished at Harrow, where he won several prizes and was a splendid all-round games player. At Clare College, Cambridge, he was a powerful rower, regularly representing the college, not least in the triumphant May Bumps of 1907, the year he graduated in classics with a BA. His family had moved by this time to 'Brook Lodge' in Holmwood, another leafy part of Surrey. When twenty-three, he opted to train for the Church at Ridley Hall, and, when twenty-six, to devote himself to the London slums.

Sometime before, he had become involved in the Cambridge University Medical Mission, a ground-breaking residential youth centre with a dispensary, manned by volunteer medical students, addressing prevalent diseases like tuberculosis. It had been set up by the vicar of St James' Church, Bermondsey, whose honorary curate Edward had become. He proved an effective social worker, especially on the sporting side. By 1912 the CUMM was fielding no less than four cricket elevens with Edward the star batsman and coach. He also helped in the excursions the CUMM organised for children from the slums to enjoy fresh air in the countryside.

The work was interrupted by the First World War. By April 1915 Edward was an army padre, ministering to front-line troops in France. Though he won the MC, he would speak little about the war in later life. Both his younger brothers, officers in the same rifle brigade, died on active service, and in August 1916 he himself was wounded and gassed so seriously that he nearly died.

When peace came, Edward returned to Southwark and Bermondsey, working in another slum parish for four years, but still helping out the CUMM whenever he could.

* * *

He was thirty-seven when he arrived at Stowe in September 1923. It would seem to have been a startling career volte-face, from the underprivileged to the privileged, but Edward's Christian links with the public schools had been running in parallel with his work in Bermondsey. Even before the war, as a keen mountaineer, he was organising holidays to Swiss resorts like Andermatt, Savognin and Lenzerheide via the Public Schools' Student Christian Movement. It is possible that the regular London smogs of the 1920s, particularly injurious after his wartime gassing, may have been a deciding issue.

In applying to Stowe, he was probably encouraged by a fellow Cambridge Christian, Theodore 'Charlie' Acland, also involved in the Cambridge University Medical Mission. The highly personable Acland (who would soon be Cobham's first Housemaster) started at Stowe at the same time as Edward, and it can surely have been no coincidence that two active supporters of the CUMM should arrive together. Acland, whose double first in Natural Sciences had led to wartime work in munitions research, was to take up Holy Orders late in life, after a headmastership.

Edward's Stowe interview had been a difficult one. Sitting beside Roxburgh was the Revd. Percy Warrington, whose role as one of Stowe's founders had stemmed from a crusade to counter high-church frippery in the public schools with doughty new evangelical institutions. Legend has it that Edward was struggling on being challenged by Warrington about the literal truth of Old Testament highlights, when Roxburgh intervened and changed the subject, determined not lose Edward Habershon over Jonah and the whale.[16]

It was a good appointment. Although Edward lacked any classroom experience, he proved himself a highly approachable, popular figure. It helped his cause, of course, that he was devoted to outdoor pursuits, much in evidence on the games field with his enthusiastic coaching and officiating, not least in cricket, rugby and boxing. It helped, too, that he was a keen mountaineer, obsessed by Everest and other famous peaks.

A devotee of missionary camps, Edward swiftly embraced Stowe outdoor life. In the summer of 1924, for example, he was helping Hugh Heckstall-Smith create a somewhat basic swimming enclosure on the Temple of Venus side of the 11-acre. Edward happily knocked a succession of thick poles deep into the bottom of the lake, before fixing two wooden doors on top to form a little island within the enclosure. 'When one jumps off it,' wrote Heckstall, 'it staggers; but, as we go to press, it is still intact.'

One of Edward's more lasting creations was a new cricket scoring box, based on one at Lord's. Located on the east side of the North Front for several years, it was quickly dubbed 'The Habernacle'.[17] Similarly, in the spring and summer of 1929, he led the creation of a tall wooden hut, the size of a house, in the field at the back of Lord Cobham's pillar. Built on a concrete foundation, 'the Habitation' was to serve as the camping headquarters for the Stowe Boys' Club and other visiting youth groups for several years. One section provided quarters for those running the camps, with a larder partitioned off in a corner. The main part acted as a dining room, and, in wet weather, also became a recreation room and dormitory. It is not known for how long 'the Habitation' survived. There is a photograph of it (described as 'the Pineapple Hut') in *The Stoic* of December 1931, looking a solid but somewhat bizarre neighbour to the high and mighty Lord Cobham. Edward had been centrally involved in the formation of a 'Stowe Club for Working Boys' in London. He recalled years later:

---

16 The final word on the chaplaincy, however, was to be largely Warrington's. Responding to one of Habershon's referees, 6 June 1923, J.F. wrote: 'Personally I think he is first rate and I hope very much that the Governors will agree to his appointment.'

17 The invention of new 'Hab' words became a Stowe obsession. A silver sugar-sifter, for example, donated by him to the masters' dining room, was at once named 'the Haberdasher'.

I spent some time trying to find a suitable place in the Edgware Road-Harrow Road district. Eventually I contacted the Portman Estate which suggested a dilapidated former pub called 'The Pineapple'.

The tired three-storey building needed much work and the appointment of a residential warden. The recently-arrived master in charge of woodwork and metal work, Robert Hole, promised a big interest-free loan. Other Common Room members collected £250. Edward raised the rest. In July 1927 the Pineapple Club was opened with J.F. and Edward, as President and Vice-President, heading a committee involving Humphrey Playford (secretary), Fritz Clifford (treasurer) and Hugh Heckstall-Smith.

Edward used to pay visits by car most weeks. Arrangements were soon formalised so that each House sent five boys down on a Friday evening, to return the next morning. Groups of club members came up from London on Sundays, taking part in games against scratch school teams, and during school holidays there would be as many as fifty camping around 'the Habitation' for a week.

The Pineapple Club was to have an honourable history. After the building was bombed in 1942, other venues followed. In retirement Edward maintained interest, being fully involved in the first of many fund-raising Pineapple Balls. Eventually, however, the school handed the Pineapple over to the Westminster Council. A superb new 'Stowe Centre' for the whole local community was opened in 2006 and still flourishes today.

* * *

In the fullness of time, well after he had retired from teaching, Edward was to feature in a book of monographs[18] written by an Old Stoic, Richard Heron Ward. The portrait has long gone unrecognised, for Ward disguised his subjects with false names, but Ward's 'Rev M.P. Corringham MC' was, in fact, none other than his old school chaplain:

He had a large athletic body (he had been a rowing man at university and was still a fanatical footballer), large hands and feet, and a large face. But just as

---

18 *A Gallery of Mirrors*, 1956

his large body was at the same time spare, his large face was at the same time handsome, with strong clear features; and his eyes in particular were remarkable, for they were peculiarly direct, gentle and affectionate.

Ward remembered with affection how Edward soon acquired 'Om' as a popular nickname. When in class he would preface almost every remark by 'er' or 'om'; in discussion there was 'omming' before every reply. Though in his early forties, Om, were are told, was still boyish. He was also kindly, sensible and well-disposed. Deep-eyed and deep-voiced, he had a florid complexion and blushed with embarrassing ease. His sitting-room, meanwhile, was of 'comfortably masculine disorder'. It had Minty chairs (then the epitome of quality and comfort), oars on the wall above the door, an ample roll-top desk, pipe racks and tobacco jars with the Clare College crest, and books everywhere. A large tea-table was 'as often as not laden with bread and honey'.

Ward also recalled the way Om would stride up and down the aisle in Chapel with great purposefulness, and wrote highly of his faith. Only once or twice in his life had he ever come across 'a Christian so aware of the example of Christ and of the necessity for imitating it'. But the more Ward explored, the greater the paradoxes he found in his chaplain:

I often used to get the impression, without being able to be sure why, that Om was not a happy man, in spite of his almost unfailing outward cheerfulness. Once or twice, he astonished me by breaking his rule of not speaking about himself, and although even then he would break it only for a moment, and speak of himself only obliquely, it was possible at such times to see that he was given much more than one would have expected to introspection, self-criticism and self-disappointment.

Ward discovered that Om, though superficially seeming 'thoroughly ordinary' and 'middling', had fascinating hidden depths:

He was not a good preacher, but he was not a bad one; he was a good rugby player, but not very good. He had rowed for his college but not his university. With Om there were no heights and no depths or none that you would notice. In intellectual matters he was decidedly middle-brow; he admired the stories in C.E. Montague's 'Action', Henry Ford's autobiography and any book written by

F.S. Smythe.[19] *He was a broad churchman. He even taught, for the most part, the middle forms of the school. Yet there was a certain quality of light within him which shone out upon the material existence and, in the most unspectacular way imaginable, added to it another dimension.*

Ward delighted in probing for more of his chaplain's 'light'. During confirmation classes, for example:

Something prompted me unwittingly to lead Om into theological byways in which his footing was unsure, though his honesty and courage in going forward were unfailing... The amount of effort he put into the search for the right words, the right explanations, to say nothing of the amount of 'omming', was astounding; it was also touching...

There was one particularly fascinating encounter: Ward had left Cobham during prep and come out onto the South Front, en route to Om's study. He stopped under the portico.

The remoteness of the stars, the grandeur and magnitude of the universe they proclaimed, the immensity of the stone pillars, the infinite smallness of myself beneath them, who yet bore some infinitesimal part in the totality of universal being, these realizations produced in me a sense of awe and wonder, of gratitude towards that 'love which moves the sun and all the stars'...

Ward was still in a strange state of awe and wonder when he reached Om's room:

Without a word he rose from his chair, went to a bookshelf and took down The Oxford Book of English Verse. He handed it to me, open at number 433, which is Addison's hymn, 'The spacious firmament on high'. When I had read to its triumphant conclusion that the hand that made us, the love that moves the sun and all the stars is divine, Om sat down again and presently we began to talk... He used one phrase, the exact words of which I have always remembered. 'You see, Dick,' he said in his large, slow voice, 'you're a bit of a mystic.' Om went on

---

19   A popular mountaineer and botanist

to say he thought it regrettable that the church, or at least many churchmen, disapproved of mystics and distrusted them... He said I 'must hang on to' what I had understood that evening. 'If you are a bit of a mystic,' he said, 'wonder and awe may overtake you anywhere, and may continue to do so when you are a grown-up man, since the reason for it is everywhere, not only in the solitude of starry nights, in mountain fastnesses or desert wastes, not only in music or poetry, but in many places where you would not expect to find it, in clamorous cities and public places, on board ship or in a prison or on a battlefield. But always,' he continued, 'it is only in one place – where you found it just now – in yourself.'

Ward offered a striking conclusion:

Om was a mystic whose mystical depths were largely overshadowed by the outward personality life and his training had imposed on him, the training of the muscular Christian, the conscientious schoolmaster, the loyal churchman. Real as these things were, they were unreal by comparison with the soul hidden beneath them, which one day had suddenly, and with the soul's clarity of understanding, grasped the meaning of the words, 'Behold, I stand at the door and knock', and, ever since, though that meaning had faded again to little more than the formula of the words themselves, had treated its experience of them as a touchstone. There were moments, I think, when those of us who knew and loved Om were witnesses, without knowing it, of that soul's struggle to escape, of his dark side's desire to break free into the light of consciousness. And, at those moments, when the darkness to which it was condemned was dispelled, the man's soul took fire; Om's wonderful understanding, intuition and compassion blazed forth; the door was again opened to the knocking...

* * *

In 1929 Om's life dramatically changed. At forty-two he suddenly found a bride, fifteen years younger than himself. The wedding with Norah Dobbs, who had spent much of her early life in India as daughter of an Army Colonel, took place that April at St Barnabas', Kensington. Om had clearly met her through church connections – perhaps even the CUMM, for Charlie Acland was his Best Man.

The lack of any married accommodation at Stowe meant they began life together in Buckingham, renting Hill House in Castle Street. Their first Stowe term together was notable for the Service of Dedication of the new Chapel in July 1929 with the presence of the future Duke of Kent, Prince George. As with Queen Mary laying the Foundation Stone in 1927, Om had little to do except look on amiably.

Unfortunately, the coming of the new Chapel had brought with it even more pressure for Om and J.F. from Percy Warrington. There were many intolerable demands, like the absence not only of any candles but also of any cross. Roxburgh was close to resignation. ('I do not think that I can go on indefinitely serving under men whose bigotry and virulence make me ashamed.') Om and his young wife were no doubt similarly unsettled.

The arrival of their first child, Margaret, in November 1930, highlighted accommodation needs. J.F. had assured Om that he was next in line for a boarding house. A new building (to be called Walpole) was on the cards, though funds were frustratingly not yet in place… Then, in 1930, Cobham suddenly came up when Charlie Acland was appointed headmaster of Norwich School. There was disappointment for Om and Norah, however, when it was given instead to John Hankinson, a more forthright personality than Om, but distinctly less stable.

It was Charlie Acland, responsible for Om coming to Stowe, who now initiated his departure, alerting him to the chaplaincy of Gresham's, Holt, twenty miles north of Norwich. Om was duly appointed. 'I was very fond of Stowe,' he would later write. 'It was a great wrench to drag ourselves away.'

It would have been a relief, however, to start a new life away from Percy Warrington, whose reputation was to scare away possible successors to the chaplaincy. It was not until 1933, when Warrington made a dramatic exit on the collapse of his financial empire, that a new chaplain was finally appointed.

* * *

Edward and Norah Habershon flourished at Gresham's. In 1936 they bought a house on the outskirts of Holt, and by the outbreak of war had three children. In a letter to J.F. during 'the Phoney War', Om wrote of his hopes that common sense would yet prevail and bring a speedy peace. Roxburgh responded:

> *I wish I could share your optimism. Hitler may be as mad as you please, but he is no fool and he would not have gone in for this war if he had not thought that*

he could win it. That does not mean that he will win it, but it does mean that he will have a very good try and is capable of going pretty near to success. At least that is the way that strikes me.

Eight months later, in June 1940, with invasion seemingly imminent, Gresham's evacuated to Cornwall and the Habershons rented a house outside Newquay. Om was soon taking services in a hotel ballroom, with Sunday Evensongs in a remote café overlooking the Gannel Estuary. Water seeped in at high tide, but the views were absolutely splendid.

By the summer of 1941 he was reporting the skies full of planes and the daily wailing of sirens. The war, he told J.F., had intensified his feelings about the past:

It has given me a still deeper disgust at the attitude of the last twenty years – our love of comfort, 'luxury' everything, artificial existence, restless dashing about and complete absence of any really worthy motive in life.

When I contemplate the end of the war, I shudder at the possibility that we go back to much of the old life... Did you read Rauschning's last book, 'Beast from the Abyss'?[20]

J.F. replied in some detail:

I am inclined to agree with you that there has been something profoundly wrong with European civilization – American too, doubtless – for at least forty years of this century. I can even believe that Hitler might act not only as a 'scourge of God' but also as a reformer and re-inspirer of the world, if he didn't happen to be so unutterably devilish in himself. He turned what might have been a real conversion to idealism and service of German youth into a crusade of cruelty and abomination. But he needn't have done.

We have lost 19 out of a staff of 40, and we have had to fill up with elderly men and actually with women... The men who have been here for years and have not yet been called up, such as Fritz, Capel and Wiggels [Harold Kinvig], are doing about three times as much as they ought to be doing, but carrying their burdens surprisingly lightly...

---

20   A German refugee's memoir about the Blitz

There was further contact between the two in December 1944 when, on Gresham's return to Norfolk, the Habershons stayed overnight in Buckingham, entertaining J.F. to dinner at the White Hart. Two years later, Om was telling J.F. of his retirement:

The boys gave us an amazing goodbye on Monday evening, a 'do' in Big School. Speeches from the H.M. and Head Boy and presentation... 'Goodbye Mr Chips' atmosphere – I could hardly speak in reply.

* * *

As he approached sixty, Om had looked round for possible country parish livings. He found one in the Wiltshire village of Coombe Bissett. Three years into it, writing to J.F., he confessed that, though he found parish work 'interesting', he missed the cut and thrust of schools.

Stowe at the time was bracing itself for the end of the Roxburgh era. In March 1949, three months before his retirement, J.F. wrote to Om:

I am more and more convinced that it is time the school had someone younger and fresher in charge of it. We have secured an extremely good man who is, I think, a good deal more than the conventional Rugby housemaster, though I trust he has the virtues of that uninteresting but effective type. We are full, and I believe I am handing over to Eric Reynolds what may reasonably be called a prosperous concern.

Om was present at Old Stoic Day that July, when J.F.'s retirement was marked by moving speeches and presentations. He later wrote to him:

The place as a whole seemed to me more wonderful than ever. You have completely thrown off the wartime features, noticeable in 1944. What a contrast between the rabbit warren on the South Front lawn in 1927 and its present state!

More than once I contemplated walking along to your study during the evening. But it did not seem fair, as I realized how tired you must be at the end of the last term...

Om himself, though J.F.'s senior, still had two more years as Vicar of Coombe Bissett before moving with Norah thirty miles to Milford-on-Sea.

* * *

They were to spend a final twelve years together there, at Hurst Barn, Ravens' Way, enjoying delightful views of the English Channel. They had the careers of their three children to follow with interest and much enjoyed helping out at services at St Mark's, Pennington. Om also used his new leisure hours for further study of spiritualism, a topic that had long interested him. He became a member of The Churches' Fellowship in Psychical and Spiritual Studies, attending conferences and corresponding with leading experts. Eventually, towards the end of his life, Om wrote a slim booklet for The Churches' Fellowship, modestly titled *Research*:

> *Some fifteen years ago, I set out to see what could be found out... I had no idea that the search would lead to such a great change in Christian outlook. Much that I learnt confirmed what I had professed to believe, but without conviction. I came to see the significance of many passages and incidents in the New Testament, which I had not treated seriously before...*

He was sure that if thirty years ago he had known what he knew now, his ministry would have been more effective. Very confidently Om outlined the 'factual knowledge' to which his researches had led:

> *Death itself is painless and without fear. Those who die a natural death rest for a few days and are met by helpers, often relations, who show them how to become accustomed to their new life.*

Everyone, he wrote, would find the new life at his or her own level:

> *The majority find themselves in planes, generally called Paradise, where they will have useful occupations, according to gifts and temperament.*

Richard Heron Ward's mystic had journeyed on...

* * *

Om still kept in occasional touch with Stowe. In July 1963 he accepted an invitation to the 40th Anniversary Commemoration Dinner. It was Donald Crichton-Miller's last summer at Stowe, hardly an easy time for the school, but for Om it was a reassuring occasion. He wrote to Crichton-Miller afterwards:

I came to feel strongly that I was not qualified to cope with the difficulties which boys now feel about Christian belief; and that a public school padre ought to have a science degree. I never evaded a difficulty, but often failed to find adequate answers. Since about 1930 many books have appeared which make it easier for us. However, it was a distinct relief to be told several times on Friday that such limitations had not quite wrecked what I tried to do…

Crichton-Miller invited him up for the weekend of the Old Stoic rugger match that October, to stay the night in Kinloss and preach in Chapel. Afterwards, he wrote to express his pleasure at a sermon 'so rooted in the 1930s'.

In his last years Om helped out at the little church of St Mary's, Everton, a late-Victorian confection of wood and corrugated iron at the back of Milford-on-Sea. Perhaps it reminded him of some of the Thames-side mission halls of his younger days.

Om was to die at Milford-on-Sea, just as two other Legends, Herbert Neville and Ernest Earle, had done before him. It was October 1968 and he was eighty-two. A whole thirty-seven years had passed since he had left Stowe, but he had maintained happy memories of his first teaching post to the last. It was to the Stowe Boys' Club, still close to his heart, that he had asked Norah for any donations in his memory to be forwarded.

7

MAJOR RICHARD HAWORTH

A gentlemanly soldier who founded Chandos & the O.T.C.
Stowe 1923-47

Richard Haworth, who was Housemaster of Chandos for twenty-four of Roxburgh's twenty-six years, came from a prosperous background. His grandfather had risen from rags to riches, creating Richard Haworth & Co., a Lancashire cotton mill business, which at its peak had a workforce of four thousand. Soon after Richard's birth, in August 1882, his father retired early from the family mills to 'Ashley Green', a house in the Lake district looking down on Ambleside[21], becoming a Colonel in the territorials and a leading member of the Royal Windermere Yacht Club.

Richard's early Prep School years, marred by the death of his younger brother, ended happily enough at Horton Hall, a large mansion just south of Northampton, from where he passed into Charterhouse. He was a popular figure there, but no scholar, only reaching 'Fifth C', a form of seven boys being prepared for the army, and he needed a couple of terms in a crammer before managing to pass into Sandhurst. In February 1902, aged nineteen, he duly became a soldier, commissioned into the Royal Lancashire Fusiliers. Much of his military service prior to the First World War was spent in India, notably in several campaigns in the Punjab around the North-West Frontier. On the Great War's outbreak, Richard and his Fusiliers immediately sailed back to England.

---

21   In the foothills of Loughrigg Fell

* * *

Promoted to Captain, he found himself in March 1915 embarking with a newly-formed Mediterranean Expeditionary Force. The Lancashire Fusiliers were to land on the peninsula of Gallipoli, part of a plan intended to knock Turkey from the war at one stroke.

'Beach W', a wide strip of sand, backed by crumbling cliffs with headlands either end, was the Fusiliers' landing place. At 4.00 am they approached in assault vessels, with the guns of the battleships behind them firing furiously but, in fact, doing little damage to the beach's barbed wire and the heavily entrenched Turkish positions. The letter that Richard wrote to his father afterwards gives a sombre insight into the kind of wartime nightmares a fair number of Stowe's early masters had had to endure:

> *About 300 yards from the beach the pinnaces stopped their tows, and the seamen in each boat rowed us in. Almost directly an awful rifle and maxim-gun fire broke out from the cliffs each side of our little bay. The sailors were splendid. Pulling on under awful fire, while they and our men were being hit. Eventually the boat grounded about 50 yards out, and I shouted to the men to get out. A good many were finished, and I jumped out up to my chest in the water. We were carrying two days' rations, 200 rounds and full packs, which was the cause of several poor fellows, who were hit while in the water, being drowned. I fell down twice before reaching the beach, when I found we were under terrific crossfire.*

Somehow he penetrated the barbed wire entanglement, but the company's Captain was killed. Richard took over, intent on attacking the nearest damaging source of fire:

> *I got together about 30 men, and we were climbing up the cliff when Porter, who was by my side, was shot through the head and died almost at once. We were soon in sight of the Turks in the trench, and one let fly at me and took the very top off my ear, but I am glad to say I got him with my revolver the moment after, right in the head. Just as I reached the trench there was a terrific explosion – the trench was mined, and I and those near me were sent bustling down to the bottom of the cliff again.*

After gathering a second group together, Richard led them up another part of the cliff, until finding the barbed wire defences of a large redoubt. There they stayed, responding as best they could under heavy sniper fire, waiting for support, but the hoped-for reinforcements were unable to get through for many hours. Face to face with the enemy and isolated, they clung on, numbers steadily lessening:

About four pm they got me. I had been crawling up and down the line, and the beggar followed me all the time. The bullet entered about three inches to the left of my spine, and came out about four inches to the right, having gone right through behind the spine without touching anything. Of course, this jar paralysed my legs for a bit, and I thought I was a 'goner' but the feeling came back.

Two hours later reinforcements finally reached them. Richard was helped down to a dressing station on the beach.

There I spent the night. There were crowds of wounded lying there, and some ghastly sights. I lay between a fellow hit in his wind pipe, and another poor chap with a bullet wound in the stomach.

Three days later he was on board a hospital ship that took him to Alexandria. Further hospitalisation in Malta followed. Over 600 Lancashire Fusiliers had been killed or wounded on 'Beach W'. Six Victoria Crosses were won. Dick was awarded the DSO for leading the attack on the redoubt, 'continuing to command with a bullet through his back' and 'refusing to accept medical treatment until reinforcements arrived'. 'Beach W' was to become a British base for the next eight months, right up to the ignominious evacuation.

* * *

Richard's subsequent hospitalisation probably saved his life, for he missed the Fusiliers' return to the Western Front. When promoted to Major in January 1917, he was still far from fully recovered and accordingly posted to Sandhurst. He was still there in 1923.

J.F. had known about Richard for some time, for a close Old Carthusian friend, Edwin 'Ted' Pye, had married Richard's sister, Mildred Haworth. Knowing that

Richard was unsettled about his post-war future, the Pyes mentioned him to J.F. A letter, enclosing a prospectus, was swiftly posted to Sandhurst with a warm conclusion:

I seem to have been assuming that you would like to come to Stowe in some capacity, but in fact I realise that I have no right to assume that whatever. But from my own point of view it would be very delightful to get you to share the struggles and triumphs (if there are any) of Stowe...

Richard responded:

I am at the moment working at Sandhurst as an instructor (and sort of house tutor), for nothing except free quarters, light and fuel. I am doing this simply because it is an occupation that suits me. The financial question does not worry me... I fear that my mathematics are not and never have been a strong point with me. In fact, I feel rather diffident about taking on any teaching except possibly Geography and History of an elementary kind... Mere administrative work (bursarial) does not appeal to me, but if you want someone to help with a House or to help you in the general running of the school I should be glad to consider the question...

'How I wish,' replied J.F little vaguely, 'that you would say that you were an expert mathematician, but I am hoping that it might be possible to ask you to join us in September, as a general master, Commander of the O.T.C. and prospective Housemaster.' Alarming news that Wellington College were also interested in Richard led to J.F. clinching Richard's arrival in September 1923 in charge of Chandos, one of the two new Houses to be opened that term in the mansion's east wing. 'You need not disturb yourself at all about the teaching required of you here,' J.F. reassured him, urging a summer reconnaissance:

You will find the whole place desperately incomplete and to anyone who has formed high hopes of it perhaps rather depressing, but I think that if you will look at everything with 'the eye of faith' you will see what possibilities there are here of ultimate greatness. I am sure no-one is likely to help more effectively to realise these possibilities than you...

The annual salary would be £300. 'Not a princely sum I am afraid, but I know your chief interests do not lie on the financial side…'

When Richard visited towards the end of Stowe's first term, Roxburgh invited Andrew Croft, Temple's Head of House, to join the two of them for dinner. Significantly, the champagne was served in J.F.'s very best Venetian glasses. This was always a sign that something delicate was going to be discussed. And so it was. Over dinner Andrew Croft, who had been finding the atmosphere in Temple 'rather oppressive', was so impressed by the new housemaster that he agreed to change from being Head of Temple to Head of Chandos. The Venetian glasses had worked their usual magic.

* * *

Fifty-six Chandosians arrived in September, virtually all straight out of Prep School. Richard had far less difficulties than might have been the case without the efficient Andrew Croft. But the teaching of geography in a twenty-seven-period timetable proved a struggle. J.F., who devised the timetable himself, was full of apology at Christmas:

> I have done my very best to cut down your teaching hours this time. You actually have 16 periods – the lowest to which I could get it – and I hope that this will ease matters a little for you. On Fridays you get a whole holiday and I hope that you will be able to take a slack day then and perhaps even go away when you feel like it.

Richard's reply suggests his Head of House may have been anxious about discipline:

> I have made rather a big reshuffle in the dormitories for next term (approved of in detail by Andrew Croft!) which will, I hope, mean better discipline… Many thanks for your kind remarks – I only wish that I could feel that I had really deserved them …

Aware of his unique want of academic qualifications, in late 1924 Richard was writing to J.F a little anxiously:

> I have been through the School Certificate Geography syllabus and papers and

I think that we can cope with them. It would make an enormous difference if I could have a geography classroom where I could keep and display my goods. I rather have my eye on the east top room of the newest block nearest the garage!

I wish you would tell me candidly if you think that Chandos is run on too free and easy lines. I'm all for having a cheery show, but I realise such shows are apt to get out of hand unless carefully watched.

There are hints in Stowe histories that, though his own courtesy and friendliness inspired considerable personal loyalty, the 'show' did indeed get somewhat out of hand: 'The Major, as a gentleman of the old school was the reverse of a martinet.' 'Chandos was not noted for meticulous discipline.' Six years on, when the Major should have been completely on top of things, a note from J.F., though couched very cautiously, suggests Chandos behaviour left much to be desired:

I am endeavouring to get some painting done in the holidays and I have been round with Bannister making a list of the worst places. The appearance of your Lower Hall suggests that the users are not excessively careful of the decoration! It almost looks as though they played some game like the 'Darts' of the village pub. At any rate the doors, lockers and all the woodwork are covered with little holes. I will try and get new paint put on if you will prevent it being stripped off again by the Wild Men.

One of the Major's problems, of course, throughout his Stowe career was ongoing pain and discomfort in his back from his wartime injuries. The 'bromide mixture', supplied by his doctor, would only have minimal effect when he was tired. Few ever knew, however. The Major made little fuss about it all.

* * *

By the autumn of 1924 Richard had fully established the Officers' Training Corps, which he would command for another nine years. In *The Stoic* of July 1924, he wrote strongly in its support. Though accepting that many of a cadet's acquisitions would fade with time, he argued there was long-lasting importance in 'the power, as an N.C.O. or cadet officer, of command'. It had, he declared, been crucial to platoon commanders in 1914-18. It might – Heaven forbid – prove crucial again… The

O.T.C. was of such importance to Richard, that when, in the 1930's, its future was seriously threatened, he subscribed a large sum of money to ensure its survival.

One of his early triumphs was the O.T.C.'s acquisition of the Gothic Temple. By March 1925 he was reporting that 'a most unsuitable building at first sight, for military purposes' had been transformed into 'a reasonably good armoury'. A photograph shows rifles neatly in place all round the circular walkway on the first floor. Hawkwell Field was soon known as Armoury Field. At its top end, directly in front of the steps of the derelict Queen's Temple, a miniature outdoor rifle range was soon constructed.

Shooting was always one of Richard's keenest concerns. For years he regularly took parties to Bicester and Bisley and coached on the miniature range at Stowe, where he presided week after week over Saturday 'spoon-shoots'. That the Stowe shooting teams regularly distinguished themselves at Bisley was extremely helpful for the school's reputation. In 1932 J.F. wrote to him:

> At yesterday's meeting of the governing board a resolution was adopted asking me to convey to you the congratulations of the governors on the notable success of the Eight in winning the Cusack-Smith Bowl at Bisley and their thanks for the skill and care which must have gone to the training of the boys.

The Major remained a good shot himself through his school career. Even in his last term he was captaining the masters against the school.

His camps were often memorable. One of Richard's typical pieces of enthusiasm was recalled many years later:

> The Major had taken the corps on manoeuvres to Newbury Downs, when the weather closed in. He made us march for hours through terrible rain until he formed us up around him, wet through and very mutinous, to tell us 'I've brought you here to see the view'.

* * *

The Stowe Sailing Club, like the O.T.C., was one of the central features of the Roxburgh success story, thanks to Richard's enthusiasm, expertise and generosity. In 1926 he reported in The *Stoic*:

We were fortunate enough to obtain permission to occupy one of the two islands on the eleven-acre lake, and last term work was begun on clearing the island and establishing connection with the mainland. As regards the latter work, the original amateur production, though suitable for light-weighters and gymnasts, was replaced this term by a more substantial professionally-built bridge. A building, for use as a clubhouse and store, has been most generously provided by the father of one of the members of the club.

The boats were the last to arrive, owing to the General Strike. The fleet consists of four 10-foot one-design pram dinghies, rigged with a 'gunter-lug' and built by G.E. Watts of Gosport...

The club began with twenty-five members and a long waiting-list. Racing on the 11-Acre took place on Sundays. There were separate classes for experts and novices, members drawing for boats. Fixtures were arranged against Oxford and Cambridge University sailing teams, and the Major himself sometimes participated in the School's team of four boats.

* * *

It was often of the greatest value to the Common Room that Richard was able to use his friendly relationship with J.F. to raise sensitive issues. In 1931, for example, he aired the inadequate living conditions under which most masters, including himself, were living. Roxburgh's response showed his frustrations with the penny-pinching atmosphere in which he had to operate:

I understand your feelings very well about the apparent indifference of the authorities to the personal comfort of the Masters. I will have one more try to get better service and more consideration for you. But my own position here is not an easy one because it involves responsibility without power. I am expected to keep my Masters and bring in a good type of boy but I am not able to spend the money necessary to make those things possible.

I will go on trying a little longer, but like you I sometimes feel that we cannot go on indefinitely...

Richard's response could not have been more supportive:

I realise entirely your position and am most extremely sorry for you. In fact I feel a brute for bringing the matter up at all. I cannot help feeling that it is time that P.E.W. had a pistol held to his head – I am sure that you would have a good many of your staff behind you.

A year later, in 1932, the Major was again giving Roxburgh quiet support:

I looked in yesterday before I left but you were out. I just wanted to express my sympathy with you in your weariness of mind and my hope that you were going to get away from Stowe very soon and for as long as possible. Shyness and a dislike of 'butting in' on another's private affairs have kept me from saying anything before this, but I have been most awfully sorry for you. With best wishes for a Happy Christmas free from worries.

The correspondence from time to time veered away from school business. 'If you want some holiday literature,' wrote Richard, 'read Desmond Coke's new school story *Stanton*. I found it most interesting and amusing.' Desmond Coke, author of spirited tales like '*The Worst House at Sherborough* and *The House Prefect*, was unlikely to have been usual reading for J.F. In Coke's latest yarn, however, Stanton was a private school where an idealist had distanced himself from conventional educational thinking…

Richard's role as a confidante of J.F. blended easily with that of Common Room pater familias. Robert Timberlake, a young classicist and early Grafton Housemaster, recalled:

Much respected, he became a kind of arbiter of taste and presided as a kind of Mess President at our table where, without the refinements of a real Officers' Mess, he contrived to make dinner, if not breakfast, a comparatively seemly meal, at which it was customary to apologise to him if one was late and only to smoke with his permission… A little gentle restraint from someone like the Major did no harm, as we younger men were rather a riotous party, still undergraduates at heart…

Perhaps it was to calm the young Timberlake down that the Major enlisted his help in a fairly hazardous enterprise:

Richard Haworth asked me to help with a fire practice in Chandos. He took
me up to the dormitory on the top floor about sixty feet from the ground and
pointed to the fire chute. He explained that when the alarm went I had to climb
out of the window and slide down the hollow cylinder using my elbows and
knees as brakes...[22]

* * *

The Major naturally made good copy for the satirical school magazine, *The Epicurean*.
Early on he had acquired the nickname 'The Merch', so there were soon extracts from
an 'undiscovered play of Shakespeare: *Richard the Fifth* or *The Merchant of Chandos*,
in which 'The Merch', supported by the Duke of Dadford (Bill McElwee) and Lord
MacDuff (Ian Clarke), led an army of too many N.C.O.s and too few privates. A few
issues later he featured in a long Chaucerian take-off that mentioned any number of
his interests (like playing the double bass in the school orchestra) and nicknames.
(He was sometimes known as 'Chin', presumably because his receded.) The Sailing
Club naturally received a mention, too:

> And in the somer time he will not fail
> With yongé laddés on the lake to sail,
> In shippés smale with sailés broun or whyt:
> In soothe it is a verray perty sight.

* * *

At the outbreak of the Second World War, the Major at once took control of the
North Buckinghamshire Local Defence Volunteers, which he somehow combined
with his Stowe commitments. These increased in 1944, when he volunteered to lead
a newly formed Naval Section of the corps. Soon there were over fifty cadets, but
it had a harrowing start when a former Leading Seaman, appointed as the corps'
naval instructor, was tragically drowned in the Eleven Acre. From press reports he
was victim of his own rash desire to show off to his girl-friend. Out on a date with

---

22   Over fifty years later many chutes of Roxburgh vintage were still in place. Even as late as January 1980
     Chatham House had them. Thankfully, by February 1980 they had gone.

a sixteen-year-old Stowe waitress, he had taken her to the boathouse, from which he took out various vessels to entertain her. Half way across the lake in a canoe, he overturned and, not being able to swim, was drowned.

Though the tragedy was a shocking setback, the new Naval Section continued to grow, not least because of the Major's continuing generosity. Despite petrol restrictions, the cadets were somehow taken on any manner of interesting expeditions. By the coming of peace in late 1945 the Eleven Acre was embellished with a 27ft service whaler…

* * *

At the time of VE Day Richard was three years past the normal retirement age of sixty. From Ambleside in the summer holidays of 1945, he wrote tactfully to J.F:

> *Now that hostilities have ceased you will naturally be thinking of finding a younger man for my place. This is only to be expected and I am fully prepared to accept the inevitable. It will be a sorrowful moment when it comes!*

J.F., however, urged him to stay on. Both shared a deep desire to mark appropriately the appalling loss of so many Old Stoics in active service, and by 1946 a War Memorial Fund was well under way. On receiving a contribution from the Major's sister and brother-in-law, Mildred and Ted Pye, J.F. responded:

> *If we can educate the children of the boys who have been killed and found a small War Memorial Bursary, in addition to the Chapel Screen, that will be something.*
>
> *Dick appears to be flourishing, and all Old Stoics are agreed that he doesn't look a day older than he did in 1923.*

Mildred responded equally warmly:

> *We have memories of so much fun and happiness, such beauty for one's eyes in the days before the war, before short petrol and hard work controlled our visits to Stowe. Then there are all the happy lives that Stowe has made – another source of thanksgiving. And, not least, the Stowe that has given Dick the very best years of his life.*

He finally retired in the summer of 1947 when nearly sixty-five, with increasing deafness very much the clinching issue. He had remained the Chandos Housemaster to the last, though clearly no longer at this best. Brian Stephan, who succeeded the Major, having worked as his underhousemaster during his three final years, was amused by some of his gentlemanly idiosyncrasies: 'He remained a soldier at heart, the only schoolmaster I have known to have a batman!' His memories, however, were mixed. On the one hand, he accepted the Major's 'immense influence in moulding the original ethos of the school'. On the other, there was the Major's sketchy teaching of Geography, 'in which he made no great claim to competence', and the unsettled atmosphere he found in Chandos.

He was running the House with military precision tempered by his essential gentleness. Every night he would make the round of the ten dormitories, accompanied by a Monitor as his Adjutant... His humanity and good humour were still undimmed, but I found it distressing that some of the less worthy members of the House took advantage of his increasing deafness and that a certain indifference, amounting in some cases almost to cynicism, had appeared among some members of the House.

J.F., by contrast, allowed no hint of criticism to mar his long and affectionate eulogy in *The Stoic*. The School, he concluded, was losing not just one of its principal creators, but a great figure as well. 'We who remain are losing something even more precious – an old and well-loved friend.' Writing from her Chelwood Gate home, Mildred Pye thanked him gratefully:

What an absolutely dear thing you have written in The Stoic about Dick! It is so perfectly charming and so full of truth. I am sure it warmed his poor heart, when he left Stowe – I know he did mind... He was so happy. It was his whole life... I feel resignedly sad too...

* * *

He retired to the Lakes. His father had died, and though his step-mother would always welcome him at Ashley Green, he moved into a house nearby, shared with his faithful batman and housekeeper. On the first day of the autumn term 1947, he sent

J.F. a friendly telegram. 'It feels very strange to be starting a new term without you,' responded Roxburgh.

The annual dinners of the Old Stoics, like those of his old Regiment, were to bring him to London, where he would always stay at the Army and Navy Club. He would pay Stowe occasional visits too. Alasdair Macdonald would recall 'the tall, slim figure striding down to the Lake, to the range and every other scene of his former activities'.

But he was happy to be back in Westmorland. Besides much sailing, he gardened and went for long walks in the hills. J.F. recalled:

Though never interested in the more spectacular form of climbing, he knew and regularly visited every peak, tarn and valley within range of his home and delighted in taking his visitors to see his favourite haunts and views.

On the school's 25th anniversary on 11 May 1948, the Major duly sent J.F. congratulations. J.F. responded:

It was very good of you to send us a telegram yesterday. The day would not have been complete without something to link up R.H. and Stowe again.

We did not do anything to celebrate the birthday, although an eccentric but kind parent provided vast quantities of iced cake for the school and some champagne for the masters, and we are not proposing to have any celebrations at all this year... I could not secure any royal person to give us a date in 1948, and in view of the shortage of petrol, food and paint I did not think that a large gathering was practicable.

But we shall be having a Thanksgiving Service in Chapel on the morning of Saturday July 10th – the day of the Old Stoic cricket match. There will be a great many Old Stoics here during the day and, if you think you could bear it, a visit from you would give great pleasure to them as well as all of us.

The Major accepted the invitation and thoroughly enjoyed the reunion.

In 1948, he began light work at Huyton Hill, a Prep School in a mock Tudor mansion on the north-west corner of Lake Windermere, only two miles from Ambleside. Despite his deafness, he was to maintain this pleasant and undemanding role for five years, every day happily sailing across Windermere to and from work.

In 1949 Roxburgh himself retired. Shortly beforehand, Richard wrote to J.F, expressing pleasure that his successor, Eric Reynolds, seemed to have been a good choice, 'thoroughly sound and level-headed'. J.F. agreed that the appointment was excellent. Reynolds was well spoken of by everyone at Rugby. 'As you say, thank God he is a bachelor!'

That July, the Major wrote again, expressing most sincere gratitude for the countless acts of kindness and guidance he had received from J.F. during his time at Stowe:

From the very start I realised that I could always turn to you for help, which you gave so unstintingly. I remember that you once said to me, when, for some reason, I was a trifle fractious, that you and I had never had a row. It was the happy understanding which, I like to think, always existed between us that was one of the chief factors in creating the spirit of contentment that filled my life at Stowe...

* * *

Five years later, on 6 January 1954, Richard died, aged seventy-two, at the Westmorland County Hospital, Kendal. The funeral was held at the little church of Holy Trinity, Brathay, built on a site chosen by William Wordsworth, the poet declaring that there was 'not a situation outside the Alps or among them more beautiful than this'. The ailing J.F., with only four months to live, was driven up to the Lake District by the Major's brother-in-law, Ted Pye, and read one of the lessons, though with difficulty. Stowe was also represented by Fritz Clifford, John Saunders, Edward Hart-Dyke and Brian Stephan, while a bugler from the Lancashire Fusiliers played the last post. Two weeks later Stowe's Chapel was full to overflowing for a memorial service. Richard Haworth had died a rich man, and quietly left several generous bequests.

The Major had been an impressive war hero. But it was for how he had made the very most of his years of peace, in his supremely gentlemanly way, that he would be most remembered.

Ful worthy proved he in his lordés warre:
And therfor was he fairé ranked Major.
And what he lerned in warre he did not cees
To turn to profit in the days of pees.

8

MARTIN MACLAUGHLIN

The first Head of History, a giddy star performer
Stowe 1924-32

Martin Crofton MacLaughlin arrived in January 1924, at the start of Stowe's third term. He was a twenty-three-year-old historian, but with no teaching experience other than having been a tutor in the household of the Duke of Westminster the previous year. He would teach the subject, however, with missionary certainty and zeal.

It was in his blood. His father, vicar of Burford, a sleepy parish on the Worcestershire side of the Welsh border, had an Oxford degree in Modern History. Martin grew up in a rambling Tudor rectory beside a church boasting a full-length effigy of a fourteenth-century knight in full armour, dramatic enough to fire any imagination, let alone his particularly vivid one.

He was sent off early to various small schools. At ten, for example, he was with five other boys in a house near Stockport, where a Miss Pacy ruled supreme. He was at Repton by the start of the First World War, at the very last part of which he became a private in the Air Force. He entered Keble College, Oxford, in January 1919 and left in the summer of 1922. The second-class degree was a disappointment, but history still a consuming passion. He was President of Keble's history society and the University's Irish Society – all his life he was obsessed with the fact that he was descended from old Irish kings. One of his pupils, Terence Prittie, was later to write of him in *A Stowe Miscellany*:

He was an Irish eccentric, and they come pretty eccentric in those parts. He claimed descent from the O'Melaghlins, Kings of Meath in the Dark Ages, which the Irish persist in believing were gay and golden. He would sometimes sing 'When Malachy wore the collar of gold' in a light and quavering tenor, and the Fenians and the heroes of Easter Week were close to his heart. Certainly, he had plenty of the characteristics of the Celt – charm, enthusiasm, gaiety and an aptitude for giving conviviality to proceedings otherwise mundane. He had, too, the bardic gift of the gab, and he believed in both fairies and leprechauns.

Inspired by his royal forebears, whenever Martin MacLaughlin sent a letter, instead of using a stamp he simply wrote on the envelope ON HIS MAJESTY'S SERVICE, having found, to his delight, free delivery would ensue.

That Roxburgh appointed such an eccentric – swiftly known around the school as 'Cluffy' – reflected the importance he placed on surrounding himself with lively characters. Youth and vitality were all-important. An unpromising degree could be offset, as in Martin MacLaughlin's case, by promising incidentals, like a few months at the Sorbonne and a connection with the Duke of Westminster.

* * *

From the start he captured attention. Gavin Maxwell wrote of him as 'weirdly hunched', stalking down a corridor 'in the manner of Napoleon'. Terence Prittie likewise found him distinctly striking:

A beak of a nose, a piercingly pale blue eye, an unimpressively small cranium, the stamping, swinging gait of a man who was always in a hurry, and the high cackle of laughter which left an echo behind him – these are things that one remembers about the man. He was ceaselessly on the move, preferring to address his class from the front of his desk, uneasily, jiving, hustling across North and South Fronts on his way to the classrooms, and sometimes breaking into a shambling lope en route for the tennis courts by the shop – where he hoisted lobs in the manner of old King Gustav of Sweden.

Cluffy made his mark early by founding the highly successful Debating Society that he ran throughout his Stowe years. Masters would regularly participate, he and physicist Hugh Heckstall-Smith leading the way with 'This House views with concern the possibility of a Conservative victory at the polls'. Cluffy, the proposer, was seconded by the future politician John Boyd-Carpenter; Heckstall by the future writer James Reeves. Though Baldwin was later to defeat Ramsay MacDonald, Cluffy won a great victory. He was an irresistible debater, 'always ready to take to the floor' and 'displaying Celtic wit in a gobbling voice with a long carry'.

Cluffy also started the Senior Essay Society and the Twelve Club, where he was soon holding forth on 'A Prologue to the World War' and appointing John Boyd-Carpenter as his secretary. Whenever other groups were looking for a speaker, he would be quick to oblige. One of the Arts Club's first talks featured Cluffy's reminiscences of Pompeii.

Within two years he was History Tutor, holding sway in one of the red-brick teaching blocks just inside Cobham Court. Roxburgh's hunch had paid off. Cluffy not only knew his subject well but was articulate and imaginative, insisting on the boldest of essay writing. Stowe House's own history was naturally a useful asset, and he was soon writing about it in *The Stoic*. As ever, facts were useful, but secondary to richly confident language:

The society of Vanbrugh's time was more experienced, more sound in the fundamentals of taste and learning than our own. For these very reasons it is a society which cannot be easily understood. The tyro of a democratic age takes the majestic for the effete, the uncomfortable for the undesirable. My Lord Pierglass[23] and my Lady Girandole saw their stately unpractical houses in another way. The absence of bath-rooms, the lack of bed-chambers did not trouble them. But they did esteem a house of great reception rooms and classic beauty, grottoes worthy of the nymphs, lawns where Mr Pitt might play cricket, and shaded alleyways where the wits could jest and the poets meditate. These immense houses had faults, but they were the faults of immense men, the aristocrats, who, if they lost America, gave to Britain the best and most prosperous period in its history...

Cluffy was a teacher for top sixth-form sets. Understandably, he was less effective with lower forms. There was also the problem of his wild appearance that 'encouraged

---

23   There were, of course, no such persons. Cluffy was showing off his erudition. A pierglass (a large mirror between two windows) and a girandole (an elaborate candle-holder) were eighteenth-century luxuries.

gibes and misbehaviour', even though he was 'by no means unable to compete with unruliness'. He chose carefully the few he thought might make historians and was brilliant with them. His panache brought history alive. He could make the dullest of historical characters seem hugely interesting. In achieving all this, as Heckstall-Smith was to observe, he often resorted to an unusual technique:

> He used to make the most outrageous assertions, but chose assertions too complex to be refuted without a good deal of research. He managed to make the boys so indignant at times that they felt inclined to do almost anything to prove him wrong; and this could only be done by ferreting among the history shelves in the library...

Of the first twenty-four university scholarships and exhibitions Stowe obtained, twelve were for history.

Cluffy taught some French and German as well. He was a well-travelled polymath, delighting in sharing his enthusiasms in school trips to Europe. One disaster in Sicily, however, soon became legendary:

> We had lunched on salami in a humble taverna close to Catania railway station. Unwisely, we had drunk rich, golden local wine as if it were cider. In the train to Noto we began to argue furiously, but Cluffy magnanimously 'made it up' as we drew into the station. 'Come on,' he said, 'let's have no truck with these Italian porters.' He flung the door open imperiously. Unfortunately, he had forgotten that he was not in England and the platform was four feet below him. He bounced off the top step into two porters and an old lady carrying a basket of oranges, and all four went down on the platform, with oranges running and bouncing onto the line.

Italy featured strongly in Cluffy's great coup, *Newest Europe*, a book offering his views on the contemporary political scene, published by Longmans in 1931. He was sympathetic to the advent of Fascism in Italy. It was 'one of Italy's contributions to civilisation' on a par with its gifts of 'the medieval church, the first European banks and the beginnings of world commerce'. Just as in the past Italian fascism had produced great people from Virgil to Leonardo, so now, in the present, it had produced Marconi and Mussolini:

No doubt there has been a loss to individualism and an expulsion of liberal ideas. But the first duty of any Englishman or American who wishes to understand other countries is to forget all about his own.

In discussing Germany, he was confident there should be no alarm at the Nazis' recent election success:

Despite the sensational growth of Herr Hitler's National Socialists, the Parliamentary majority of the Social Democrats and kindred Parties has not been upset. Government in Germany for the present is likely to be of the same mild red political hue which it has been since the war.

Around Stowe, however, *Newest Europe* consolidated Cluffy's scholarly status. *The Epicurean* was soon offering it an affectionate salute:

The glory of Stowe is a master I know,
Who possesses a nose like a vulture,
And a head that contains quite magnificent brains,
Which he keeps to disseminate Culture.

The way he has taken our minds to awaken,
And to lift up our eyes from the mud is
A way, I have heard, not unwise; in a word,
To encourage Historical Studies.

Army Class exercises he wholly despises,
In Physics he puts no reliance,
Or in methods designed for training the mind,
Such as Euclid or Classics or Science.

But to learn about things like the habits of kings,
And the method of floating the dollar,
And treaties and sieges and monarchs and lieges –
Now that is the job for a Scholar!

To judge like a sage the Mind of an Age,
To classify countries with caution,
To slay reputations of prominent nations,
To view everything in Proportion –

This noble endeavour he will further for ever;
And indeed it is needless to tell him,
That in every section of mental perfection
No man can be found to excel him.

Cluffy's other remarkable achievement was to establish Stowe as one of the best fencing schools in the country. Early on, he advertised its attractions by operating at the bottom of the South Front steps. By July 1926 it had become so important a sport that he was able to announce proudly:

We now have a 'salle d'armes' of our own. Completed at the close of the Seven Years War, the Temple of Concord and Victory is a fine relic to the great days of swordsmanship.

It was damp inside, for there was no heating, and two smelly lamps provided only modest illumination. Fencing in Concord's portico accordingly became the norm. Cluffy's passion for the sport meant that Stowe in his time, 'with one doubtful exception', never lost against another school. His achievements long remained vivid:

His own fencing was mediocre. The secrets of his success were his discrimination in picking talent, his bounding enthusiasm, his abilities as a coach and his readiness to give praise to the members of his team. One should mention, perhaps one other factor: he was a brilliant advocate of his own side. In school matches there would be a clash of foils, and one umpire would claim a hit – against the Stoic. Cluffy would mince into the arena. 'I'm not …quite …sure,' he would say, the last word on a high nasal note. 'I rather think the attack came from here' – indicating the member of the home side. He generally got his way.

Getting his own way had become somewhat obsessive. It was even mirrored in his driving. The roads of the period were charmingly sleepy, but the egotistical Cluffy, it seems, did his best to liven things up. Hunched over the wheel of his Morris Oxford, he would pretend to be Guglio Ramponi, winner of the Mille Miglia, hugging the crown of the road, crowding out cars that came his way, and bitterly complaining at the same time of the decline in driving standards. His control of his machinery, meanwhile, was only fitful. On one occasion, when he reversed into his narrow Stowe garage under the guidance of Major Haworth, Cluffy so confused clutch and brake that the unfortunate Haworth ended up pinned against the back wall, anxiously urging him to engage first gear.

In 1931 Cluffy's sense of self-worth, already considerable, had received an unfortunate boost when he spent the Easter term in the USA lecturing at the American University in Washington and acting as Associate Professor of Modern History at Rollins College, Florida. On return he seemed more combative than ever. One flaw he inherited from the O'Melaghlins was 'that less amiable Celtic trait of feuding'. The barbed comments he was making about one or two senior masters, whom he considered pompous drones, went down very badly. The matter was taken to J.F. The feud swiftly escalated. Cluffy finally decided to win the argument by handing in his resignation. J.F., under immense pressure from the opponents of the MacLaughlin empire, sorrowfully accepted it.

No other master in the 1920s had done more for the reputation of the new school than Cluffy. He had basked in J.F.'s favour. When Queen Mary laid the Chapel's foundation stone in 1927 he was one of the handful of masters presented to her in J.F.'s garden.[24] But in 1932 he had finally overstepped the mark.

His last fencing match, against a skilful team brought to Stowe by Sir Oswald Mosley, proved particularly poignant, ending as it did in that unheard of eventuality for Cluffy, defeat. Despite Cluffy's best efforts, the leader of the British Union of Fascists managed six wins himself. In the light of later events, the surprise defeat was distinctly ominous.

* * *

In January 1933, against Roxburgh's best advice, Martin MacLaughlin followed Browne and Arnold into the Inspectorate. He did not last long there. When he began

---

24 The others were Earle, Clarke, Acland, Arnold, Hole and Capel Cure.

applying for school posts, J.F. supported him strongly, though admitting he was 'highly-strung and fine-drawn':

> *In some ways I regarded his departure as a disaster. But he had certainly been quarrelling with some of the more elderly and hard-bitten housemasters and I think he had got tired of the struggle. You would see for yourself that he is a bit temperamental and inclined to exaggerate things… Actually I had a good deal of sympathy with him because there is no type I deplore more than the diehard Housemaster… Personally I have always got on extremely well with MacLaughlin and I enjoy his conversation greatly when he dines here.*

By October 1934 he was having to mention Cluffy's rising mental health problems. 'The wretched man spoils every chance he is offered by his preposterous affectations.' After a succession of jobs failed to work out, in 1938 he somehow persuaded his rich, elderly father to buy him his own school in Scotland. He was full of confidence. Finally, he could create his own Stowe …

* * *

Newstead School for Boys was an amazing gift. Its current pupils were housed in a nineteenth-century mansion (Deanston House) in fifty-five acres. A grand entrance led to a building gleaming like a small castle, dominated by a five-storey entrance tower. MacLaughlin's predecessor as owner-headmaster bequeathed forty boarders of all ages.

At first, it looked as if he might make a success of things. He began marketing Newstead defiantly as a Public School with all the usual exams and inspections. In addition to the usual games there would be skating on the lake, riding, golf and fishing. He courted the local gentry with enthusiasm, retaining Lady Margaret Sackville, poet and cousin of Vita Sackville-West, as the School's 'Visitor'. On his first Speech Day (in summer 1938), the chief guest was the Countess of Tankersville; on his second, Scottish playwright James Bridie. Numbers, however, continued to fluctuate around forty.

J.F. found himself badgered for support and gallantly came up to Cluffy's Speech Days. He also allowed his name to be used as one of four educational experts who had become Newstead's official 'Advisers'. He found Cluffy (whose father had just died) emotional on the Speech Day of 1939. Afterwards J.F. wrote encouragingly: 'As soon as Hitler starts, you will be full up with boys from the towns.' 'It is nice to think that Hitler may be of some use,' replied Cluffy mid-July, 'but I am inclined to think that nothing will happen… Hitler wants to break up Poland and Rumania but does not want a major war, and will not risk it, if we make it perfectly clear we are going to fight …' The confident author of *Modern Europe* had again got things wrong.

Each week as headmaster he would give an afternoon's lecture on the current developments in Europe. In the summer of 1939, only a month or so before the outbreak of war, he took a school party to Germany. They all gazed in awe at the Siegfried Line, the deep fortifications that the Nazis were to bypass. On his return, Newstead School created its own 'Brownshirts', a quasi-military squad that built bridges and repaired walls.

Cluffy's school was not unimaginative. The boys had allotments within a walled vegetable garden and complete freedom of the school grounds; educational visits took in any number of cotton mills and iron foundries, often with Cluffy to the fore. At Killiecrankie, for example, he would give lectures about a Redcoat who leapt across the River Garry, fleeing from the victorious Jacobites. Even the more traditional things like crocodiles to and from a distant church and early morning runs and cold baths might have been tolerated but for one thing. Cluffy had become an alcoholic. Indeed, he was often 'incapable for days at a time'.

In September 1940, he rang up a parent and abusively demanded money. The news swiftly spread. Pupils were withdrawn. He somehow kept going into 1941, but the end was already in sight, and when the Army suddenly requisitioned the house and grounds, he accepted that, after less than three years, his school was finished. Only in his early forties, he took refuge with his widowed mother in Cheltenham.

* * *

Drink and drugs gained further hold. Jobs proved elusive. He lasted no more than twenty-four hours at Uppingham. An Old Stoic, coming across him in a Cheltenham pub in 1943, wrote to Roxburgh in distress:

A bowed figure shambled in, with torn overcoat, unbrushed hair and shaking hands. For a moment I did not do more than glance in that direction, but when

I heard him speak I looked again. Could it be? Yes, it was Cluffy, obviously in the throes of a terrific drinking bout. I hesitated, and finally spoke to him. It took some time for my presence to penetrate a very fuddled brain. I was really horrified at the state he was in. I took him to his home where I met his mother stoking up the hot water boiler. It was all very tragic. What is more tragic is that their home is full of treasures – silver, regency ornaments, pictures (I spotted a Ruysdael) and this besotted creature showing them off. I believe he is lecturing the troops, though what on, and with what results, I dare not think.

Only months later Cluffy was informing Roxburgh of his intention to return to Stowe:

It is now ten years since I left and just more than twenty since I came to help you. These last 10 years have only strengthened my faith – I know that Stowe has the right idea and I think I know how great it is that have developed it. [sic] My illness is over and I shall come back to teach in the autumn. Preferably, I would settle at Stowe and write and lecture and teach – that is, if you care to find a sword for your First Lieutenant…

It soon became clear that his illness wasn't over. J.F. replied with his usual courtesy, sadly but firmly declaring his lack of vacancies. Cluffy responded by sending a gift for the School, a Watkin Williams-Wynn drawing[25], which he had just come across. Roxburgh had it framed and hung in the Aurelian Room. For Cluffy there were to be further short teaching debacles; occasional glimpses, too, of the promising past, like the chapter on 'Nationalism and Internationalism' he somehow managed to contribute to *A History of the World*, published in 1944.

In 1948, the year before Roxburgh retired, he learnt that Cluffy had been sectioned and was now in a mental home, unlikely ever to recover his senses.

Sixteen years of appalling anguish followed, mainly spent in institutions. Garbled letters were sent to Roxburgh's successors, in one of which Cluffy asked whether he might be buried at Stowe. But the tragic circumstances of his lonely death in March 1964 precluded this. Having slipped away from his Oxford institution, the penniless Cluffy had headed for the area in which he had grown up, though neither his sister

---

25 Probably the scene in the Grenville Room, as illustrated in Michael Bevington's *Stowe House*, 2002

nor his parents were still alive. Found sleeping in a Shropshire ditch, he was taken for shelter to Shrewsbury Police Station, where he collapsed and died.

The antique desk the school had gifted Cluffy on his departure in December 1932 had been bequeathed to Stowe in his will.

9

THE REVD. HUMPHREY PLAYFORD

Bruce Housemaster for twenty-five years
Stowe 1925–58

Humphrey Blake Playford arrived at Stowe in 1925. An imposing figure of nearly six and a half feet, he had been an outstanding oarsman at Cambridge in an age when rowing Blues could be national sporting celebrities. He was to be a towering presence in the Common Room until the late Fifties, synonymous with Bruce, the House he ran like a breakaway baron, seemingly answerable to no-one.

He was born in 1896 at Hampton-on-Thames into a famous rowing family. His father, a stockbroker, had been a star at Henley in the 1870s; his grandfather in the 1840s. Humphrey, however, initially resisted the sport during his five years at St Paul's.

His schooldays ended in July 1914, the month the First World War began, and he joined the Army in 1915, first as a driver in the Army Service Corps and subsequently a Second Lieutenant in charge of Horse Transport. Having survived two years of fighting on the Western Front, in early 1918 he transferred into the fledgling Royal Air Force. Posted to 70 Wing at Felixstowe, for the last three months of the war he scoured the seas in flimsy flying-boats.

On the coming of peace he joined the London Rowing Club and studied for an accelerated Pass Degree at Jesus College, Cambridge. For four successful years he rowed for Jesus. He was also the heaviest crew member and powerhouse in the winning Cambridge crews in the first three Boat Races to be held since the war (1920-22). 'There is something about rowing that makes it impossible for anyone, who takes it up, willingly to drop it,' he wrote in 1922, when President of the University's Boat Club. 'There are some who would put it down to insanity.'

Rowing may well have played a part in the decisions to stay on after his degree to study theology at Ridley Hall, and, after his ordination, to return as Chaplain to Jesus College. It was then, in early 1923, that the Cambridge grapevine encouraged Roxburgh to write to Humphrey Playford in exploratory fashion:

My dear sir,

A friend – I fear an exceedingly optimistic friend – has told me that you might consider coming to Stowe as our Chaplain. You probably know that Stowe is a new public school, which is to open its doors in May. The work there will at the first be rather small, but it will rapidly grow and the destiny of the school will depend, I think, as much upon the first Chaplain as upon any other single man...

Humphrey duly met up with J.F., but decided not to give up the college chaplaincy and his rowing. He won some famous victories in 1923 and a year later coached the Jesus first boat to Head of the River. He also equalled the triumphs of his father and grandfather by winning the Grand Challenge Cup, the most prestigious event at the Henley Regatta. At Henley, too, he was captain of the Leander Club.

In 1925 Humphrey had just accepted the curacy of Christ Church, East Greenwich, when Roxburgh, though no longer needing a chaplain, invited him 'to look us over'. Ever a keen motorist, Humphrey conceded 'a run to Stowe' might be fun. The car flew, the visit prospered and Roxburgh offered him a job:

The salary sounds low, but I have got to weigh your Blue, your age and your Parson's work against the fact of your Pass Degree and your lack of teaching experience. I do hope, however, that you will not regard £230 as a sweated wage...

And so, at the age of twenty-nine, Humphrey joined Stowe for its eighth term.

* * *

His accommodation initially was in the uncomfortable White Horse Block, but, when it was re-developed and opened as Grafton in 1926, Humphrey moved in as

Underhousemaster. The first Grafton log book contains Humphrey's explanation of the choice of two Latin words, *virtus* and *integritas*, for the House's motto:

> It is hoped that all generations of Graftonians will be able to say, 'The lot is fallen unto me in a fair ground: yea, I have a goodly heritage.' This will only be possible if those qualities of perfect manhood signified by virtus and integritas are the aspirations of Grafton. Both words can be translated as 'virtue', yet virtus also means 'manliness' and integritas 'purity', without which no true manliness is attainable.

The Log Book also has a 1927 holiday snap of Humphrey at the tiller of a small boat in Scotland alongside the short-serving Grafton Housemaster, P.B. Freeman. At thirty, with his square chin, jet-black hair and clean-shaven good looks, Humphrey would not have seemed out of place on the cover of *Film Weekly*. In 1929 he was asked to take over Bruce, whose housemaster, Francis Arnold, was leaving for the inspectorate. 'It is a house,' J.F. warned him, 'which somewhat needs pulling together.'

Like his predecessors, Humphrey found the chaotic geography of Bruce a challenge. For his own Spartan accommodation Humphrey at once ordered himself a seven-foot bath. (His successor, Chris Deacon, on the short side, was said to have nearly drowned in it and had it swiftly replaced.) The Music Room, of course, acted as Bruce's Houseroom. George Clarke was to wince at the memory:

> How it survived so well the rough and tumble of a junior day room I can't think. In my time as Humphrey's underhousemaster, they used the cupboards down at the far end as dart boards and once a year they built a charming indoor auditorium with tiered seats on scaffolding poles to put on entertainments in the alcove.

Although not a disciplinarian by nature – he was before his time in refusing to use a cane – Humphrey found the new job to his liking. Bruce quickly rallied and numbers increased from 65 to 75. When in 1930 another headmaster tried to poach Humphrey, J.F. responded spiritedly: 'Playford is quite first-class and if you take him away from me, I shall go for you with a revolver...' The pair enjoyed a good rapport through the early 1930s.

Humphrey was also a sympathetic presence in the classroom, where he taught History, Elementary Maths and English to the less gifted forms. In 1931, moreover, he stood in during the lack of a chaplain, and was soon putting to rights (as he believed) the first chaplain's open-minded approach:

> At present we are too much influenced by criticism and too un-enterprising in our efforts. The boys are too vague in their beliefs, too apathetic about their religion and too much encouraged to be sceptical and unorthodox...

Among his suggestions were a pupils' Chapel committee, less outside sermons, more instructional addresses and two confirmations a year.

Everything he touched went well. His participation in the Gilbert and Sullivan society was said to have raised the standard considerably.

* * *

By the mid-1930s the Common Room was strongly polarized, with Humphrey and Eddie Capel Cure leading the Liberals (recently reinforced by T.H. White and Bill McElwee) against the growingly influential Conservatives. Humphrey infuriated the latter, but he was impregnable, commanding much respect within the community, ever active, enthusiastically driving tractors, chopping down trees, clearing undergrowth and even building his own garage. The Conservatives complained to Roxburgh that Humphrey shut his ears regarding any discipline problems involving Bruce boys. They also felt he delegated too much to his seniors. J.F. smiled sympathetically but did nothing.

A sense of fun flourished in Bruce in the pre-war years with Humphrey's Lancia often a central participant. Boys unable to go home at half-term often found themselves speeding all over England in it. On the outbreak of war, Humphrey filled it up with all the copies of paperback novels he could find in the Cambridge bookshops. The Lancia regularly ventured abroad with parties of Stoics, all navigating, diary-keeping and wine-tasting. In 1935 he enlisted David Brown and Donald Crichton-Miller to help take a party of sixth-formers, during which they somehow sped through the Turkish army, out on manoeuvres.

For many years he was an integral part of Bill McElwee's trips to the continent with the historians. In April 1938, for example, the two took eight Stoics to study the buildings and literature of Normandy. One of the party, Edmund Neville-Rolfe, later painted the group sitting outside a café in the Cathedral Square at Coutances, 'blissfully unaware of the hostilities about to commence'. The painting encapsulates the relaxed and civilized values inculcated by Humphrey and Bill.

Humphrey's continued passion for flying was exemplified by his acquisition in July 1934 of his Royal Aero Club Aviator's Certificate, and most terms in the mid-thirties *The Stoic* included his enthusiastic reports:

> *We have made several expeditions to Halton for flights in dual Avros. All members have been able to handle machines in the air, and some have shown considerable aptitude after a little tuition. We have been to Bicester again, this time to see and fly Sidestrands.*

English Tutor Tim White, ten years younger than Humphrey, was soon utilising Humphrey's expertise, particularly at the Finmere airstrip. White's flying had begun in April 1934 when he and Capel Cure took their first lessons at Sywell Aerodome, Northampton, in 'an incredibly ancient Avro held together with pieces of insulating tape'. Humphrey ferried them there and back in his Lancia and, on the outward journey, held forth on the intricacies of a plane's controls. White reported (in *England Have My Bones*):

> *Humphrey said: 'Movement's almost imperceptible, and you won't feel in contact with your aeroplane at all during the first hour.' It was a piece of luck he said this, because I had been reading a book and had got it into my head that one pushed things about by numbers.*

Delighted by outperforming Capel in their first gentle attempts under professional instruction, the extravagantly jubilant White upset Humphrey by his loud singing in the back seat on the way back to Stowe – his 'songs' apparently including an out-of-tune version of the scherzo from the Brahms Quintet in F Minor. Humphrey was quite amused the next day, however, when he received a note from White challenging him to a cross-Atlantic flight. The two usually got on well. Two years later, Humphrey was to receive a copy of *England Have My Bones* inscribed 'with love from Tim'.

Although as Hon. Secretary Humphrey spent much of his leisure time at the Pineapple, the school's London Boys' Club, his liberal views were inevitably in regular conflict with those of the equally opinionated Fritz Clifford, the Club's Hon. Treasurer. The conservatives' grip on the Common Room had increased perceptibly in 1933 with the appointment of Patrick Hunter in the new role of Senior Tutor. Notes in Hunter's neat hand began speeding to J.F., suggesting things could be made 'tighter', particularly in Bruce. Prep was one of his vexations:

> *I frankly feel that our chief weakness here is that nothing like 100, or even 50, per cent is done of what might be done in preparation. Much, I am sure, depends on what is demanded by the Masters for the whom the prep is done. But could more perhaps be done by Housemasters to ensure that the state of things is better than at present in studies?*

Under Hunter's influence J.F. began to ask more of his housemaster barons. With an unusual terseness he wrote to Humphrey:

> *On Monday Bruce will be provided with a complete set of new Houseroom chairs. These are fresh and strong and cannot be broken except through rough usage. I very much hope that they will be treated with reasonable care and that if any breakage does occur the boy or boys responsible will be reported to you and charged by the Bursar.*

Humphrey was outraged. Almost as prolific in his notes to J.F. as Patrick Hunter, he quickly sought to regain the moral high ground with a complaint that £2 12s 6d had been deducted from his salary. Such penny-pinching, he declared, was intolerable. Just because he had been forced to spend time in the San, why should the sum required to pay his deputy be charged against his salary? He had only spent time in the San because of an accident, through no fault of his own, in the discharge of his duties! J.F. was forced to apologise. 'I am afraid I had not remembered,' he conceded, 'that your illness was due to the blow you received when demonstrating the use of your long fire chute.'

The relationship started to change. J.F., under pressure from Patrick Hunter, began to confide to others that Humphrey was 'not an easy man to manage'. By the late 1930s Humphrey was regularly penning unrepentant explanations for being out of school, forgetting lessons and being absent from chapel services and meals. All too aware of his elder brother's country mansion, he remained on the attack, meanwhile, about school food and the mean accommodation of Stowe resident masters. It made him all the keener to live well in the holidays, happily accepting regular invitations from Bruce parents. He often stayed, too, with the Fremantles at Swanbourne.

* * *

The coming of the Second World War allowed him to forget the inadequacies of the Stowe kitchens and play a brief but vigorous part in the war effort at the age of forty-four. In May 1940, two days before the evacuation from Dunkirk began, Roxburgh was hastily explaining to Pickard-Cambridge, his Chairman of Governors:

> *Playford has been invited to take charge of a number of ambulances which are being sent out by the Anglo-French Ambulance Corps to deal with the French wounded, by whom the French organisation have been completely overflowed. I advised him to take the job, for which he seems admirably qualified. He is a remarkable motorist and he has many times motored the whole length of France under conditions of every sort. He knows more about motor cars and keeping them on the road than any ordinary mechanic, and he has plenty of drive and organising power. He has been fretting to do something active for some time...*

By 1 June 1940 he had headed off on this courageous enterprise. He was still there when Paris fell on 14 June and only just made good his return to England before the surrender of France later that month. Back on home soil, he continued to work with the Anglo-French resistance movement before returning to Stowe in January 1941.

He now found himself, on Tim Brook's departure, in the role of stop-gap Chaplain for the second time. J.F.'s feelings were distinctly mixed when he broke the news to his Chairman of Governors:

> *I do not think it is an ideal arrangement to have a Housemaster as a Chaplain, nor do I think that Playford is the ideal man for the job. But he will do better when he is in charge than he did when he was working under Brook (with whom he did not always agree) and we could hardly hope to get a first-class man in wartime.*

In the holidays, most masters were timetabled to do bouts of fire-watching. Humphrey, however, preferred to work on the land. Wade's at Barton Stacey, a Georgian farmhouse just north of Winchester, was his regular haunt. He cut 160 acres of various crops one summer and innumerable dead trees one Christmas.

Ivor Cross, in charge of the organisation of holiday fire-watching, protested to J.F., without success, at Humphrey's absence.

When news came of Ivor Cross's imminent departure from Stowe, Humphrey eyed the private side of Chatham with interest, raising with J.F. the possibility of a move there from Bruce. Told that it was a married master's house and so Alasdair Macdonald was in line for it, Humphrey responded enigmatically that he might well soon qualify. When J.F. tried to clarify this, Humphrey told him he was off to London on Wednesday and hoped to make some progress then. It would seem that Humphrey's marriage proposal, if made, proved unsuccessful, for by the Easter of 1942 the admirable Alasdair Macdonald had gone into Chatham.

Humphrey's strong response to this upset was to apply for the headship of Rondebosch High School for Boys in South Africa, a rowing school close to a long-established rowing club. J.F.'s testimonial was hardly one to impress:

He is a man with whom it is not easy to become really intimate. I do not know as much as one might have expected after all these years about the spiritual side of his life. His churchmanship is best described as moderate and tolerant. The spiritual tempo of the place quickened under him, when he was Chaplain here, with a pleasing increase in the numbers taking Holy Communion. As regards his sermons, the best are good and his worst never fall below a fair standard...

Many Old Stoics, including those outside Bruce, would have disagreed with this lukewarm assessment. Peter Anstey, for example, was to write of Humphrey's 'unforgettable sermons'. A *Buckingham Advertiser* report also survives of a Playford sermon at Buckingham Parish Church on the Easter Day, 1943, showing him both direct and thought-provoking:

The presence of the Risen Lord with his Disciples during the walk to Emmaus emphasizes to us that in these dark days the presence of Christ could be as real as it was on that first Easter evening.

The Resurrection, he told the attentive congregation, meant that they could firmly believe in life after death. However, they should not be led away 'by the unfortunate words' of some of their hymns to construct in their minds a picture-book idea of heaven:

Peter Anstey also offered an anecdote suggesting Humphrey's interpersonal skills were much livelier than J.F. was intimating. Both were on Scafell Pike when Anstey suddenly became aware of a tall and somehow familiar figure descending the pathway above him, immaculately turned out in plus fours, windcheater, woolly hat and heavy climbing boots:

> *Humphrey, as he turned out to be, was full of helpful advice for the completion of my hare-brained venture onto the high fells. He subsequently entertained me royally at the Dungeon Ghyll Hotel (where it transpired he was a frequent and honoured guest).*
>
> *When I returned this summer to the Lake District, I happened to meet the daughter of the former proprietor of the Dungeon Ghyll. I diffidently mentioned Humphrey's name and her face lit up. She recalled his all-encompassing friendliness, his love of the mountains, the generations of Stoics to whom he had introduced them…*

* * *

The coming of peace meant the return of competitive rowing, still the centre of Humphrey's existence. Henley had always been his Mecca, and in January 1946 he was invited to become a Steward of the Regatta. For once, he made a cautious approach to J.F.:

> *It is the highest honour that they can confer and indeed one of the highest honours in the rowing world. I should very much like to accept, but I feel that I ought to ask your permission since it would necessitate my attendance at the regatta more regularly than in the past. The regatta comes in the middle of the summer term, during the last week in June or the first week in July.*

Colleagues struggled to appreciate his status in the rowing world. The idea of him prowling around 'with that absurd pink Leander cap perched on his head' caused amusement. J.F., however, appreciating the positive spin-off for the school, told him to accept 'promptly and emphatically'.

Roxburgh's final Stowe years were not easy. Even before the war, he had started visiting Harley Street in connection with occasional blackouts, and so, in 1947, to help himself cope, he created the post of Second Master, giving it to the scrupulously efficient Fritz Clifford. In a careful and sympathetic letter to Capel Cure and Humphrey, both of whom had served Stowe longer than Clifford, he explained how, at fifty-nine and after all the strain of the war, his blackouts were getting worse:

I have lately been ill with disconcerting frequency and for inconveniently long periods, nor does [Dr] Bostock hold out much hope of better things in the future... In considering whom I should nominate I have, of course, thought over the arguments as to seniority, but it has seemed to me that small differences could not be decisive...

Humphrey was disappointed. He understood 'the many admirable qualities of Clifford'. The disappointment, he told J.F., went deeper than that:

It seems to signalize a complete change of policy and an end of the Stowe I had hoped for. Clifford stands for the stern disciplinarian and the traditional Public School system: Stowe, one had hoped, was aiming at something more free, more friendly, more enlightened. Had you chosen Capel or me, at least the way to that would still have been open... The bias is bound to be towards a rigid and stereotyped educational system. I cannot do other than to deplore that.

It was fair comment. The well-balanced enlightened atmosphere, 'the spirit of 1923', could be said to have gone missing for a while, though house and grounds were always there, urging its return.

Inevitably, Humphrey became one of the Second Master's chief targets. In May 1948, for example, Clifford was providing J.F. with 'a considered statement of the difficulties Humphrey Playford creates here', citing the old chestnut of not supporting colleagues who wanted to discipline a Bruce boy as one of his 'four major failings'. The other complaints were either petty (not taking enough interest in the Pineapple Club) or ludicrous: 'There was an unseemly difference of opinion between him and the Chaplain about the Easter flowers, in which, unfortunately, he got his way'.

The Senior Tutor, Patrick Hunter, supported Clifford, using Humphrey as an illustration of why the Stowe work ethic had disintegrated. 'He had two periods and missed one by collusion (getting another master to take it) and the other by bloody-minded obstinacy... I write in no spirit of grievance...'.

Roxburgh must have longed for retirement. Humphrey, however, was finding the prospect of his own retirement unsettling. He felt far from secure about leaving Stowe. One grey morning, he aired his anxieties with J.F.:

> *What does the future hold for me? We are told that salaries will be revised – but I shall be too old to benefit. I ought to be saving now, but I can't... I was horrified to discover that the L&G[26] policies do not produce a pension of £200, the sum specified, but something less...*
>
> *Stowe does not provide a home for me, and it does not pay me enough to provide one for myself; it apparently assumes that my family will provide one for me – but I have no family to do it.*

J.F. responded with one last piece of generosity: a formal agreement that when the time came for Humphrey to retire at 60, Stowe would allow him to stay on an extra two years, to boost his pension.

* * *

Humphrey's last nine Stowe years coincided with the uneasy headmastership of Eric Reynolds. Like most of the older masters, Humphrey no doubt viewed the newcomer with some misgivings, though they had much in common. Both had been long-serving bachelor housemasters. Reynolds, too, was a staunch Christian who enjoyed the outdoor life and was witty, cultured and liberally inclined.

It was not long before Patrick Hunter was urging Reynolds to cancel the tradition of allowing Humphrey time off school for the Henley Regatta:

> *... The whole story of his attitude to his responsibilities in teaching is, in my opinion, a sordid one, with a degree of meanness, self-deception and neglect of duty which it would be hard to surpass... This is a 'racket' which must end.*

---

26 In 1934 Stowe and other schools of Warrington's fragile Martyrs' Memorial Trust were saved by the Legal and General Assurance Company.

Reynolds, to his credit, upheld the status quo.

One of Reynold's early initiatives was to limit a housemaster's tenure to fifteen years. This, of course, put Humphrey's position in Bruce under some pressure. By 1951 he had already notched up twenty-three years. Eventually, soon after the Queen's Coronation, in December 1953, despite the staunchest of rearguard actions, the baron had to leave his castle.

Humphrey would loom large over his successor, Chris Deacon, for the next four and a half years. His would be a hard act to follow. He was already a legend in Bruce. Stories were legion: his celebratory suppers in the Green Man for all the cup-winning teams; the trip to London for George VI's Coronation; and the one, at the speed of light, to Fenner's, purely to watch Bradman bat, only for the great man to get out seconds before their arrival… Every Old Stoic seemed to have a Humphrey Playford story. For Jos Nicholl it was the House Prayers that started with 'I don't mind "Humphrey" and I don't mind "Humph", but I absolutely won't stand for "Bumph" – let us pray'

* * *

Briefly, Humphrey thought about Prep School Headships. 'He was a very good housemaster,' wrote Reynolds on his behalf. 'He is an impressive figure and has about 6 foot 6 of bolt uprightness without a grey hair. I am sure he would inspire parents with confidence… His academic qualifications are very poor.'

No interview followed.

Commuting from Fringford Lodge, near Stratton Audley, he was a less noticeable presence around Stowe. The baron was suddenly cutting a forlorn figure, tending to keep himself to himself. As the year agreed for his departure drew nearer, he began angling with Reynolds for a further stay of execution. Old stagers hanging on, particularly of the more liberal variety, were not what Reynolds needed to help overcome mounting difficulties. 'I know how much you have the interests of Stowe at heart,' he responded gently, 'and that you are anxious in your vigour to stay with us, but I am afraid that it cannot be managed.'

In the event, he and Reynolds both left together in the tumultuous summer of 1958. He was one of seven departing members of Common Room whose cumulative length of service was an awesome two hundred and twenty years. Patrick Hunter, old tensions forgotten, gave him a friendly send-off in *The Stoic*:

For twenty-five years he made Bruce a House of outstanding quality: a good, often very good games House, but one which produced scholars too, a House whose particular stamp was one of gentleness and self-restraint, of tolerance and culture, a House that exemplified the civilized values at which Stowe has always aimed. He was, too, a good man at a crisis; self-possessed, calm and effective.

A Bruce dinner with a generous presentation was held in his honour in London. Many members of Bruce would keep in touch over the following years. He would officiate at several Old Stoic weddings.

Within the Common Room, past and present, he would retain many strong friendships. Typically, his departure from Stowe coincided with the gift from Bill McElwee of his latest book, *The Wisest Fool in Christendom*, inscribed 'with love and gratitude'.

* * *

For many decades he was talked about in the Stowe Common Room. Brian Stephan took the Hunter line, thinking him 'a remote, aloof man', showing 'little apparent interest in the school's activities, except for the Chapel when he was Chaplain'. George Clarke agreed:

He was aloof! Urbane, but thick-skinned and bloody-minded. It has to be said that he ran a very good House for so lazy a man, but he did what he wanted. Lots of Bill McElwee's historians tended to be at the top of the House, perhaps helping its tone. I don't remember him ever getting angry or even raising his voice. He seemed above that, with a lofty disregard for the worries and objections of others. To me personally he was always very friendly, but never a close companion. He was not very obviously Christian. It's said that early on in the War, when there was talk of the Germans dropping paratroopers disguised as nuns, one of the Common Room wags (probably Ratcliffe) suggested 'Why don't they drop Playford into France disguised as a clergyman?'

And there was one very special excursion:

He took me out to a pub for a meal one Saturday. It must have been one of the first Silverstone meetings, when all the little roads of North Bucks were overwhelmed with traffic. On the way back, we were confronted by an endless stream of traffic taking up most of the road to Chackmore. 'There are two ways we can deal with this,' said Humphrey. 'We can crawl past them, hugging our side of the road, or we can put our headlights on and drive down the middle, and they will get out of the way. Which shall we do?' I said we should drive down the middle. So he switched on the headlights and we did – and all the traffic gave way to him, right up to the Oxford Lodge. I suppose that he was taking the way he dealt with the problems of life, with sublime self-confidence.

There was, however, another viewpoint, an important one, that centred around the care and concern Humphrey quietly showed for those around him. Liz Zettl knew him well, for her late husband, Ewald, a modern linguist, long shared with Humphrey a practical interest in cars and car mechanics and had participated in some of the McElwee-Playford tours. Liz recalled him as someone of great kindness, citing as an example the many times he drove her to hospital when her husband suffered a severe illness:

He took me over to Oxford once a week for ten weeks. He would speak to Ewald and then discreetly leave us alone. He always took me to his brother's house for supper on the way home.

His innate modesty always impressed her. He kept very quiet about his encyclopaedic knowledge of the rowing world and the period when he regularly commentated on the Boat Race for the BBC beside the great John Snagge. 'He never "sold" himself the way others do. I always found him very sensitive.' Liz smiled to remember Humphrey's unsuccessful wooing of the formidable Sister of the School San, Miss Quennell.

* * *

But Humphrey's retirement began sensationally with a love affair. It is not known when he first met Elizabeth Bickersteth Birks, but she was the daughter of an illustrious Bedford doctor and granddaughter of a judge, had taught in Prep Schools all her life, and was currently at King's College School, Cambridge. They celebrated their engagement with a trip to New York on the Queen Mary in the summer of 1959 and, that October, the 63-year-old Humphrey married the 45-year-old Betty in Cambridge.

For much of the 1960s they were based at Epsom, while Humphrey and his wife taught at Prep Schools, first at Kingswood House, near the old town centre, and then at Woolpit, in the heart of countryside north of Ewhurst, where Humphrey was chaplain. In his spare time Humphrey wrote a history of the Jesus College Rowing Club, published in 1962. This was followed by two massive books recording the Henley Royal Regatta's history, for which he had at last found a sympathetic publisher and generous subscribers.

When the teaching came to an end, holidays abroad proliferated. Humphrey loved Switzerland but also guided Betty round France and Germany with dexterity. Betty was to recall that one of their final adventures was 'a very happy Wings week in Athens, getting to Delphi and all the classical sites'.

She only visited Stowe twice, Humphrey thinking it wrong for retired masters to 'haunt' the school. On the first occasion, in 1967, they had been invited by Bob Drayson to attend a Thanksgiving Service on the fortieth anniversary of the laying of the Chapel's foundation stone by Queen Mary. During the post-service lunch in the library, Humphrey reminisced about the clearing away of a yew tree and the Temple of Bacchus to make way for the new building, and how, during its construction, on many an evening after the builders left, he had 'crawled all over the site' in excitement. The Thanksgiving proved a heartening day, with Humphrey 'convinced that Stowe had got the right headmaster this time'.

His final Stowe visit was in 1970, to visit a relation of Betty's. She recalled with amusement:

> *He shocked my nephew by driving so far past a notice which said 'No cars beyond this point' that he reached somewhere in the grounds that the boy had never visited! On the way back, Humphrey saw a huge pile of logs and jokingly cried 'Ah! Those are just what I need!' 'You can't touch them,' cried my nephew in earnest. 'They're Mr Theobald's – for Community Service delivery!'*

By 1969 they had left Epsom for Alresford in Hampshire. Their small new home (30 West Street) dictated that all the saws and autographed oars that had embellished Humphrey's different studies at last had to be rationalised. The books, too. Among those still retained was *Harpoon at a Venture* inscribed: 'For Humphrey Playford, who gave me my first encouragement to write, Gavin Maxwell.'

The move to Alresford was connected with Humphrey's opportunity to help at the little church in the village of Bighton, situated within the grounds of Bighton House, a Regency mansion. Here, at last, he could feel at peace both with the tranquillity of the historic building and the strong reminders, all around, of Stowe.

* * *

By the late 1970s the towering figure that once had been so upright was no longer so. Humphrey's last year, indeed, had to be spent in the geriatric ward of Basingstoke Hospital. 'When age and sickness deprived him of speech,' commented one friend, 'he could still communicate with his serene and lovely smile.' One former Bruce pupil visited him regularly there:

> *Although he could not say more than 'yes' and 'no', he still beamed at one on arrival, and the staff said he was always a true gentleman. The essential goodness of the man was there to the end.*

In the late summer of 1981, when *The Times* and *Telegraph* announced his death at the age of eighty-five, the brief notice very aptly ended with the past tense of the school motto: *Perstabat et praestabat.* 'He stood firm and he stood out.'

The funeral duly took place at Bighton. The little church was absolutely full. There were half-a-dozen Old Stoics there, a number of contemporaries from his Oxford days, and a large body of fellow Henley enthusiasts. The address was given by a fellow Pauline, the Right Reverend C.J. Patterson, who had first met Humphrey sixty years ago at a Christian camp.

Betty later wrote to Jos Nicholl:

> *We sang lustily 'Praise My Soul' and 'The King of Love' and read Psalm 84. It really seemed gladsome and more like a memorial service than a sad funeral. The ashes were buried in the churchyard later.*
>
> *The last year was not as trying as it might have been because Humphrey accepted the fate of hospitalization and was loved and respected by the staff. Better looked after than I could manage at home, alone, and he really was an influence for good on his surroundings till the very end.*

In his letter to Betty, as Stowe's headmaster at the time of Humphrey's death,

Christopher Turner (who had met Humphrey at Henley and was a rowing Blue himself) mentioned how he was still talked about at the school 'in fond remembrance and not a little awe'. 'Thank you very much for your kind letter about Humphrey,' Betty replied. 'I am glad to think he has become a Stowe legend.'

10

CHARLES SPENCER

The first Head of English, dynamic & fragile
Stowe 1926-32

It is likely that Philip Browne, Stowe's first Head of Music, recommended Charles Spencer to Roxburgh. Not only had they been friends and teammates at Magdalen College, Oxford, they had holidayed together abroad in 1926, the year of Spencer's arrival. Roxburgh may well have had stronger candidates on paper. The twenty-three-year-old Spencer had a second class degree and no teaching experience. However, he quickly impressed and was soon given the special title of 'Universal Tutor to the Upper School'. In 1930, thanks to his efforts, English was elevated to parity with the other leading 'sides' or departments, with Spencer becoming the first English 'Tutor'. By 1932 he was widely regarded as one of 'the most vigorous and exciting' of all the early masters.

Alas, Charles Spencer's flair, like that of Martin MacLaughlin, was matched by emotional fragility. The two would both raise the profile of their subject significantly only to discover, on leaving Stowe, that life without the sympathetic support of J.F. could be seriously problematic. The lives of both men would eventually be overtaken by tragedy.

* * *

Charles Richard Spencer was a Welshman, son of a successful solicitor in Cardiff.

The Spencer home for several generations, Llwyn-yr-Eryr, his birthplace, stood by itself in many acres of grounds just outside the village of Llandough.

He was eleven and at Prep School (Brightlands, Gloucestershire) when the First World War broke out. In 1916, when his brother was twice awarded an MC for conspicuous bravery on the Western front, he began six years at Clifton College, where his sporting talents were soon in evidence. He was lucky that in his later Clifton years his Housemaster was the notable former county cricketer and international hockey player, R.P. Keigwin. Scholastically, however, he seems to have underperformed for some time, the summaries in his reports reflecting a distinctly volatile temperament: 'Must take things more seriously. Promising, but most unscholarly.' 'Not thorough – thinks too well of himself. Wants industry and teachableness.' 'Better progress – more humility.' And finally, 'Good progress. Has done very well – still an inane scholar.'

Inane or not, in the end Charles achieved a Demy Scholarship to Magdalen College, Oxford, and there he continued to impress on the cricket, rugby and hockey fields. Although, disappointingly, he did not win a cricket Blue, he made his first-class debut in 1923, playing for Oxford as a wicket-keeper against the touring West Indians. Other University appearances included one against the powerful Middlesex side. In the vacations he played regularly for the strong Penarth Cricket Club as well as for the Glamorgan Club and Ground XI, and, in his penultimate Oxford year, he made his county debut for Glamorgan. It was only a single appearance, but it certainly did much for the standing of Stowe's new arrival. County cricket in 1926 enjoyed a very high profile.

* * *

Charles Spencer proved, as Roxburgh had expected, 'a turbulent, restless spirit' who was not particularly appreciated by the conservative elements in the Common Room. 'His violent and strenuous manner,' conceded Philip Browne, 'naturally did not endear him to all he came in contact with.' Stoics, however, responded well to 'his frank enthusiasm and warm-hearted sincerity', delighting in his unpredictability and disdain for convention. Patrick Hunter, Senior Tutor for many years, later recalled that he would wander into a classroom between lessons, hold up his hand and say, 'I'm not taking you, but wait a minute. Just listen to this!' He would then read out a poem which he had recently discovered and admired. Noel Annan, a star pupil of the period, was a staunch supporter. 'His delight in paradox jabbed into activity minds which otherwise might not have stirred.'[27]

Philip Browne was impressed by the vitality he brought to everything:

He took endless trouble thinking out what to teach his form, and how best to present it. As Universal Tutor to the Upper School he made the impractical commitment of setting two major essays for each boy in the Upper School each term and going over them individually. If he sometimes became overwhelmed by the accumulation of uncorrected exercises that lay on his table, it is still true to say that energy and thoroughness were the keynotes to all his school work.

It was not long before Charles had founded a Literary Society, which soon became, albeit a little erratically, one of the jewels in the Roxburgh crown. In the Society's first year those who read papers included John Masefield, Edith Sitwell, Walter de la Mare, Ronald Knox and M.R. Ridley.

The poet who perished young in the Spanish Civil War, John Cornford, was a member, and his development could not but have been helped by all the new poetry that Charles brought to the attention of the Society. Particularly impressed by one Cornford poem, Charles sent it off to a young friend of his from his Oxford days, W.H. Auden. Cornford was much encouraged by Auden's long and encouraging response.

Big dramas accompanied many of Charles' activities. The Lit. Soc's success, for example, made Martin MacLaughlin so anxious for his History empire that he took to seeing Roxburgh every evening to lodge complaints about it. On learning this, Charles dramatically terminated the Lit. Soc. Cajoled by friends, however, he soon re-started it and the MacLaughlin-Spencer feud raged on. Ironically, MacLaughlin's uncle had been the headmaster of Spencer's Prep School.

Spencer spread his talents more widely than MacLaughlin. *The Stoic* captured him playing for the Masters (as scrum-half, wicket-keeper-batsman and golfer);

---

27 But as Patrick Hunter wrote most of *Roxburgh of Stowe*, this might have been Hunter's assessment too. 'Patrick was asked to write a biography of J.F.,' recalled Roger Rawcliffe, 'which was to be issued as the work of Noel Annan. Annan altered it or approved it, and set it in context, but it was substantially Patrick's work.' Years earlier, Roger had read Hunter's whole manuscript when his wife Elizabeth was typing it out for Annan.

painting and playing bridge, billiards and the piano; as an O.T.C. Second Lieutenant; setting questions for the General Paper; acting as Vice-President of the Debating Society and lecturing to the classical Society on 'Realism in Art'. Herbert Neville, the first Head of Art, wrote of Spencer's talk:

> *He is an able advocate on behalf of the more advanced school of modern art, and his remarks, which were stimulating, and, as he himself said, 'provocative', must have given his audience food for thought. If he did not quite convince us that scarlet skies and blue hair, or black skies and yellow seas, were an improvement on the old realism, he made an eloquent plea for toleration in our judgment of the 'left wing' of art today.*

Charles also helped Anthony Radice research Stowe's history, the resultant paperback ('by a member of the Sixth Form') coming out on his final Speech Day.

He was much liked. He put smiles on faces. The school's satirical magazine, *The Epicurean* loved him, and, after Leslie Huggins' arrival, the evident camaraderie between the two soon led to his nickname of 'Spuggins'. His car became 'the Spuggernaut', its deeds regularly a source of interest. 'At moderate speeds the car holds the road well,' ran one *Epicurean* road test, 'but at anything over 2 m.p.h. she is apt to become bumpy… The journey from Stowe to Buckingham in 24 hours is easily within the car's capabilities…'

* * *

Drama was a passionate interest. In his first term Spuggins was involved in J.F.'s Modern Play Reading Society, participating in Drinkwater's *Abraham Lincoln*. J.F. himself naturally read Lincoln; Spencer and Heckstall-Smith read the Chroniclers. Soon he was masterminding small, individual form plays, usually put on in the Gym but sometimes outdoors; also trips to theatres, with Stratford a seeming favourite. He acquired an ally in 1929, when John Saunders arrived, full of enthusiasm for practical music, drama and folk dancing. In July 1930 Spuggins's Oxford actor friend Gyles Isham brought his OUDS production of *Twelfth Night* to Stowe, presented in front of the Temple of British Worthies, with the audience on the far side of the Styx. George Devine and Lionel Hale were among the distinguished cast. 'It was easy to imagine that the play was being performed against the wall of some mellowed sixteenth-century manor house,' wrote Spuggins in *The Stoic*, 'with Shakespeare himself taking one of the minor parts.'

This was followed by the first staff play, when 'Mr Spencer and a cast of masters and matrons presented A.A. Milne's ironic comedy about marriage *The Dover Road* in the Gym. A year later came Spuggins' great Stowe achievement – Milton's masque *Comus*, the poet's first dramatizing of his great theme, the conflict of good and evil, acted in 1931 in front of the British Worthies. Leslie Huggins' orchestra played Thomas Arne's score, seated in moored punts on the Styx.

There is a nostalgic account in *Roxburgh of Stowe* of the way in which the preparations for *Comus* invaded the life of the whole school. Thirty-four years had elapsed since, but memories were still vivid:

Spencer requested that every form in the school should be taken through the masque; he viva-ed them all personally; set them tasks and examined them all. They had to supply the missing word in any line of the text. He would quote: 'Thus I hurl my --- Spells into the --- ayr, Of power to --- the eye with --- illusion'; the forms were expected to supply the highly poetic words dazzling, spongy, cheat, blear. After several whirlwind visitations by Spencer one aspect of the nature of poetry dawned upon them; the school hummed to the sound of boys testing each other's memory... This was the kind of teaching that Roxburgh encouraged, whatever havoc it played with the timetable.

It was a lengthy process. Four months before the masque took place, *The Epicurean* was amusedly relating Spuggins' agonised reactions towards those slow to embrace the delights of seventeenth-century verse.

There were several performances, the final one starting at 9.30 on the evening of Speech Day, allowing spectacular effects from blazing torches and strategically placed floodlights. There was much brave acting. The review in *The Stoic* picked out for particular praise Comus (played by Noel Annan's elder brother), the villainous god of revelry and would-be seducer of The Lady: 'T.Q. Annan's acting of an extraordinarily difficult part was always good and often brilliant, as with the passage of stichomythia with The Lady.'

It was an inspired setting, ideal for making the most of the masque's processions and tableaux. There was a magical occasion, for example, when the British Worthies was transformed into 'a stately Palace, set out with all manner of deliciousness; soft

Musick, Tables spred with all dainties' with 'Comus and his rabble' on one side and 'The Lady, seated in an enchanted chair' on the other. 'This was the finest tableau in the whole performance!' enthused *The Stoic*. 'The grouping was magnificent and the reflection of the torches in the still waters gave an added splendour.'

Another outstanding section featured the arrival of the water nymph Sabrina, patron goddess of the River Severn and Milton's symbol of unity, who frees the Lady from the evil Comus:

> *Sabrina's entry was perhaps the most striking moment of the performance, and P. F. Baker made the best of a difficult task of making himself heard by the audience while speaking to the other characters. It was here that the lighting effects really became astounding, and with Sabrina's solemn departure, the whole scene became infused with beauty to an extraordinary degree. The stage emptied, to be refilled with the country dancers...*

A procession followed that led, across the Styx, through the audience and into the Temple of Ancient Virtue, allowing 'The angel', 'an ethereal vision in the floodlights' to bring the masque to its strongly moral conclusion. The production could not have ended more powerfully. 'Perhaps, among the British Worthies,' reflected *The Stoic* wryly, 'the stern features of John Milton might have been seen to relax a little.'

* * *

Spuggins was too restless and too self-demanding to stay anywhere very long. By 1932 he had spent six years at Stowe. He had learnt much, he believed, and it was time to move on. As Spuggins' chief confidante, Philip Browne had mixed feelings. He himself had already moved on from teaching after six years at Stowe. However, he knew too well that, though on the surface Spuggins was almost ruthlessly self-confident, deep down he was not at all sure of himself. He had once written to him in deep despair:

> *I am fed up with myself because I teach without knowing anything, without knowing how to teach, without knowing anything about the minds of the boys I teach, without knowing anything about the world so as to know what ought to be taught.*

These moods of black depression were in stark contrast to his usual vitality and enthusiasm. 'He was motivated by a divine discontent,' reflected Browne, 'never satisfied with what he was doing, always wishing to improve.'

A poem of farewell in the *Epicurean* of July 1932 shows something of the amused affection in which Spuggins was held. He might have struggled to return his marking on time, have driven a succession of old bangers and taught over the heads of even the cleverest, but his passionate approach to life would not be quickly forgotten:

O thou who entered with a rush,
Who made the noisy classroom hush,
Who forced attention on the wand'rer,
Who puzzled e'en the hardest pond'rer –
Farewell!

O thou, with ever-smoothéd hair,
Who never moment had to spare
Who when annoyed thy hands did clap,
Who in remorse thy brow did slap –
Farewell!

O thou, who with thy cars was mocked,
Who by our ignorance was shocked,
Who ran a Literary Soc.
By fits and starts –
Farewell!

O thou, who by this frequent gem:
'Oh, heavens! I've forgotten them;
Do please forgive me, gentlemen.'
Made us to laugh –
Farewell!

We may have scoffed at Spuggernauts,
We may have laughed at your best thoughts,
We may have e'en decried your tasks,

But e'er in our affection basks
That name whose passage here we tell –
S---------r[28], farewell!

* * *

Five chaotic years followed full of enthusiastic projects and lost jobs. He began by signing on at the London Day Training College (later London University's Institute of Education) to improve his teaching skills. At the same time he worked feverishly on a scheme for an ideal Public School. He apparently came close to putting these ideas into practice, when offered the Headship of a new establishment in Iraq only for it to fall through at the last moment. Instead, funded as a Commonwealth Fund Fellow in Education, he went to the USA, travelling widely, though based chiefly at a progressive school in Chicago. By early 1935 he was back in England, teaching at Charterhouse, his outspoken manner leading to his departure after six months. A job at the BBC talks department ended quickly for similar reasons. So, too, appearances at Bryanston and Eastbourne College. As Philip Browne recorded, his restless idealism was always his downfall:

> *He saw what he thought was right with too fierce and logical a clarity to allow himself to be convinced that what he wanted might be more effectively attained by a slower and more roundabout approach. This impatience naturally, but most unfortunately, had an adverse effect on his career... There were few institutions tolerant enough to give him the rope he needed.*

So there were periods of unemployment. There was also much despondency when, in the summer of 1936, with his father dying, the family home in Wales was auctioned off at its lowest reserve. Llwyn-yr-Eryr, his dependable sanctuary, was suddenly no more.

In 1937 he re-found some brief stability with a return to America, this time as a History teacher and resident assistant housemaster at the old-established Lawrenceville School, located on a campus of 700 acres near Princeton, New Jersey.

---

28 The blank for 'Spencer' in the poem was a reminder, perhaps, of the *Comus* tests he set in class when blanks had to be filled in.

There, Philip Browne, on a sabbatical from the inspectorate, visited him several times, finding his enthusiasms and ambitions undimmed. He was still expounding brilliant new panaceas for the world's ills; still debating with anxiety points of detail and principle in his teaching; and still organising interesting visitors for his pupils from the outside world. (Alistair Cooke, when a famous radio host at NBC, was one of his many guest speakers.) By the summer of 1939, however, with war with Hitler clearly imminent, Spuggins dutifully returned to England, and, in November 1939, only two months after hostilities began, he was commissioned as a Temporary Second Lieutenant in the Royal Marines at the age of thirty-six.

* * *

After training in 1940 with a Royal Marine Brigade, Spuggins joined a newly founded Commandos unit under the charismatic Robert Laycock. Shortly before embarkation, he called in at Stowe, as forceful and ebullient as ever. He was sighted in Egypt (where he was described as 'a very capable officer who gave infinite thought to the welfare of his men') and was in action in Crete, including the shambolic Allied evacuation. For Spuggins there was the extra excitement that Evelyn Waugh was one of his fellow officers and, on the journey back to Britain from Crete, was writing *Put Out More Flags*.

Laycock's commando group was shortly disbanded, relocated in various new units. For some reason, however, a new posting was withheld for a while from Spuggins. When it eventually did come, he was disappointed to find it was to a Mobile Defence Organisation in the Portsmouth area, an important job, though a seeming comedown after the Commandos. Three days after his arrival at the Hayling Island headquarters in late September 1941, he was dining with a fellow officer at nearby Havant. His companion remembered:

> *For a short period Captain Spencer had made reference to some worries about being dissatisfied with his present position, but he did not harp on it. It seemed that when he came down here he was not expected, and this rather upset him.*

They parted at 9.00 p.m. What happened the rest of that evening and night was known to nobody. At 6.15 the next morning, a soldier reported hearing a distant gunshot in Havant's Park Road South, but it was too dark to see anything. Half an hour later, however, a policeman came across a body, lying on the pavement. There was a bullet wound in the head. A service revolver lay close by. Spuggins' death had apparently been instantaneous.

A verdict of 'Suicide while balance of mind was disturbed' was duly returned at the Havant inquest. The contents of a four-page letter in an envelope beside the body, addressed to Spuggins' former commander and apparently referring 'to his previous service', were not read out. No light at all was shed on the tragedy. Spuggins' brother, Major James Spencer, said he knew of 'no worries that Charles might have had', though he had not seen him for five months. He was quietly buried in the Haslar Royal Naval Cemetery, Gosport.

Writing to Hugh Heckstall-Smith after the war, Evelyn Waugh recalled:

I knew him only as a Marine, but saw quite a lot of him. He was a keen officer but full of frustrated ambitions (I thought). As far as I know, he was in no disciplinary trouble and his death came as a surprise to all in the Corps.

* * *

For Roxburgh, there was much fending off of painful enquiries. Martin MacLaughlin was one of the first who wrote, his Stowe rivalry with Spuggins long forgotten. 'We do not know much about Spuggins,' responded Roxburgh carefully. 'I think he had overdone himself…'

Philip Browne wrote of him with rueful affection in *The Stoic*:

He would never be content to work to an established routine, or to allow that what should be altered should not necessarily be altered at once and completely. He saw what he thought right with too fierce and logical a clarity.

Of all the many tributes, Spuggins would surely have been moved by a poem written by a former pupil, Robin Atthill. Having begun with a stanza on the sadness of learning that his 'thousand lights of living, that glittered like frosty stars in the northern night' had been blotted out 'in the monotone of death', it continued:

For you entered our lives with the freshness
Of a clean wind that sets the leaves dancing

And stipples the grey streams with passing
Beauty that never dies, and though the windows,
Where you looked in and smiled, may be closed
Against the business of life and the shadow of age,
Your laughter lingers in the worn pages of books,
And the pictures on the classroom wall, your bright
Glance illuminates the sudden recess of thought
By the winter fire, when thought was strange
Adventure into Elysian fields of truth.
There across the midsummer river you threw
The magic dust into our eyes, stronger
Than Comus's spells, but not for death.

So, at this moment of your death,
I do not rebel at the event, but only pray
That the daemon reminded you of our debt
Outstanding, that none can now repay.

* * *

There were two other tragedies connected with the sadly-missed Spuggins. The first, only a year earlier, had involved the multi-talented Peter Fyfe Baker, who had acted Sabrina in *Comus*. He was subsequently to become Head of School, take a First in History at Cambridge, and teach for a term at Stowe before joining the Army. But in February 1940, when a second Lieutenant in the Royal Artillery, he mysteriously vanished when driving along the south coast, returning after leave to his unit at Gravesend. To everyone's deep distress, he was never seen again.

For the Spencer family, too, worse was to come. In 1947 his elder brother, the much-decorated Major James Spencer, was discovered dead, alone on the downs near his Hampshire home. A double-barrelled shotgun lay beside him. It was thought he may have stumbled.

11

LESLIE HUGGINS

Head of Music, Huntsman & Tingewick Legend
Stowe 1929-52

Stowe's early masters often enjoyed private means. Dr Leslie Parry Huggins, however, the second Director of Music, may well have outstripped them all, for his father owned several lucrative family businesses, not least those producing metal tubing in Birmingham. When his father died in 1932, Leslie and his three siblings each inherited what, in today's terms, would be well over £1 million. He was never, however, ostentatious with his wealth

Similarly, as a Director of Music – for six years at Radley and eighteen at Stowe – he led small teams achieving splendid results with the minimum of fuss, a natural teacher as well as a high-class organist, pianist, conductor, choir master and composer, somehow coping with facilities that in modern days would be thought intolerable. Inconspicuously generous in any number of good causes, not least through his commitment to the British Legion and his Christian faith, Leslie generated fun and happiness all around him. 'He was good at everything he did,' remembered one friend. 'He had not an enemy in the world, and with it all was so modest and unassuming.' 'Those of us who knew him,' wrote *The Stoic*'s obituarist, 'will always thank God upon every remembrance of him.' His Stowe nickname, 'Hug', could not have been more appropriate.

* * *

Hug was born in April 1896. Soon afterwards, the family moved from Olton (his birthplace, south of Solihull) to the similarly rural Blackdown (north of Leamington Spa). Their home, Wicksted, was a sizeable mansion in thirty acres beside the River Avon. Hug's parents hunted with the North Warwickshire Hounds, and the Warwickshire Beagles often met up at Wicksted. Hug learnt the piano and organ early. In his teens, indeed, he was the village church's organist and helped his father run a choral society there.

His Prep School was nearby Packwood Haugh – it was only later to move to Shropshire – and in 1910 he began five years at Rugby. There his music flourished, bringing him several prizes, and he also made a mark as a sportsman, representing the school in athletics and cross-country. In his last year he was taught by the composer George Dyson, his lifelong friend and mentor. The organ scholarship he won to Balliol College, Oxford, came as no surprise.

The First World War, however, intervened, and he duly enlisted at eighteen in November 1914. Posted as a 2nd Lieutenant to the 2nd Warwickshire Battery of the Royal Horse Artillery, he served in France and Belgium from July 1915, before being transferred in 1917 to the RHA's elite Chestnut Troop, with whom he saw out the rest of the war. In May 1918, just after his twenty-second birthday, he was awarded the Military Cross: 'When Acting Captain, he on two occasions brought up teams through a gas barrage and throughout the recent operations has displayed the utmost energy and courage.' His last action took place on 4 November 1918 at Ors-Sambre, where, on the very same day, Wilfred Owen was killed. After the armistice, Hug moved on to the Rhine, briefly participating with the Army of Occupation.

* * *

Demobilised in April 1920, Hug spent four years at Balliol, obtaining a B.Mus in 1923 and BA the year later. His studies were all the more appreciated for allowing him some serious hunting. He also helped a friend from his Rugby days, Robert Hole (who was to join the Stowe Common Room three years before him) in the running of a Scout Troop.

In 1920 the family had moved to Harbury Hall, south of Leamington Spa, situated in a first-class hunting district (close to the Warwickshire Hunt headquarters) with stabling for ten horses. Most conveniently, Harbury Hall backed onto the village church, where Hug was soon busy helping his father build up the church choir.

Throughout his Balliol days he would motor up to Harbury on Sundays to play the organ, occasionally giving organ and violin recitals with one of his sisters at the services' conclusion.

In 1923 he became Precentor of Music at Radley College. Pupil numbers there at the time were low, and music facilities negligible until, in 1928, a fine new building arose, the top floor providing Radley's first custom-built music school, the lower floor becoming headquarters for his other passion, the Officers' Training Corps. While at Radley Hug somehow found time to achieve an Oxford D.Mus., no mean achievement, for the doctorate would have required 'the composition of a major orchestral work such as a symphony; the ability to write 8-part counterpoint and the knowledge of 12 substantial set works, one alone of which was liable to be the full score of Wagner's *Tristan und Isolde*.'[29]

There was much disappointment when news of his impending departure to Stowe in January 1929 was announced. 'Alone and unaided he has made the Radley music what it is,' stated *The Radleian*. There was also an affectionate salute to his faithful dog, Rusty. 'We wish them both the very best of luck at Stowe!'

* * *

Hug's arrival involved the loss of Sydney Watson, who took over from Hug at Radley. Hug was disappointed to leave the new Radley music school so soon, but Stowe was better for hunting, closer to Berkswell Grange (his brother's Warwickshire home) and warmly recommended by his friend and fellow scouting enthusiast, Robert Hole. There was also the possibility of a magnificent organ in the newly-built chapel. When, shortly before arrival, he learnt from Roxburgh that a shortage of money might preclude the acquisition of the promised Rushworth and Dreaper, he swiftly arranged for his father to lend a large sum without interest or repayment schedule. Hug did not reveal the benefactor's identity. 'It is rather hard to thank an anonymous abstraction,' Roxburgh wrote to him, 'but I am full of thankfulness towards the impersonal source of this unexpected help – and also, as you know, towards you.'

Hug swiftly made his mark as Director of Music, overcoming the disadvantages: singing and orchestral practices taking place in random classrooms; pianos scattered

---

29   As former Stowe classicist Stephen Suttle pointed out, when disputing a comment J.F. had once made that Huggins was 'not an intellectual man'. (*The Corinthian*, 2015)

in odd nooks; and visiting music teachers working from his room in the Hostel. There were compensations: grand concert settings like the Marble Hall and library; an admirable new assistant, Bill Snowdon; and the superb chapel organ. Musical activities quickly proliferated, he and Snowdon usually giving weekly two-piano recitals. In 1930, for example, they gave sparkling performances of Brahms' *St Anthony Variations* and Ravel's *Mother Goose Suite*. From the start Hug enjoyed an easy rapport with his pupils. 'He had a rare combination of great gentleness and the most daemonic energy,' remembered one colleague. 'He possesses enthusiasm without intensity,' wrote another, 'and that priceless possession can produce power and drive with an infectious quality.'

J.F. was delighted with all Hug was achieving. On Speech Day 1930 he told everyone about 'the remarkable effect which the arrival of Mr Huggins has had', rejoicing in the outputs of musical society, choral society, madrigal society, two orchestras, a band and a panatrope (a state-of-the-art home entertainment system). A Music School was also about to happen:

> *The Governors are giving us a new set of practising rooms at the back of the classrooms now being built. The big top room of the new building can be used for small concerts and orchestral practices, and I think that with these additions to our equipment, the music of the school (so long as Dr Huggins stays with us) should go from strength to strength.*

Alas for his optimism, incorporating a music school in the new classroom block beside the Chapel did not prove feasible.

Another disappointment was the attitude of the Housemasters. At one of their meetings in 1933, for example, outrage was expressed about boys returning late to their Houses in the evenings from music lessons. At the same meeting 'it was decided to ask L.P.H. to discontinue the annual House Musical Competitions, both vocal and instrumental', yet, shortly afterwards, came the launch of a House PT Competition.

* * *

Unsuprisingly, Hug began to look around for other jobs. One in particular interested him, and he wrote to Roxburgh:

The Music School is excellent at Marlborough. I am not applying because Marlborough is a better school than Stowe. I feel quite sure that while you are at Stowe the school will continue to flourish and prosper... I know what efforts you are making to obtain a Music School for us. I'm afraid I feel rather pessimistic about it, however.

Roxburgh, alarmed though he was, wrote honourably in support of the application:

Huggins is an absolutely first-rate fellow and he has done wonders for the singing in our chapel... I am not competent to judge the quality of his school concerts, being almost completely unmusical, but I am told he has made much more than was to be expected out of the orchestral material he has to deal with. The part of the music here I most enjoy is the unaccompanied singing by the Madrigal Society, one of Huggins' creations...

Hug's lack of artistic temperament was also a huge appeal: 'It is a blessing to find anyone who, though being so musical, is at the same time easy to live with and so normal...'[30]

J.F. celebrated Hug's eventual decision to stay by suddenly revealing, during the Prince of Wales' visit on the tenth anniversary Speech Day, a scheme for the restoration of the derelict Queen's Temple as a Music School. The QT's open, arcaded ground floor would be enclosed, creating a few practice rooms. Hug had not been party to any discussion of such an idea, however, and was soon writing in some alarm to Roxburgh of the 'numerous disadvantages', citing chiefly the distance away from the rest of the school. He wondered whether the Temple of Concord and Victory might not represent a better option, but preferred something purpose-built:

The ideal Music School would be a brick building of one-storey, shaped rather like an army hut, but wider and longer, with a central passage and practising and teaching rooms leading off on either side. At one end of the building would be a large room for orchestral and singing practices. The ideal site for it would be somewhere in the centre of the school, e.g. the Stone Yard or in the trees

---

30 A comment, suggesting, perhaps, that his first Director of Music, Philip Browne, may have given him a harder time than history relates.

behind the Gymnasium. I don't think a building of this type would cost more than £1,000... I am very willing to help all I can for such a scheme, but I am dead against the Queen's Temple plan.

Roxburgh was shocked:

Your verdict on the QT is rather shattering. The appeals have already been printed and several subscriptions have been received. Personally, I am still convinced that the scheme is a good one. If it goes through, you will have a most beautiful little Music School in the country with a real character of its own. Dodd assures me that there is plenty of room for seven or eight well-lit practising rooms in the basement of the Temple, besides teaching rooms and that two more biggish rooms could be provided by adding 'blisters' at the side...

Hug gave in with dignity, telling the Bursar, indeed, that the final third of the organ loan need never be repaid, but perhaps a similar sum could be invested in the Queen's Temple Restoration Fund. That autumn Hug also announced the first of what would become an annual Subscription Concert series, aimed at raising money for the Queen's Temple. The series, which hugely widened the school's cultural horizons by bringing in many famous instrumentalists and orchestras, would be quietly and regularly subsidised over the coming years by Hug himself.

Stowe's own music flourished in tandem. Helped by strong singers on the staff like Saunders, Clarke, Todd and Cross, Hug was able to offer (in chapel) works like *The Messiah*, while his friendship with Spencer led to the outdoor production of *Comus*, and, with Saunders, splendid performances (in the gym) of *Boris Godunov* and *Der Freischütz*. And it was not long, of course, before Bill McElwee, fully supported by Hug, began using the Queen's Temple for his annual outdoor Shakespeare.

* * *

Hug's creative talents found expression in the many hymn tunes he wrote in the 1930s for services. (Ten of them would later be included in the revised version of *Cantata Stoica* that in 1953 would update the original publication of 1927.) Among the names he allocated to his melodies was 'Jeremy', awarded to 'Father of all, to

Thee'[31] in celebration of a nephew, born in 1933. In time a very close relationship was to spring up between Jeremy Huggins and Hug. Both were devotees of riding and music. Whenever Hug called in on his brother at Berkswell Grange, his young nephew would always urge him to give an immediate concert in the drawing room. Whenever Jeremy, as he grew older, visited his uncle at Stowe, there would always be a horse for him to ride, or even hunt. Alas, Hug would not live long enough to witness the great success his nephew would make as an actor, not least as television's Sherlock Holmes, having taken the stage name of Jeremy Brett.

* * *

Hug's personal life, outside school, was always important to him. He was often down in London as a member of the Cavalry Club. His parents had moved there, too, by the time he arrived at Stowe.

By 1930 he had left the Hostel and acquired the delightfully thatched 'Wood Lane Cottage' in Upper Street, Tingewick, which a housekeeper-cook and a gardener-handyman helped him run. With a small paddock and outhouses at the back, it was ideal for his purposes once he had built an extension to the sitting room to accommodate the two grand pianos he needed for duets.

Hug's arrival from Radley had coincided with the start his friend Robert Hole had been making with the creation of the Stowe scouts. Hole was probably the inspiration behind Hug's swift accreditation as a scoutmaster, leading, in May 1930, to his re-forming of the 1st Tingewick troop, whose activities were swiftly to blossom. Four months later the troop had erected its own scout hut in the grounds of the Rectory, Hug no doubt being helped in this by Edward Habershon (who had just built Stowe's camping headquarters building behind the Cobham Pillar) and Robert Hole (Stowe's first Head of Workshops and also the Assistant Commissioner for Bucks Scouts).

Hug was to run his scout troop vigorously throughout the 1930s. It operated on two levels, partly as an adventure playground for young people, learning the concept of service to others, and partly as an adult social club, for whom whist drives, dances and entertainments were regularly devised. He was a hugely popular figure. One of the earliest members of the troop, Fred Raynor, declared many years later:

---

31 To several other of his tunes he gave personal names: Stowe ('Say not the struggle naught availeth'), Grafton Regis (saluting the Grafton Hunt), Berkswell (saluting his brother), Queen's Temple ('O Brother Man') and Chatham (saluting Ivor Cross).

Mr Huggins was ever so well loved. He was a friend of everybody's. He'd got something about him. He was rather religious, but as straight as a gun barrel. He tried ever so hard to help people. He taught all us boys lots of things – how to behave, what life was all about. He taught me so many things.

Music, of course, was central to Hug's scouting. He was soon to be appointed Commissioner for Music for the whole national Boy Scout movement.

* * *

Stowe's music continued to flourish, somewhat against the odds. There were three orchestras, the top one capable of tackling complete symphonies with seeming assurance. Exciting contemporary music was included, Hug conducting the 140-strong orchestra and choral society in superb performances of Constant Lambert's symphonic jazz hit, *Rio Grande*. In addition, Hug's self-funded Subscription Concerts were reaching new peaks. Applause for the distinguished pianist Moiseiwitsch 'shook the Gymnasium to its rickety foundations', and tickets for Mozart's 39th Symphony, played by Beecham and the L.P.O., created a Stowe black market. At the same time as all this, however, in his fight against philistinism Hug was writing in *The Stoic* of 'the devastating effect of the numerous extra parades for the Drill and PT competitions'.

Meanwhile, J.F., having accepted the inadequacy of the Queen's Temple, yet struggling for viable alternatives, kept Hug in play as best he could:

The original plan for the development of the School includes a building for music on a site not far from the present Workshops. But there is nothing final about that, and if you prefer the site beyond the hostel I expect that the Governors will agree to that quite happily.

The idea was good – the second site, ironically, being that of the future Roxburgh Hall – but money was unavailable. Eventually Hug offered to fund a purpose-built Music School himself, with a non-interest loan of indefinite length. For some reason, hard to fathom, the governors turned it down. Later he wrote despondently to J.F.:

I obtained an excellent plan for an inexpensive Music School the other day. I have not submitted it to you because I know that it will be turned down... It won't fit in with the architect's grandiose schemes... The Queen's Temple is all right as far as it goes, but there are only four small rooms up there, and the distance from the school is a real handicap.

In July 1937 the frustrated Roxburgh wrote ironically to Hug:

Dear Director-of-Music-without-a-Music-School,
    You know that if it depended on me you would have had a Music School long ago. At present I cannot even get a kitchen range for Kinvig, although it would cost only a few pounds...

Hug responded:

Is there any chance of the Electric Drying System being installed in the QT during the holidays? The damp there is awful...

There was also a dearth of reliable chairs:

At a concert in the Queen's Temple tonight nearly all the boys had to sit on the floor... Rather a large distinguished lady collapsed onto the floor as the chair gave way beneath her at a concert recently!

He could not help sharing some of his frustrations in *The Stoic*:

Stowe, the proud possessor of many fine buildings, both ancient and modern, must be the only big public school in the country which lacks a music school and a concert hall. It is a somewhat depressing outlook that there appears to be no chance of either building materialising for many years to come...

* * *

Fortunately for Hug, there were his own passionate equestrian pursuits that more than compensated for professional disappointments. He always had a couple of horses stabled at Thomas Connor's stables by the Corinthian Arch, Mary Connor, his daughter, remembering one particularly fine hunter called Avondale. He had also bought and paid for the stabling of several more, so that Stoics could enjoy a school Riding Club. He himself not only rode with the Grafton but hunted in Leicestershire and his native Warwickshire. It was an elaborate business. When riding with the Quorn, for example, he would have his horse brought from Stowe to Buckingham Station and put on a train for Melton Mowbray, where he would meet it. Later the same evening, the process would be reversed, his gardener-handyman, Fred Raynor, collecting his hunter from Buckingham Station often quite late at night.

It was helpful that Fred Raynor, one of Hug's most devoted Tingewick scouts, had gradually turned his job at Wood Lane Cottage into that of an army batman. It had all started, as Fred was later to recall, from fairly unpromising beginnings:

When I started work, I was on a coal cart with old Bill Turner. I was helping old Bill carry some coal in, and Dr Huggins come up and asked me if I'd like a job. I was getting ten shillings a week off Ernie Frost, the coal merchant. And he offered me a pound a week. So I said, 'Yes'. I was ever so busy, and had a lot to do. He relied on me for everything... He knowed I could do it.

He saw me all right. He'd say 'Come and have a glass of wine or someat' or 'Come and have some supper'. Mrs Stewart cooked for him. She'd say, 'Come and have a bit of supper'. She was a good cook.

Fred Raynor's support for the hunting became stronger and stronger:

You get wide breeches, a red coat and boots and everything, and you've got to keep that lot absolutely bang on, for five days a week. It takes a bit of doing. I worked till 12 or 2 in the morning getting his tack ready for the next day.

In due course, too, he was to become a useful chauffeur:

All his big singers and so on used to come to Brackley Station, and I'd pick them up and take them to Stowe, and then, if it was too late for the train, I used to take them down to London... I gave the Prince of Monaco a ride once.

He also acted as chauffeur on a holiday trip with Hug to Monaco, 'over the Alps and all'. Hug's sports cars were probably his greatest luxury:

First car he had was a Lea Francis; then a MG; then he had an Alvis Speed 20 - that was the best one, that was a beautiful car.

Eventually, he was to invest in 'one of the fastest production cars of the time':

I don't know how it come about, but he had a Railton – with a Hudson straight eight engine. So he sent me on a course to Hudson Motors, top of Western Avenue, Brentford, for 3 months to learn about Railtons. While there I'd be going to Brooklands, and taking Railtons down the course. They made a Railton Special that were a 2-seater. That couldn't half go! And I was no more than twenty!

There was one motoring near-disaster, when Fred was nineteen:

He liked a bit of fun. He was all for having a good time... He said, 'We'll get a motor-bike, Fred.' I used to ride it about and one night at Yardley Gobion...I had a bad accident – came off his motor bike – I broke my thigh, wrist, shoulder, and fractured my skull – unconscious for a fortnight. I was in Northampton Hospital for thirteen weeks.

Dr Huggins comes over and fetched me from hospital. We got halfway home. He said, 'Think you can drive, Fred?' Despite the caliper on my leg! 'Come and have a try! ' I drove the car all right... and we got home!

Hug responded to Fred's misfortunes by taking him and a friend across the Atlantic and much of north America.

* * *

In late 1937 Hug toyed with the idea of a move to Winchester, to follow George Dyson there as Head of Music. J.F. wrote dutifully in support:

Although I hate the idea of losing him, he certainly deserves a move up. He has been making bricks without straw here for nine years, and extremely good bricks they have been. We cannot afford to give him a proper Music School or even proper practising rooms, and yet music of every kind flourishes in the place... He is a first-rate organist and choirmaster. Everyone here loves him dearly.

In 1938 George Dyson, as the new Principal of the Royal College of Music, tried to interest Hug in becoming the R.C.M.'s Registrar. 'We want a distinguished musician,' he explained to Roxburgh, 'and Huggins is that in every respect.' London was not good hunting country. Hug stayed on, and Adrian Boult and the L.P.O. visited the school that autumn, as if in celebration.

* * *

The Thirties proved a golden time for Hug's Tingewick scout troop, which, in numbering well over fifty, eclipsed most local rivals. He maintained, too, a full programme of social events. At a fund-raising tennis tournament he was able to award himself one of the prizes he had provided, as winner of the Men's Singles.

In 1936 Hug oversaw a new scout hut, this time professionally built, with a stage at one end to facilitate the various entertainments he would be directing. The building, gifted by Hug to the village in 1946, still functions today as the local hall. It was there, most appropriately, that Hug was presented in 1938 with a Medal of Merit by the scouts' District Commissioner.

Hug's other out-of-school activity involved the Buckingham Music Festivals, started by his predecessor Philip Browne. Hug was a regular supporter, usually as conductor and adjudicator, but often as a soloist. In 1936, for example, his playing of a Brahms' Intermezzo, a Schubert Impromptu and a Chopin Mazurka and Polonaise was 'one of the musical treats of the evening'. Another year, there was similar success with Debussy's *La Cathédrale Engloutie* and Poulenc's *Movement Perpetuel*. 'No Festival is complete without the delightful playing of Dr Huggins', noted the *Buckingham Advertiser*.

The Thirties, however, were coming to an anxious end. Shortly after the Munich crisis, Hug was again in Buckingham Town Hall, this time addressing the Bucks and District Scout Association on the troubled political situation

In 1939 the arrival of the long-promised music school at last seemed imminent. On Speech Day the Chairman of Governors announced that funds for one were at last in place, 'the result of a very generous donation from an anonymous donor'. It was surely Hug. But war came, only weeks later, and the whole project had to be shelved.

* * *

In May 1939, four months before the outbreak of hostilities, Hug had rejoined the Territorials. Helpfully, his brother was a Colonel in a territorial Artillery Field Regiment and the pair had spent the summer encamped and training with the regiment. When war was declared on 1 September, their 120th Field Regiment was automatically incorporated into the regular army. Hug, now Major Huggins, took responsibility for one of the Regiment's batteries, charged with both defending the country's southern and eastern shores and, at the same time, training up young soldiers for the fighting abroad. Fred Raynor would soon join him as a lance-corporal, serving as his army batman throughout the war.

At the time of the outbreak, confusion reigned, and Roxburgh anxiously sent the forty-three-year-old Hug details of the start of the coming autumn term:

> *I don't know how far the war will affect you, because I don't know whether you are back in the Army again 'for the duration', or whether we are to have you here next term as usual. If you have any knowledge on this subject yourself, I wish you would let me know.*

Hug swiftly gave J.F. the news that a replacement would be needed. He was stationed on the Lincolnshire coast, commanding his Home Defence unit. Major Huggins was in the war 'for the duration'.

Five grim years passed. Towards the end of 1944, when second-in-command of the 173rd Field Regiment at Cromer, Hug received a letter from Roxburgh, querying the possibilities of his release. Hug, however, although worn out by his relentless duties and now forty-eight, was all for seeing things through:

> *In view of the somewhat unfavourable turn the war situation has taken, I think it is extremely unlikely that any application you have made for my release from the army will be granted. Also, after thinking things over, I think it will be better if I remain in the army a little longer, at any rate till next summer, when things have taken a turn for the better... I feel that I may be wanted to go and fight before the show is finished...*

Demobilisation finally came after VE Day, in the summer of 1945. There were soon new challenges for Hug of a rather more attractive nature. As if in reward for his tough wartime years, he was appointed Joint Master of the Grafton Hunt.

* * *

Musical standards in the immediate post-war period even transcended what had gone before. The glorious Subscription Concerts returned. In 1946 they were notable for a recital by Solomon and another visit by the L.P.O., this time conducted by Ernest Ansermet. The school's own music-making excelled. The choir was at its peak and in high spirits. One Old Stoic remembered:

Food rationing was still on, and we yearned for rich cream cakes. So we loved Dr Huggins taking the choir to sing in local villages for the feasts afterwards.

One notable orchestral concert in Assembly featured Haydn's 'Surprise' Symphony, Beethoven's *Coriolan Overture* and Rachmaninoff's 2nd Piano Concerto. A year later Temple House pianist Michael Harding again distinguished himself, this time in Frank's *Symphonic Variations*, when George Weldon and the City of Birmingham Orchestra visited. By 1948 over 60% of the school were members of the Music Society, its concerts packed to overflowing. One highlight was a recital given in the Library by Andrés Segovia. Yet more operas were attempted by the team of Saunders and Huggins. In 1949 it was the turn of *The Marriage of Figaro*.

It was a time of financial retrenchment, however, so there was no possibility of a new Music School. Roxburgh's twenty-six year reign was now over, but the emotional celebrations on his retirement in the summer of 1949 largely passed Hug by, for he was absent that term for several weeks, undergoing radio-therapy for the illness which would in due course kill him. In 1950 a serious riding accident forced him to resign as Master of the Grafton.

There were some final musical highlights: conducting his orchestra and choral society in Brahms' *Requiem* in the Chapel; a Christmas performance of Mozart's 'Jupiter' symphony; and German's *Merrie England* in the Marble Hall. His final summer concert, including Elgar's 'Nimrod' and the *Andante* from Mendelssohn's 'Italian' Symphony was an absolute sell-out. 'Never before at Stowe,' declared *The Stoic*, 'has there been such a demand for encores.' The final Huggins Subscription Concerts included Dennis Brain and his Wind Ensemble, Denis Matthews and Alan Loveday.

Visits to external concerts somehow continued. In 1951, for example, Hug and Humphrey Playford filled their cars with boys for a trip to Oxford where Barbirolli was conducting the Hallé. Talks for the Music Society continued, too. One was later written up in *The Stoic*:

> … *We reclined on sofas in Dr Huggins' room, while he gave us a lecture on the music of Bach and Handel. He illustrated his points with a very well chosen selection of gramophone records.*

Hug was ill and staying with his brother at Berkswell Grange, when John Saunders mounted his last opera, *Carmen*, but he still managed, out of his own pocket of course, to take the entire cast to see Anna Pollak in the leading role at the Royal Opera House, after lunch nearby at the smart Boulestin Restaurant, founded by the very first television chef. The productions of *Carmen* and *The Marriage of Figaro* in consecutive years brought the performing arts in the Huggins era to a triumphant peak.

* * *

The swiftness of Hug's final illness appalled the school. Fred Raynor was shocked to be told by Hug in Oxford's Acland Hospital that he had been given only six weeks to live.

> *I got in touch with the old Colonel. He said 'What we'll do is get him over to Berkswell. So I took the front seat out of the motor and I got him in there and drove him over to Berkswell.*

Hug's sister-in-law took over. Chaplain Cyril Windsor-Richards orchestrated support from Stowe as best he could. Fred Raynor was magnificent.

> *I used to go over there every day and take him out. But then it got bad, and that was it… He said he was going to be buried at Stowe. He says to me, 'You'll have to do everything. Can you do it?*

Though in great pain, Hug was uncomplaining and accepting. He died just short of his fifty-sixth birthday. Shortly afterwards, on 17 April 1952, Colonel Huggins wrote to Eric Reynolds:

Throughout his illness a host of loving friends from Stowe have helped him through – and it has surely been given to few men to know how much they are loved and appreciated in this life. To my mind he was a greater man in his going than ever before in his life. He shewed heroic patience and courage and unselfishness to the very end – and I feel that all the prayers and love of all his friends made that possible. My wife and I are deeply grateful.

Half an hour before his death, when we feared he was too far gone to understand – we assured him we were with him; and he broke through the dark clouds – smiled and said 'Thank you – sorry to be so much trouble'. Not one word of complaint ever crossed his lips. And he died with complete certainty in his faith – without fear.

* * *

The funeral took place in Chapel. Windsor-Richards took the service, with Bill Snowdon on the organ. Hug had chosen 'The God of Love my Shepherd is', the 121ˢᵗ psalm ('I will lift up mine eyes unto the hills') and 'Praise, my soul, the King of heaven', all of which he knew the school enjoyed singing. The service ended with two of Hug's own hymns, 'Say not the Struggle naught availeth' and 'Sunset and Evening Star'.

Afterwards, through Chapel Court and across the South Front to Stowe Church 'a long and a solemn procession passed in the sunshine of a perfect April afternoon'. Fred Raynor led the procession, as requested. The pallbearers included Alasdair Macdonald, Ainger Negus, John Saunders and Raymond Walker. Silence reigned long in the churchyard as it slowly filled to overflowing.

Hug had asked Fred Raynor that, if possible, his grave should face across the Elysian Fields towards the Queen's Temple. Fred had ensured it did. The Revd. Clifford Fernihough, Vicar of Stowe, said a prayer of blessing of the grave and Windsor Richards performed the last rites. Finally, Will Pope, Huntsman of the Grafton, sounded 'The Gone Away'.

Hug's brother and two married sisters led the mourners. His nephew, Jeremy Brett, was there. So, too, many local dignitaries. But perhaps the most notable figure at the graveside was J.F. It was his first visit since his retirement and self-imposed exile at Great Brickhill, and he would not visit again. But Hug was special.

A week later, Colonel Huggins wrote again to Eric Reynolds:

It was a wonderful tribute to him... Leslie's spirit was indeed there and I am confident that he would not have had one thing altered... And I am sure he marvelled at such homage... It is a matter of very great pride to us – his family – that the service took place in Stowe Chapel, in the very heart of your great school that he had loved so much. It is also a joy to us that he is buried in that lovely little churchyard in the school grounds within hearing of the playing fields. Stowe has indeed taken him to herself.

Today Hug's splendid monument, topped by the largest cross in the churchyard, still proudly chronicles the dates of his time as Director of Music. The inscription, too, reads clearly: 'He showed the way in peace and war, and in his passing.'

* * *

Hug left the school a large sum to put towards a purpose-built music school, but J.F's death and bequest to Stowe, two years later, slightly blurred the issue. When an appeal for another pressing need, a school hall, failed to meet its target, Hug's bequest went into the 'Roxburgh Hall', which was given some music practice and teaching rooms. The Hall was to remain a music and drama battleground from 1959 until the building of the superb Chung Music School in 2014. That year, the painting of Hug, which had largely hung in the Roxburgh Hall foyer, came to rest appropriately within the new building outside the Huggins Library.

May 1923: Front (l-r): Clarke, Earle, Roxburgh, Cross, Arnold. Back (l-r): Millner (bursar), Whitaker, Hanford, Browne, Fremantle, Neville.
Below (l-r): Earle, Roxburgh & Cross + prefects Robinson, Croft, Wilson, Butler, Bowie.

I

Top: Earle & his Bishopstrow rectory & church.
Below: Remains of his gravestone, Milton-on-Sea.

Top: Cross & the Lapley Grange entrance.
Below: His grave, Eglwys-fach.

Transport for a Neville-Whitaker trip to Oxford, 1925.
Below: Roxburgh's Overland Crossley, lent to Neville. (Edward Whitaker's photos)

Boats on the Eleven Acre in the mid-1920s (photo: Whitaker).
Below: the Haworth boat hut.

Top left: Haworth. Top right: Neville.
Below: The New Inn at the time of the Nevilles.

Top: Spencer at Clifton College & later.
Below: MacLaughlin (left) supervising a Temple of Concord fencing practice.

Top: Gilling-Lax, at Marlborough College (seated) & later.
Below: Playford between Kinvig & headmaster Reynolds, 1955

White and Brownie, Stowe c.1933

An old photo of Josephine & Bob Wheeler of Blackpit Farm.
Below: the pair, years later.

Above: Josephine Wheeler & son Terence.
Below: her side of White's Ridings cottage, the famous barn on the right.

Top: Wilson Knight as himself and King Lear.
Below: Zettl (left) & Todd (right)

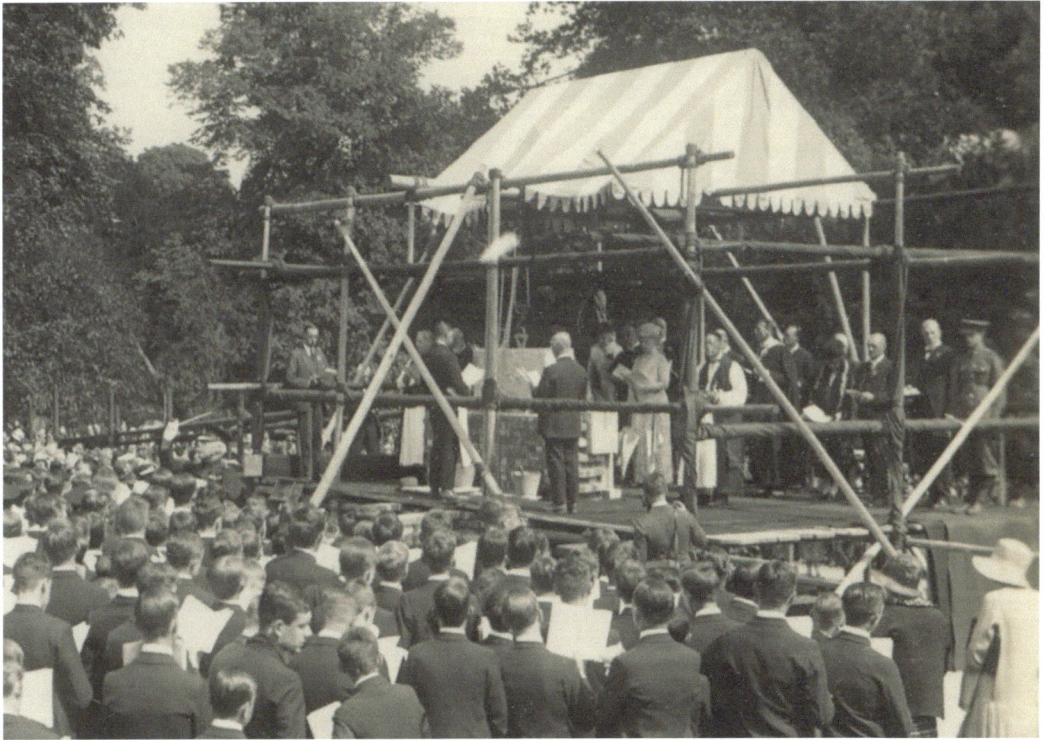

Queen Mary laying the Chapel's foundation stone, June 1927

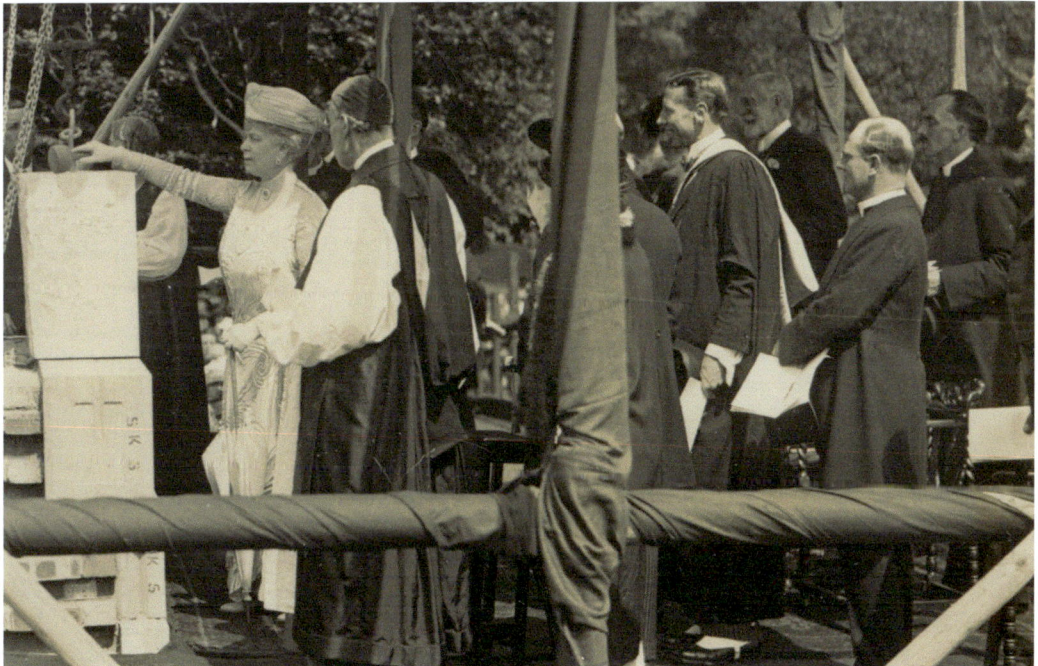

Prince George (with Gisborough, Roxburgh and Warrington) before & after
the Chapel Dedication, July 1929

The Prince of Wales en route to planting a tenth-birthday copper beech in 1933.
Below: watched by Warrington, Roxburgh, Clarke & Gisborough.

John Fergusson Roxburgh in 1929, 1939 (with Pickard-Cambridge) & 1949 (on retirement).

12

T. H. WHITE

Novelist whose time at Stowe proved his major inspiration
Stowe 1932-36, Stowe Ridings 1936-39

When he became Stowe's English Tutor at only twenty-six, Terence ('Tim') Hanbury White was already a published poet and novelist. It was an exciting appointment for the school and a reassuring one for Tim White himself. He had overcome some difficult early years.

His adventures had begun in India. An only child, he had been born in Bombay in 1906 and christened at All Saints, Malabar Hill, the church where, two years earlier, his parents had been married. Both sides of his family had deep Indian connections. Tim's father (Garrick White) was an assistant district superintendent in the Indian Imperial Police. Tim's mother, Constance White, was the daughter of Harold Aston, a Bombay High Court Judge.

The Astons lived on Malabar Hill, the most exclusive part of Bombay, and Constance's wedding had been a great social occasion, a distinguished morning gathering in a church aglow with decorative ferns, palms and flowers supplied by Government House, Malabar Hill, and Government House, Poona, on orders of the Bombay Governor's wife. The service was taken by Bombay's Bishop, the organ played by the daughter of Bombay University's Vice-Chancellor. The chief bridesmaid was the daughter of another High Court Judge. Afterwards, an arresting cavalcade of new-fangled motor cars took everyone to a reception at Judge Aston's 'sprawling residence'. There the couple were toasted by the Lord Chief Justice.

By early afternoon, however, the couple had forsaken Edwardian niceties for a heat-oppressed, smoke-ridden, two-day train journey to Garrick's far-away district of Nandabar, where they were soon at odds. All the horrors of the British Raj, so graphically depicted in George Orwell's *Burmese Days*, were to engulf the pair. By the time Tim was born, his father was a violent heavy drinker, often with his pistol at the ready, fearful of assassination. The heat and horrors of the British Raj inflicted lasting personality damage on both his father and mother.

In later years Tim would muse on old photographs of 'a tragedy queen in black evening dress with a diamond star in her hair'; 'a lean man in white, sitting beside dead tigers with a rifle'; and 'a sturdy, defensive boy of five, with yellow hair and a toy sword'. The sturdy boy, both neglected and spoilt, had a mass of expensive toys and friendly servants, like Dungee, who sent him presents long after the return to England, and Chota Syce. He would later reflect:

> *What a feudal life we lived in the old days of the Empire! I was their Chora Sahib – the little lord – and I had a personal attendant of my own. If you treated them justly, you got a feudal response of real loyalty, like a clan. My Chota Syce would have come back to me, if I had gone into the Indian army when I grew up. I would have been his sahib. He would have felt possessive about his Lord. They were lovely...*

* * *

In 1911, aged five, Tim contracted a form of paratyphoid that required his urgent return to Britain. In the event, it was miraculously cured by a German doctor on the voyage home. Both parents, though at odds, accompanied Tim, and all three were to stay with Tim's grandparents, the Astons, at St Leonards-by-sea, where the retired judge had acquired a Victorian villa, West Hill House, high on a cliff overlooking the sea. It was a capacious house and already home to one of Constance's brothers and his three children.

Though Garrick lost the battle for Tim and returned to India, Constance ill-advisedly soon followed him back. For Tim, however, there were to be six happy years at St Leonards. Everyone liked the white-bearded Harry Aston. He had once entertained the Duke of Connaught at his palace, the Shahibagh (a picturesque residence near Ahmedabad), but he displayed no airs or graces. He was a charmer, a byword in St Leonards for his all-round courtesy and kindness and his great love of children. So, too, his wife, Augusta. In West Hill House, full of nostalgic trophies and furnishings from the Raj, Tim had his own playroom on the top floor with his own favourite Indian playthings. He later wrote:

Blessed and beautiful grandparents, you made a paradise for one little boy which lasted long and was lovely. I can't pass the house even now, can't bear that it should belong to somebody else. Gunga and Grannie, you darlings, whose sweetness I never really knew while you were alive, now that you are dead I know what you gave me and what has gone out from the beauty of the world.

Though Tim was a boarder at Hill House School on Fulsham Road, it was only a short walking distance away from the Astons. Housed in ample red-brick buildings with a well-used sports field attached, it was a traditional Prep School founded in the 1890s, recently taken over by a Mr and Mrs Felix Palmer.[32] There was a big drama during Tim's time at Hill House in the first World War when one of its Old Boys won a posthumous VC on the Western Front. Public School scholarships were from time to time advertised with almost equal pride. Tim himself didn't get one to Cheltenham College, but then his behaviour at Hill House would seem not always to have been scholarly. His geometry compass, for example, took flight during one lesson and, on landing, triumphantly stuck itself into Mr Palmer's desk. 'Even then,' remembered Tim, 'he had only made me stand on a chair, but I grinned and clowned at friends over his shoulder and was caught.' He also enjoyed dormitory rags: 'The H.M. had already found me out of bed and ordered me back to it so that I should not catch cold. But I got out again and was found by him while pillow fighting in another dormitory, itself a grave offence.'

The cane was not, it seems, in constant use at Hill House, but when, in 1920, he moved to Cheltenham College, he found it was. Though a new, reforming Headmaster had just arrived, (the father of actor Robert Hardy), it was Tim's bad luck to be in Cheltondale, a boarding house on College Road, run for the first three of his four years by a grim disciplinarian, Thomas Hyett. An old fogey (though only in his early fifties) surrounded by savage prefects, he possessed no interests beyond team games. He would later feature as the villain in *Mistress Masham's Repose*. Tim

---

32 By 1937 it had been taken over by the Dominican sisterhood. Though not in educational use, Hill House's main buildings still survive as part of St Dominic's.

was to write bitterly about the awful Hyett, but never mentioned that in his final year the old fogey was replaced by the admirable young Mr Pigg, who quite belied his unpromising name.

Tim was also lucky in having an inspiring English teacher, Christopher Fairfax Scott[33], who ran, among other things, a flourishing Shakespeare Society. A school history tells of Tim, in reading the role of Snug in *A Midsummer Night's Dream*, 'producing some extraordinary sounds as the Lion'. As a young man, Tim would keep in touch with Scott. Lively letters were exchanged. He and Scott would meet regularly in London, their mission often being to search out the best mussels in Soho.

Cheltenham College's staff reports suggest Tim showed academic promise throughout. In 1920-21 it was stated (cautiously, in Latin) that ongoing parental battles might damage him (*Pater materque inter se rixantur*) and that he was being given special financial aid. He was 'working well and succeeding'. In 1921-22 he had been 'getting on well and creditably', won two prizes and justified further financial help. ('He would profit by another year here.'). 1922-23, however, was interrupted by long hospitalisation with scarlet fever, but there were further prizes, positive remarks and an English poem that particularly impressed. Above all, that summer he passed his School Cert with five distinctions.

But it was a year marred by one shocking disaster. In 1922 Tim's father, in his mid-forties and no longer *persona grata* in the Indian police force, had come home to retire. He had also come to cause trouble, demanding that Constance should return to him. She not only refused, but obtained an interim court order for Tim's custody. Garrick White thereupon petitioned the courts for a decree of restitution of conjugal rights, to which Constance pleaded that she had just cause for refusing to live with her husband (whom she had not seen for eight years). She, in turn, petitioned for a judicial separation on the ground of his cruelty. When the case reached the courts in January 1923, it received sensational media coverage. There were, for example, photographs of both Tim's parents on the front page of the *Daily Mirror*. For a few days the anguish and drama of their private lives become salacious public entertainment, and Tim himself was enmeshed in it:

---

33   Christopher Scott (1894-1958) had been a senior at Lancing College when Roxburgh first arrived there to teach. He served throughout WW1 in a rifle brigade. After six years (1921-27) at Cheltenham, he became an outstanding headmaster. He could well have been influential in the arrival of Tim White at Stowe in 1932.

Mrs White stated that on one occasion her husband tried to get into bed with a loaded revolver and a lighted lamp in his hands. He said he would shoot her and the boy, or he would shoot himself so that the insurance companies would not pay.

Mr White said his object in bringing proceedings was to be able to educate the boy, as he could not afford separate establishments. He did not love his wife after what had happened, but he wanted her back for the sake of the boy.

This produced further exchanges about Tim:

His Lordship: Then I don't understand the object of these proceedings.
Garrick White: The question of the boy necessitates her coming back to me.
Counsel: Is not the real object an attempt to avoid supporting your wife?
Garrick White: My object is to educate the boy.

In the final judgement, Constance White emerged victorious. The defeated Garrick White also paid all the costs. Tim, however, was probably the greatest loser.

The ill-judged shenanigans were reflected in the school reports of 1923-24. Though Tim still managed to win a French prize and pass Cert A in the corps, his work was suddenly uneven. Remarks like 'good but florid' and 'good but wild' (in English) were supported by comments like 'he must avoid a suggestion of being temperamental'. Meanwhile, a cash crisis at home meant that he now left Cheltenham, a year early. It was unthinkable, wrote the school to his mother, that he should miss out on university entrance, and it resourcefully managed to get him accepted at a coaching establishment, where, for a year, he could both earn money as a tutor and be coached for entrance to Queen's College, Cambridge.

* * *

He duly blossomed at Cambridge in the widest of ways. In his first year, for example, he became one of the editors of the Queen's College magazine, *The Dial* and also became a leading figure in The Erasmus, the college history society (with literary leanings). In the summer of 1926 *The Dial* recorded a particular excitement:

An informal meeting was held in Mr Potts' rooms at a late hour one evening, when Mr T.S. Eliot, who was the Clark Lecturer for 1926, came and spoke to us about future developments in prose, poetry and the drama. The meeting did not end till midnight.

Leonard Potts, a young married English don and a prime mover of *The Dial*, was to become Tim's lifetime mentor and friend, his influence no doubt contributing to the First that Tim won in the 'Mays', his first-year exams.

Tim's poetic skills were soon flourishing in the strongly competitive Cambridge atmosphere. Of the promising Ian Parsons, he was soon commenting in cheerful awe:

He writes what will be supreme poetry when he learns restraint, and his enthusiasm is not of this earth. To hear him read Flecker or Faust's last speech in Chris Marlowe is an education. He disheartens me more than anybody I have ever known...

But Tim was having his own successes. All the ambitious undergraduate poets were making for 'Henn's Monday Evenings', meetings with an exciting young English don, newly arrived at St Catharine's. Tim wrote to a friend in February 1926:

There was a sort of poetic contest of the Greek type a couple of weeks ago chez my beloved don in Catz. All the genius of the university (except two) competed, and I suppose in order to cheer me up, for they are godly people, the success was adjudicated to me.[34]

Tom Henn himself was later to write of Tim's contributions:

He very rapidly established himself as one of the group: original and even violent in argument, delighting in various iconoclasms, full of recent reading, particularly Eliot. Great gaiety, a very strong personality, apt to dramatize himself, strong desire to épater la bourgeoisie...[35]

---

34   His poem was to feature as 'Lament' in *Loved Helen*
35   Writing to White's biographer, Sylvia Townsend Warner, in the 1960s

Tim more or less took over *The Dial* in his second year, high-spiritedly lightening the tone with undergraduate humour. 'If all the clergy produced by Queen's were placed end to end, they would stretch from Geneva to Rome,' he wrote typically. 'If all the dog-collars worn by them were ironed out flat and placed end to end, they would provide the Ministry of Transport with white lines for the roads of England for a month.' Important Queen's figures became gentle targets for his short light verses. Of the popular but slightly fussy chaplain, the Revd Robin Laffan, he wrote:

Mr Laffan
Lends books to any man
Upon condition and
On receipt of note-of-hand.
For
(Though nobody could be politer than Mr Laffan),
One always likes to be sure.

In April 1927, towards the end of his second year, all the fun came to a sudden end. He wrote starkly to a friend[36]:

I have tuberculosis, slightly, curable. They are letting me take my Tripos (in May) so long as I retire to bed to rest for six months after. As they originally hinted that I might not be curable, it has been rather unbalancing and decentralising and I find I can't work…
PS What price Keats and James Flecker?

In addition to the frightening illness, he also 'got beastly drunk' in the middle of Tripos week. A second class Second resulted, despite a fine essay on Malory.

The illness interrupted his studies for a whole year, the first four months being spent in a Sanatorium, the next seven in the Italian sun. His mother (now divorced) was going through hard times and would have been unable to fund any such recuperation. (Indeed, Tim only survived at Cambridge by tutoring in the holidays.) However, a group of dons, led by Robin Laffan and Leonard Potts, funded the entire seven months.

---

36 Ronald McNair Scott, a friend from Cheltenham College, studying at Oxford (Harry Ransom Center collection)

Fully recovered, Tim returned for his final year of 1928-29, hugely grateful and passionately determined to prove his worth. He did so magnificently, putting to rights the traumas of the first part of his English Tripos with a First with Distinction in the second. As a poet, too, he consolidated his name, he and William Empson dominating *Cambridge Poetry, 1929,* published by the Hogarth Press. Other featured undergraduates included John Lehmann, Michael Redgrave, Jacob Bronowski, Julian Bell and the Old Stoic James Reeves.

Even more impressive was a whole volume of poems, *Loved Helen,* published by Chatto & Windus and dedicated, with huge affection, to his mother:

MATER MEA

PRINCIPIUM ET FINIS

VITA CORPUS CAPUT

FELICITATIS MEAE

ACCIPE HUNC LIBRUM

QUI SINE TE

NIHIL ESSET[37]

Tim's Cambridge finale was a splendid review of *Loved Helen* in the Queen's College magazine, which also interviewed and photographed him for its 'Man of the Moment' feature.

* * *

Friends were surprised when, for two years after graduation, he taught Latin at St David's, a Reigate Prep School, but it was his means of having time to write some novels. His first one, *Dead Mr Nixon,* was a one-off collaboration with a Cheltenham College friend, Ronald Macnair Scott. Its proceeds enabled him to buy one of Macnair Scott's cars, a beautiful 1926 Bentley. Another thriller, *Darkness at Pemberley,* partly set in the home of Jane Austen's Mr Darcy, he claimed to have dashed off in not much more than three weeks. Two further novels, written under the pseudonym of James Aston and the influence of Aldous Huxley, were both published in the summer of 1932. That September, he arrived at Stowe.

---

37 Mother mine, my beginning and my end, the very sum total of my happiness, please accept this book, which, without you, would not exist.

* * *

Few new masters could have caused such an initial stir. Not only was he a writer, but a bizarrely Byronic figure. Within a week it was being whispered in studies that the tall and handsome Mr White had successfully propositioned a fox-hunting duchess, a barmaid, and a colleague's wife.

Not all his novels, however, proved immediate hits. A parental rumpus swiftly arose when it was learnt that the new English master was none other than 'James Aston', author of *They Winter Abroad* and *First Lesson*. Though utterly innocuous by today's standards, both novels were just a little racy for their time, and Roxburgh found himself under siege. 'Although I was told it was a filthy book,' wrote one Stowe mother of *First Lesson*, 'I felt it my duty to wade through it.' She had discovered 'the most putrid bit of beastliness' and could not believe that its perpetrator, clearly 'a depraved specimen of human garbage', was at Stowe. J.F. responded with care: He had read three-quarters of *They Winter Abroad* and 'found it too boring to finish, but quite innocuous'. The young man in question was 'a particularly nice fellow and a very healthy, manly and satisfactory person, devoted among other things to riding and hunting'.

As more florid denunciations poured in, so J.F. conceded further ground, all too aware of the damage that bad national press could do to his nine-year-old school. He had read the 'abominable' *First Lesson*, he declared, and totally agreed with all the distress. He swiftly extracted an apology from the amused Tim, who was not strong on such things: 'I can promise you there will be no second lesson.' 'I may find myself unable to do what I want to do,' responded J.F., 'namely, to keep you here as long as possible.' However, his deft interpersonal skills went smoothly into action. Hearts warmed and passions cooled.

As Stowe relaxed, the young novelist was soon dazzling his students in the classroom, and when he asked J.F. to vet *Farewell Victoria*, a nostalgic evocation of a lost era, seen through the life of a stable groom, assent was speedily given. The book was greeted in *The Stoic* less than generously by an anonymous reviewer, but the *Telegraph* thought it 'a magnificent survey' with 'all the interest of a moving picture with the deeper note of the more human contact of a play'. James Aston was never to reappear in print, but there were times when Tim White, teaching the art of essay writing, would mischievously cite examples from that undervalued novelist.

* * *

He was given no junior classes, teaching only in the Upper School (the Fifth and Sixth Forms). Essays improved all round, as his fiery pamphlet on bad writing circulated everywhere. Somehow, as English Tutor, he managed to get away with having only four or so tutees, but he was form master of the most scholarly Fifths (the XX) and also taught those struggling in VB. At all levels his teaching was stimulating. Nigel Clive recalled:

His impact was immediate. He began by telling us to scrape our memories for reminiscences of childhood – little sketches of how we had been brought up would, he thought, bring out spontaneity, a quality he valued as highly as sincerity. Later we were told to write about 'happiness'.

Tim had strong views. Literary criticism meant I. A. Richards and E.M. Tillyard. Guidelines were decidedly contentious: hearty endorsement of the Metaphysicals, Manley Hopkins, Huxley, both Lawrences and C. Day Lewis; deep caution towards the Romantics; and sheer derision for Dickens, Scott Fitzgerald and Stephen Spender.

There were more strong views when Tim contributed to 'Present Day Lectures', big occasions given in the Library to the whole of the Upper School. He would stalk around, gown billowing behind him, as he talked up Norman Douglas' *South Wind*, 'completely holding everyone's attention'. He was equally persuasive on current affairs, happily inveighing against pet hates like capital punishment and the armaments industry.

It was all heady stuff and, to J.F.'s delight, his pupils were soon winning Oxbridge scholarships. 'He expanded our minds like elastic,' wrote one. 'I largely peppered my Oxford papers with Tim's *obiter dicta*,' remembered another, 'repeating his judgements which I knew by heart and following the tricks of style which he had drilled into me'. These included a short punch line at the beginning and end of an essay, a slangy word as a commentary on a serious quotation, and the elaborate use of metaphor.

He had, indeed, as Noel Annan wrote, 'a devastating impact', but occasionally there were tantrums. Peter Orde remembered:

English was easily my best subject, and I had hopes of a literary career. My Tutor was T.H. White and he was not a natural teacher – tough, impatient, and, to my mind, obscure. I found myself floundering – unable to understand just what he expected from me and too shy to ask. Early in my third term with him, no doubt bored with my inadequacy, he said in a tutorial, 'I'm getting rid of you, Orde; better leave the room.'

Orde became a McElwee historian instead, but bore no grudges:

Tim was far more human to me when I ceased to be his pupil and we had good talks and laughs together.

Generally, however, memories were positive. An American, Lloyd McKean, was typical:

Every class was enormously entertaining. He had a great sense of the comic in life, of the ridiculous. He delighted us, for example, with his irreverence toward the Headmaster's overblown, rhetorical style with an elaborate parody. He was passionately excited by the material he was discussing; he had the most fanciful ways of explaining the most practical elements of grammar, literally illustrating them on the blackboard with drawings. I do not feel he had any sense of mission or vocation. He was simply excited by the phenomena of life, an excitement he couldn't contain. He therefore shared that excitement because he was just as young and startled by life – particularly its lunatic side – as we were.

Stephen Whitwell likewise recalled:

While the new Art School and the classrooms under it were being built, Chatham houseroom was used as a classroom. There, with Lower VB, I was first taught English by T.H. White, a memorable experience. Tim was the most impressive person I had met (impressive, in the sense of making an impression, rather than grand). He was both engaging and frightening. If you were feeling lazy, it was as well to avoid his eye. Otherwise his lessons were fun, even for the non-combatant, and passed quickly – a feeling of rather hazardous enjoyment. An added fascination was that he sometimes cut them altogether

Lessons exuded unpredictability. Cyril Croft recalled one that was largely spent on explaining and practising how to toss a coin and win by sleight of hand.

Another day he gave us advice on beer-drinking in pubs. He was a striking presence – a choleric, red-faced handsome man in a well-cut tweed hacking coat and light corduroys – and expressed himself with flair. He read poetry beautifully, as he did the Bible in Chapel. He had a fine speaking voice, modulating and varying his pitch and speed to great effect, always ready to exploit the drama in a pause.[38]

Out of class, too, he was unpredictable. Dawyck Haig, with whom he would have earnest discussions about salmon fishing, was intrigued that although he always seemed to be pursuing some pleasures of life ('be it sunbathing by the lake, practising his horse over some hurdles near the football grounds or missing pheasants around Bill McElwee's house at Vancouver Lodge'), he never actually looked happy.

He seemed to accept Stowe as something to tolerate and he was no dedicated schoolmaster, quite happy to slip away to his cottage somewhere hidden in Stowe Ridings, where one would never be allowed to visit.

* * *

Early on, Tim featured quite strongly in the pages of *The Stoic*. He seconded a Debating Society motion, for example, that 'This House Deplores the Conservative policy of the National Government'. Physicist Hugh Heckstall-Smith was his opposite number. Over two hundred packed the Library as Heckstall pleaded his cause with vigour and panache. Tim, however, in 'an unscrupulous attack upon the person, profession and possessions' of Heckstall was the star performer.

He was the obvious person to take over as President of the Twelve Club after Martin MacLaughlin's departure. Wide-ranging papers in his first term included 'Lord Byron', 'The Church in the Dark Ages' and 'The Civilization and Conquest of Mexico'. Tim himself contributed a paper on *Farewell Victoria*. Mulled ale, it seems, often tended to stimulate Twelve Club debate during Tim's brief reign.

He also soon revived the Literary Society, becoming its President, with Noel

---

38 Tim White was later to exemplify all these qualities when reading extracts from *The Sword in the Stone* for an Argo recording.

Annan, the Secretary, giving the first paper. He and Annan amusingly crossed swords over the latter's paper for the Twelve Club on 'Freudian implications in *The Duchess of Malfi*', and both clubs joined together for a talk from Tim's former Cambridge tutor, E.M. Tillyard, on 'Poetry Direct and Oblique'. Meanwhile, Tim's pacifist ideals led him to support the founding of a Stowe branch of The League of Nations Union, in which he led discussions on 'International Relationships'.

The Modern Play Reading Society, under J.F.'s chairmanship, also attracted him. At his suggestion they read *Miracle at Verdun*, a play he had seen in the West End exploring the tragedy of the Great War and about which he felt so passionately that he himself soon directed a full-scale version of it in the Gym. His programme notes explained:

The play is an answer to the question 'Have we kept faith with the dead?' A large number of people were persuaded to give their lives for their countries on certain conditions. One of those conditions was that theirs was to be a war to end war; another that post-war Europe was to be a place fit for heroes to live in. The author poses the question by raising the dead and by letting them see for themselves. They, the dead, are the heroes of this play; as we, the living, are the villains.

The narrow rostrum in the Gym could hardly hold a cast of forty, so Tim staged certain scenes directly in front of it. Experimentation was the keynote of the production. The dead, 'the real people', were acted naturalistically; the living, 'who are unreal', in a highly stylised manner. Scenery and lighting were of necessity simply done. He wrote sardonically:

If the market-place in Verdun is nothing more than a rather dark place with little light in it, the omission of the village pump need not necessarily be attributed to the wilful modernism of the producer.

There was a large cast and no shortage of hangers-on. Tim himself, who could be said to have acted for most of his life, took over at the last minute three parts from a boy with mumps. For a while Verdun was the talk of the school, ensuring that most other activities, including work, had a hard time of it.

Unsurprisingly, at the next Housemasters' meeting, the Verdun juggernaut was top of the agenda. The conservatives (led by Fritz Clifford) swept all before them, and the Minutes were crisp with asperity:

It was decided that in view of the immense expenditure of time and energy involved in the production of Miracle at Verdun and the complete dislocation of ordinary life which resulted from rehearsals etc., no productions on such a scale ought to be allowed again. Some Housemasters felt that all plays by boys should be forbidden...

* * *

Tim's growing absence from *The Stoic* in his final two years reflects the way his own ambitions edged out the usual extra-curricular activities. He did, however, maintain one sporting interest (albeit for summer terms only), as master-in-charge of the school swimming team which operated in the outdoor 'pool' created in the Eleven Acre Lake near the Temple of Venus.

In 1935 the team's success against Westminster, Rugby and Radley was said to be 'largely attributed to the energy and interest shown by Mr T. H. White' and even in his last term in the summer of 1936 'Mr White's unflagging enthusiasm' had apparently 'done much to keep the standard high'. It seems, however, that he largely relied for coaching on friends outside the school like Jimmy Blaize, the landlord of his favourite pub, The Crown in Tingewick. One of the leading swimmers, moreover, Lloyd McKean, declared that he never saw White swim a stroke; that he gave no instruction and maintained a very distant interest, preferring to sunbathe alone on the grass.

Much of Tim's spare time was devoted to the learning of new skills. He rejoiced in the opening of the purpose-built Art School in 1934 and the arrival of the Watts to run it. In 1935 he exhibited his own works in the school's summer exhibitions. *The Stoic* commended 'some good oils and a lovely large-scale lino-cut of 'Pook's Hill'. When Robin Watt's wife, Doreen, began a high-powered Puppet Club in 1936, Tim joined Patience and Bill McElwee as joint Vice-Presidents.

* * *

Tim's later Stowe years were to be recorded in some detail by an American

Chandosian, Donald Demarest[39], who, as his Sixth Form tutee in 1934-36[40], had privileged insights into White's eccentric lifestyle:

He would hold a lot of our tutorials walking around the grounds, riding in the Bentley and playing darts in local pubs. Tim used to brag that he had a 'Rolls-Bentley' i.e. a Rolls motor in a Bentley body, but experts have questioned this.

Many a tutorial was spent in The Crown, where a barmaid called Lyn was the object of Tim's persistent advances. He knew all the pubs for miles around, but the down-market Crown – alas, it closed in 2013 – was his favourite. On one famous occasion he had been left to run it on his own. He ensured the takings were good, and claimed to have slept that night with a full till underneath his bed.

Demarest's recollections featured an account of the bright September morning in 1934 when, as a fifteen-year-old, he went to see Tim in his study, to discuss becoming his tutee. He found a note on the door:

Go in. Find something to read. Make yourself comfortable. Have gone to the village to replenish my buttery. Help yourself to cigarettes in the box shaped like an aeroplane on the mantelpiece. Tim.

Ignoring the gift on the mantelpiece, Demarest made himself as comfortable as he could on a 'tan, overstuffed sofa' and tried to come to terms with the disorder around him. Hogarth and Rowlandson prints of 'elderly lechers and ladies with bosoms spilling out over their dresses' vied for attention with a large oil painting (recently by Tim) of 'naked Rubensesque she-devils tossing poor souls into a violent cauldron of vermilion flames'. Among the logs and ferns in a large fireplace was 'a murky aquarium'. A top hat, riding crop and hunting horn hung from moulting deer antlers. The mantelpiece included a stuffed jay and a ceramic goblet in the shape of a skull. Demarest nervously made a choice from one of the crammed bookcases:

---

39   In *The Once and Future Merlin*. Had his book found a publisher, it would have queried, with reasonable evidence, several of the more wayward assertions of the Sylvia Townsend Warner biography. Particular inroads were made into the book in 1986 and 1989 but well into the Nineties it was still having some rewrites. Its enthusiasm seems at times to have outweighed its factual reliability.

40   Seemingly T.H.W.'s sole tutee in 1935-36

It was a battered, extremely ancient and crumbling treatise in Latin on prehistoric or mythical animals, scribbled all over (even though it must have been rare and valuable) in clear but minute handwriting in green ink.

A few minutes later White came bursting in, wrestling with some large packages, one of which was stamped 'Younger's Scotch Ale'. His Irish setter, Brownie, bounded in after him as he handed Demarest one of a number of wrapped bottles. 'Here! Put this sherry in the cupboard under the bookcase! Sorry to be late. The Bentley was being bitchy.' His voice was deep and musical. To Demarest he seemed smaller and less awesome in his study than on a lecture platform.

He was fine-boned with small, delicate hands and feet. He was wearing a tattered tweed jacket, a fisherman's jersey and grey flannels. He had reddish curly hair, piercing blue eyes and a sweeping moustache over an astonishingly full and scarlet lower lip. He stared at me with an unwinking and benevolent curiosity.

Tim explained that the battered book was part of a long-term project – a translation of *The Bestiary's* twelfth-century Latin, complete with annotations. After opening a bottle of beer and filling two glasses, he ordered Demarest to 'get the second book on the left from the bottom shelf and open it at page 73'. Demarest found himself looking at Gerard Manley Hopkins' 'The Windhover'. 'Sit on the sofa. Read it to yourself and then read it to me.'

White listened carefully, arms stretched out across the mantelpiece, as Demarest did his best. 'Good,' he said, after a thoughtful pause. 'Now tell me what it means.' As Demarest stuttered, Tim suddenly changed the subject.

I hear you're having trouble with your father. They tell me that he kidnapped you after the divorce and brought you to England. My own parents were divorced when I was fourteen. Bit of a scandal in the papers. I didn't get over it until I went to Cambridge.

Before Demarest could reply, something grey-green, coyly undulating, came out from underneath his sofa. 'It's a grass snake. Won't do you any harm! Fascinating creatures.' Tim was soon feeding the pet snake. 'I should like you to write a paper on grass snakes, now you have met one.' Tim carefully refilled his pipe, tamping it with the tail of a model aeroplane and lighting it from the flame that came from a flick of the propeller. His eyes were gleaming brightly. 'There's no great shakes in getting a scholarship to Cambridge. I warn you, however, I'm a ferocious taskmaster. And you'll have to start back at the beginning, with grammar and punctuation.'

Demarest could not believe his good fortune:

I was fortunate that my time at Stowe coincided with the period in which Tim was planning and discussing almost every book which he was subsequently to write. Almost all the themes and a good many of the epigrams and philosophical conclusions that appear in his books were first tried on his students and then appeared in his journals, letters and eventually published writing.

All Tim White's personal relationships were possible writing fodder. One late morning Demarest went searching for his tutor, only to discover him in bed with a buxom blonde called Joyce. He was later assured that it was all in aid of research for a possible new novel. At the time it seemed quite an imaginative excuse for an embarrassing situation, but years later Demarest came across White's account of his happy encounters with Joyce, written up in one of his journals.

Demarest always maintained that the first novel in his Arthurian series, *The Sword in the Stone*, was firmly in Tim's mind at Stowe. He realised, too, in retrospect, that the only reason for Tim giving him so much time was that The Wart (the young Arthur) was to be based almost entirely on him:

He devoted four to eight hours a day to my education. We had few interests in common. I was not particularly bright nor graceful, neither a hunter nor fisherman nor country raised. I was especially clumsy – a trait he abominated. Yet his tutelage went far beyond the elements necessary to obtain a scholarship to Cambridge. He taught me a great deal about the flight of birds, and insect behaviour and the habits of fish. It was a remarkable education.[41]

* * *

---

41   In recreating in the 1980s what White had said to him in the 1930s, Donald Demarest was surely writing *in the manner of Tim*, imaginatively building upon his own memories and using comments from Tim's own books and journals as and when he could include them.

Stowe and the surrounding countryside provided Tim with constant inspiration. One day, for example, he stumbled across tales of seventeenth-century ghosts connected to Passenham Church, just outside Stony Stratford. He subsequently crafted them into a short story, *Soft Voices at Passenham*.

His three final Stowe books all took inspiration from Stowe and the local area. *Earth Stopped*, a comic fantasy, published in 1934, ending with the Bolsheviks invading England, had the subtitle of *Mr Marx's Sporting Tour*, paying homage to the great Victorian hunting novelist, R.S. Surtees. Stowe naturally provided inspiration for 'Woodmansterne', the mansion from whose North Front both the Quorn and Grafton hunts set out in the novel.

Mr Marx himself was an amalgam of two Stowe communists: Graftonian John Cornford for the physical description; George Rudé, a young modern languages master, for the mannerisms. The ill-fated Cornford, still remembered as a poet of great promise, despised the Public School system but got on well with Tim. Their friendly intellectual duelling had begun at a Twelve Club meeting, where Cornford read a paper on communism. In the summer holidays of 1933, while Tim was writing about the adventures of Mr Marx in *Earth Stopped*, he would meet up with Cornford most evenings in a Suffolk pub, close to which they both happened to be living.

George Rudé also indirectly helped inspire the follow-up, *Gone to Ground*. Rudé had formed the highly subversive Viveur Club, of which Tim was a valued member, a limited gathering of rebel masters and boys which met on and off in 1934-35, sometimes in Bill McElwee's Dadford home. In addition to gossiping, drinking and playing cards, they also read dramatic short stories. *Gone to Ground* was essentially a series of such stories, told by a group of Woodmansterne survivors as they hid underground from the cataclysm that ended *Earth Stopped*. The *Daily Mirror* thought it 'original, pleasantly satirical and vastly entertaining', possessing 'an engagingly relentless early-Evelyn Waugh kind of humour'.

England Have My Bones, published in February 1936, was a resourceful digest of the accounts Tim had been keeping of his various country pursuits (all of them, in their different ways, helpful to his future magnum opus about King Arthur). His publishers announced:

It is the journal of a young man with enormous zest for living, who in the few happy months of these diaries has experienced the pleasurable thrill of learning to fly[42], landing his first salmon, the joys of hunting, of shooting partridges in the autumn fields and who has found in the simple pleasures of the country life a philosophy of content.

Ever the opportunist, he brought his rambling country diaries to a dramatic conclusion with an account of the car crash that wrote off his Bentley (and nearly himself) in early 1935. The title was an adaptation of Prince Arthur's last words in *King John*: 'Heaven take my soul, and England keep my bones'

The book was illustrated with his own linocuts – a skill Tim had acquired from Herbert Neville in the old Art Room – and full of Stowe interest, several masters playing active parts in the text but under assumed names. He expected it to be a flop. Instead, it was selected by the *Daily Mail* and The Book Guild as their Book of the Month. By May 1936 this had made him temporarily rich, and so, having decided to risk full-time writing, he handed in his notice. He had already started renting a cottage at nearby Stowe Ridings from the well-known farmer Cyril Wheeler and his wife Lillian. It was the perfect setting for him to start on his Arthurian books, a project that had tantalised him ever since writing on Thomas Malory at Cambridge.

* * *

J.F. much regretted his departure that July, but Tim had few regrets as he bought a second-hand bicycle and unreliable Austin 10 and headed for Stowe Ridings. Indeed, he felt 'wild with freedom':

> *I was a hawk, a falcon, which had slipped its jesses. The wide air was mine again, as it ought to be in boyhood, and that year passed like a flash. I spent it writing The Sword in the Stone... It seems to me now that the book was a happy one because I was happy. Merlyn's Cottage in the book is a fairly close description of the cottage I was living in.[43] The Forest Sauvage is the woodland*

---

42   Tim was a quick learner. His first lesson was in April 1934. In July 1934 he acquired his Aviator's Certificate, flying a Tiger Moth at the Northamptonshire Aero Club's headquarters, Sywell. In 1936 he gave flights to (and thoroughly scared) both Leonard Cheshire and Donald Demarest.

43   This is only true up to a point. The charming stone-built cottage (of around 1870), which still survives and is in private ownership, is actually double the size of the one described by White and, accordingly, by all later writers. It housed two individual cottages, side by side, backing onto Stowe Ridings, each with its own front door leading to two rooms below and two above. Tim White lived in the premises that were the

which was round it. I was doing in real life the very things which occupy The Wart. I was training a couple of goshawks to hunt rabbits, I was helping farmers to make hay. I was out with the poachers at night as much as I was out in the daytime of that miraculous summer. I really did have an owl called Archimedes – he had been rescued from a pond as a baby – and the small badgers really did nip my ankles with their needle teeth until I hopped. The book wrote itself, much as Merlyn's dishes did their own washing up.

Two days after he left the school, Tim White acquired a captive goshawk. A few days later, he contacted Donald Demarest, who was currently beginning his holidays in London.

Could use some help in manning a hawk. Would you like to spend a week with me? Sufficient fare (but neither gourmand nor gourmet) and a quantity of beer promised. It will probably be your most important lesson yet. No need to acknowledge this. I shall be expecting you for High Tea on Saturday. If you do not show up that will be understood. Tim.

'Manning' a hawk meant acclimatising a bird to the human species. But Tim had greater ambitions, the taming of its independent instincts by the ancient (Arthurian) technique of 'watching': 'It involves keeping awake and keeping the bird awake on your fist until it finally gives in and accepts bondage from sheer exhaustion.' It would take anywhere from 36 to 72 hours before the hawk accepted the need of falling asleep on a human's gloved hand.

Much later[44], Donald Demarest was to write a graphic account of this visit, beginning with his Tutor's sanctuary:

The cottage had a bright blue front door with a brass knocker in shape of a dolphin. The overstuffed parlour contained most of the furnishings from his Stowe study. Books were scattered everywhere, including the floor. His desk was piled with manuscripts and bills. Either side of the door was a fox and salmon.
The tiny, old-maidish kitchen, off the parlour, had a black tiled floor. Copper

---

further of the two from the Black Pit Farm road. When he was there in the 1930s, the nearer premises to the road were probably empty.

44   All of fifty years later, in 1986…

pots hung over an old-fashioned, lion-legged wood-burning stove. A cupboard, topped with a Sèvres soup tureen, contained Wedgwood plates, his Venetian glasses and some chipped tin mugs. There was a small fireplace in a corner, fondly tended with lampblack and brasso. Water was heated on a primus stove. There were two rocking chairs beside a table, covered with oilcloth.

Upstairs, Tim's bedroom was whitewashed and unadorned; the carpet was russet; the narrow bed boasted a gold eiderdown. The guest bedroom bed likewise had a gold spread. The ceiling was mirrored, the walls sky-blue, featuring naked nymphs pursued by randy satyrs, with wisps of cloud decorously protecting their modesty. Tim called it his D.H. Lawrence room. 'The local barmaids find it an irresistible aphrodisiac.'

That first evening they dined in the kitchen on tinned pheasant from Fortnum and Mason, cheese and gooseberries. There was also madeira and an excellent bottle of hock. Later, as Tim laid out his plans, he smoked cheap Woodbines, instead of his usual Balkan Sobranies, and gulped ale from a tin mug.

The next day the watching began. Three days and nights of hell were to ensue, their scene of operations either the kitchen or an adjacent, lamplit barn.[45] Donald would sleep till three, and then relieve Tim for a few hours. Most nights, sleep was difficult. He could usually hear 'a continuous shriek from the kitchen over the quiet, patient, reiterated oaths of the substitute parent'. On the third night's vigil he read to Gos the whole of *The Taming of the Shrew*, which Tim had told him was underpinned by Shakespeare's take on falconry. Tim himself tended to recite poetry, notably Blake. Gos was receiving a privileged literary education.

Eventually, on day three, after seventy-two hours of watching, the unreal moment of victory came:

Gos was back with Tim who had been intoning poetry, like a crooner, when Gos fell asleep on his arm. After he had returned Gos to his well-deserved and ferociously fought-against sleep in the ramshackle shed, Tim came back to the kitchen and began opening cans and bottles. 'How would you fancy Fortnum's best lobster thermidor with a bottle of precious Pouilly Fuissé? With plum

---

45 Accounts of the 1930s may suggest a bigger barn than the actuality. Brick-built (and currently in a fragile state), it faces parallel, and close, to the front of the cottages. It had brick-built extensions either end for use as earth-closets.

pudding flamed in brandy to follow? Now we really have something to celebrate. Like Lawrence and Frieda, 'We Have Come Through'.

The next morning, when Donald came downstairs, Tim was nursing a glass of brandy in the kitchen, looking as if he had not been to bed. Tim fetched water from the well and made a celebratory pot of tea for the two of them, marking the triumphant occasion by using the Crown Derby teapot and best cups and saucers, laid out on a silver tray.

Tim looked exhausted. Listless. Emotionless. He made no motion toward his teacup but poured himself out another brandy from the bottle between his feet.

'I suppose my contribution is finished.' I found my voice distressingly subservient, on the verge of a stammer.

'It's up to you.' (His speech was slightly slurred.) 'I imagine your father is having a fit. I don't suppose you told him you were coming here.'

I went upstairs, made the bed, packed my rucksack. In the kitchen Tim was slumped in the same position. His glass was beside him on the floor, empty.

He got up and shook my hand formally.

'I do appreciate all the help you have provided. Truly. I hope it has been an experience that will help you. In your writing, if not in your life.'

And that was that. Tim, it seems, had no more use for The Wart. The handshake had a finality about it that Donald immediately recognised. He headed out with his rucksack, determined not to look back, but found the urge irresistible:

When I looked back from the shelter of the apple tree, my former tutor was sitting in the deckchair as I had first seen him. The hawk was on his fist. Brownie was lying beside him. They were sharply silhouetted in the morning sun.[46]

Suddenly Tim White had no responsibilities to anyone. He could give free, unfettered rein to his imagination. By October 1937 *The Sword in the Stone* was finished.

---

46 It's a moving narrative, and the geography just about fits. The building is surrounded by gardens on all four sides. On one side (the opposite end from Tim) the garden extends a long way. There Donald would easily have been able to take a distant last look at Tim and Brownie. Demarest's chapter on Gos, however, suggests quite a strong imagination at work.

* * *

In 1938, when the American Book Club chose *The Sword in the Stone*, easing Tim's finances, he acquired a superb S.S. Jaguar that he was to keep the rest of his life. He had already started his second Arthurian novel, *The Witch in the Wood*. That year, too, another idea began to surface, a book for children and adults, for which he now had a possible heroine to study.

Early on in his time at The Ridings, he had had visits from young Josephine Surete Wheeler, ambling up from nearby Black Pit Farm, run by her parents, his landlords. She became fascinated by the olde world atmosphere that pervaded Stowe Ridings. It was not everybody who had a tame owl or trained hawks. Few dogs, too, were as beautiful or loving as Brownie. From her parents' farm she would bring down pots of jam; from the surrounding fields, bunches of flowers; and from her own fertile imagination, poems. Whenever passing, she would always peer in to check whether or not he was sitting at his writing desk. Tim soon grew to enjoy her lively visits. As usual, in meeting new people, he began thinking of new books…

* * *

In late September 1938, having heard on the radio that negotiations between Chamberlain and Hitler had probably broken down, he penned a long letter to Roxburgh, of light tone but serious intent. If war came, he would be keen on a job that was 'more intelligent and useful than running about with a bayonet'. 'I am perfectly certain that you are going to be a general,' he told Roxburgh, 'and, if so, I would like to work under you.' If not, what would he suggest? J.F. did his best to respond. Tim should not be cannon fodder, he quite agreed. Something in intelligence, maybe? The Admiralty or War Office?

* * *

In February 1939, however, seven months before the start of the Second World War, Tim enjoyed a salmon fishing holiday in Ireland so much that it led to his settling there for six years to write the rest of his Arthurian novels. He and Brownie, for a cheap rent, had a couple of rooms in 'Dooliston', a lonely farmhouse in 70 acres, some thirty miles west of Dublin. He wrote to Josephine Wheeler's father:

You have no idea what a wilderness it is – no trees, hedges, houses or even stone walls in sight. It is absolutely flat for ten miles in all directions, and only one road on it.

Somehow, for the author of *England Have My Bones*, staying in Ireland for the duration of the war did not seem quite the appropriate alternative to being 'cannon fodder'. Tim had been dazzled, it seems, by the success of *The Sword in the Stone*. Invitations to Hollywood had followed Walt Disney's acquisition of the film rights.

By the end of 1940, nonetheless, two more Arthurian novels were published: *The Witch in The Wood*, featuring Queen Morgause, and *The Ill-Made Knight*, the story of Lancelot. By August 1941 he had also finished the fourth in the series (*The Candle in the Wind*, chronicling the revenge of Mordred), though it would be delayed by the war and came out some years after it.

In 1942 Tim applied for a commission in the RAF, asking Roxburgh to be kind to his 'Old Slave' and act as one of his referees. 'I have performed the necessary act of perjury,' replied J.F. by return, 'and sent off the bundle of papers.' He ended warmly: 'I wish we saw you sometimes... I only hope that your preoccupations with Hitler will not prevent you from pulling more swords from stones.' Nothing, however, came of the RAF application. Tim stayed in Ireland.

This strangely sudden attempted enlistment may well have been influenced by José[47] Wheeler, who, by giving her wrong age, had just joined the WAAFs straight from the Royal Latin School at sixteen. Her real age surfaced, however, and a swift discharge had followed. In 1942, to get her own back on the Air Force, she turned to the Navy and became a Wren, getting work for a while at Bletchley Park before being posted to Ceylon to serve at Lord Mountbatten's HQ in Colombo. She had had some exciting affairs during the war, she told Tim, but he remained very dear to her. The feelings were mutual. 'It is sweet of you to say you will have a love-affair with me after the war,' he wrote amusedly in April 1943.

Another letter, in January 1944, announced that she was to be the heroine of what would become *Mistress Masham's Repose*:

Do you know, Jose, that I am writing a book for you... The book is two-thirds finished, and it is called 'Black Maria' – that's you. I had to make your hair

---

47   Josephine used to insist she was José not Josie...

darker – and she has a futile friend called the Professor, who lives in a cottage in the Ridings on bread and butter. You may remember that you yourself wrote a few lines of The Sword and the Stone for me. Well, Black Maria is the same sort of Jose and the Professor is the same sort of me, though of course we are all long dead. The book is for children and it takes place at an estate called Malplaquet – a mixture of Stowe and Blenheim – and it is something like Gulliver's Travels. I had to make Maria only ten, which is too young, but whenever I can't think what she ought to say I say to myself what this Jose might have said, and write that... I have a wicked vicar in it, like 'Fernie'.

I must warn you that I am dedicating this book to a little girl, David Garnett's daughter, who was born about two months ago and whom I have never seen. It is to please him, because he is my best friend, but you will see as soon as you read it whom it is really written for.

David Garnett was currently giving Tim helpful feedback. 'You have stumbled upon a most beautiful subject which you will never get again,' he told Tim, 'and you have the opportunity to write a masterpiece.' Urged on by Garnett, Tim gave the book several revisions, one of which, to make the vicar more horrible, meant re-modelling him on the first of his Cheltenham housemasters. 'Fernie' (Clifford Fernihough, a Stowe master and the rector of Stowe Church) was no villain, just an amusing eccentric in real life, full of japes. On one famous occasion, having fallen out with J.F., he had got his own back by ringing the Stowe Church bells throughout speeches on the South Front during a visit by the Duke of Gloucester.

* * *

In September 1945, four months after Victory in Europe, Tim finally returned to England. He was living in a four-room cottage in Yorkshire, rented from David Garnett, when *Mistress Masham's Repose* was published in the USA, bringing him big success by becoming a Book of the Month Club choice. When it came out in Britain in 1947, John Betjeman enthused:

He is one of our best living writers and he has written a thrilling story... What a book! What a well-told story! What superb description! What wit! What poetry!

As a drawing at both ends of the book showed, Malplaquet, in the end, was totally based on Stowe. Buildings were simply moved round a little and given some new names. Mistress Masham's Repose was an island on the Eleven-Acre Lake ('the Quincunx') onto which White had moved the Rotondo. Vanbrugh's attractive folly had become the home of the descendants of the people of Lilliput, and it was there that Maria found them. José would have been amused by the number of her talents and foibles that Tim had managed to give his heroine:

Her nature was a loving one. She was one of those tough and friendly people who do things first and think about them afterward. When she met cows, however, she did not like to be alone with them... Her main accomplishment was that she enjoyed music, and played the piano well. Perhaps it was because her ear was good that she detested loud noises, and dreaded the fifth of November. This, however, was her only weakness, and she was said to be good at games.

J.F., sent a copy by Tim, wrote back thanking him for 'two of the most delightful evenings I have had in recent years':

I cannot resist telling you that Chapter XVII thrilled me more than anything else in the book – more even than the delicious description of the Vicar and Miss Brown in Cobham Monument. But apart from entertainment value the working out of the history of the People and of the way they fitted into our world is surely the most brilliant thing you have ever done.

* * *

Ironically, the huge success of the book that José had inspired came at a time of deep anxiety in his relationship with her, ending in heartbreak and final parting. Back in September 1945, when he had returned to England, aged thirty-nine, things had been so very different. José, just turned twenty, was returning from Ceylon and leaving the Wrens. Marriage was a topic of discussion between them. Tim became a regular guest at the White Hart, paying José court. In April 1946 he was telling David Garnett:

I have sort of become engaged. If I don't marry her I will never marry anybody and I am sick of the pale cast of thought. I am trying to escape with her to America... I feel quite mad...

In May he was sounding anxious: 'She says she won't marry me now, but I am hoping this is a fad.' By the end of June a rival had appeared on the scene. 'She appears to have jilted me completely. I am much distressed and still hoping against hope.' That summer, when Tim visited Stowe to give a talk to the Twelve Club on 'Ireland', among other visitors was José's new suitor, a young county cricketer, Brian Edrich, playing for Buckingham against the 1st XI and taking half their wickets. He lived locally, at Home Farm, Lillingstone Dayrell. His elder brother, Bill Edrich, an England Test cricketer, was about to have a momentous season. José could be forgiven if she was dazzled by the Edrich name.

There was to be no resolution until, in November 1946, José, understandably, opted for Edrich. The forty-year-old Tim immediately took flight, beginning a six-month drunken odyssey round the Channel Islands, unable to face reminders of his painful past. By the time José married in January 1947, shortly before *Mistress Masham*'s publication in England, Tim was about to move from Grouville, Jersey, to Guernsey. It had been decided that he and José, to give the marriage a chance, should no longer keep in touch.[48] By the time that José's baby was christened Terence, in April 1947, Tim was in Alderney, where he would soon buy a house.

* * *

Tim White's sixteen Alderney years were not blessed by great creativity. Nearly everything published after his break with José used material of the 1930s and 1940s. There would only be one more novel. In 1958, however, his Arthurian saga was given a new definitive form, as *The Once and Future King*, when the previously unpublished fourth novel, *The Candle in the Wind*, was united with its predecessors. Tim, finally, was world famous. His magnum opus, depending so much on Stowe and Stowe Ridings, was translated into innumerable languages.

In the 1950s came two books centred around eighteenth-century *mores*. One of them, *The Scandalmonger*, included a whole Stowe chapter. *The Goshawk*, a success

---

48   In a letter of 1958 to a Cambridge contemporary, John Davenport, Tim wrote: 'I believe myself to have one son... The older I get, the more pleased I am.'

in 1951, was a reworking of his Stowe Ridings diaries. Of Tim's home, rented from the Wheelers, there is little information. It is simply a Victorian workman's cottage, 'once inhabited by a gamekeeper'. One or two Wheelers are mentioned mysteriously. José herself, like Donald Demarest, does not feature at all in the narrative.

* * *

In December 1960 *Camelot*, the Lerner and Loewe musical based on *The Once and Future King*, began its two-year, 900-performance run on New York's Broadway, bringing Tim financial prosperity that, perversely, helped hasten his end. His life spiralled out of control, great happiness alternating with aching loneliness and self-destruction.

He loved the show, declaring delightedly:

I have been totally accepted by every member of the cast and every stage-hand, even by Lerner and Loewe themselves, and spend every performance crawling over every corner of the theatre to find out how the wheels go round.

Richard Burton's dressing-room, known as 'Burton's Bar', was a regular haunt. Tim and Burton, with their common drink problems, became great friends, reciting poetry together and roaring with laughter at each other's jokes. Tim saw the show seventy-three times. Shortly before he died, he circulated around his friends a self-published volume of poems, the final two of which were tributes to Richard Burton and the adored Julie Andrews.

* * *

In 1963 Tim responded to an appeal from the school for reminiscences of Roxburgh for the Annan biography. Although far from well, he responded warmly:

Roxburgh was one of the best men I have been lucky enough to meet. I can say this with my hand on my heart because, while I was employed on his staff at Stowe, I rather disliked him. 'Dislike' is not the word – it was envy, and it was my own fault. I was insubordinate. I was too proud to suffer the position of an under-officer, little as he expected it. So I searched for his weak points, hoping to emphasise my virtues...

Now that I am old myself, I know why I 'disliked' or 'envied' him. It was because I loved and admired him. I wanted to be his 'blue-eyed boy', as everybody else did. But J.F. had no favourites. He widely spread the warmth of his heart over a large part of the earth... He was a rarity. If rarity is genius, he was a genius...

Late the same year, Tim returned to the USA for a busy lecture tour, giving the kind of stimulating talks he had once given Stowe English specialists. On its conclusion, he set off for Alderney in a cruise ship that included a stop in Greece. Just after it had docked at the Piraeus, on the morning of 14 January 1964, he was found dead in his cabin. 'I expect to make a rather good death,' he had written two years earlier. 'The essence of death is loneliness, and I have had plenty of practice at this.' He was buried in Athens' Protestant Cemetery.

Far away, the sorrowful José Edrich carefully studied all the obituaries. 'Not worth doing,' she wrote of *The Guardian*'s small effort; 'Whoopee!' of the *Sunday Times*. She was soon phoning around to chivy up backsliders like *The Times* and *New Statesman* who so far had failed to produce anything.

* * *

José was to outlive Tim by fifty-five years. Her marriage worked well initially and she had a second child. In the gaps between the cricket seasons. Brian Edrich was always a popular figure helping out at Black Pit Farm, not least at harvest time on a Ransome combine, but a divorce finally came in 1965.

José was already synonymous with Stowe Ridings, surrounded by paintings and other Tim White memorabilia in the other half of the cottage that *The Sword in the Stone* and *The Goshawk* would make famous. She was at peace there, steadily turning the lengthy garden into an idyllic paradise, an Arcadia, perhaps, in which she could stroll with Merlyn and the young King Arthur. She never lost her vitality or inclination to party. Right up to the end, happy among her large and engaging family, she would give regal entertainment, almost always with a glass in one hand and a cigarette in the other.

Back in 1964, Tim's devoted literary agent, David Higham, had visited Black Pit Farm to try to discover the likelihood of José contributing to the biography that Sylvia Townsend Warner was to write. He afterwards told the Stowe School secretary:

Mrs Chubb Wheeler is the world's great charmer, and, as you'd told me, she loved Tim a great deal. She gave us a great deal of information... She very sweetly then took us on to meet Josie and that was quite an experience. I must admit to having been fascinated to see her after all I'd heard over the years. I'm afraid she's had a bad time of it.

Understandably, José did not wish to contribute, thinking it all too painful. It was a decision that José may well have regretted, after the book came out, badly misrepresenting Tim in many basic ways. Thereafter, however, she closed her doors on most of those who tried to interview her about the famous writer.

One exception was Donald Demarest in 1987, when revisiting England from the USA. He wrote about the experience:

When I visited the school, Christopher Turner suggested I get in touch with Bob Wheeler. I called at the farm to find he was in Europe. His wife, however, suggested that her sister-in-law, living in Stowe Ridings, might see me. At first Josephine refused. She then said I might come in for a few minutes ('but keep the cab'). I suppose I impressed her with how fond I had been of Tim and how much I owed to him. We talked for four hours and she finally admitted that she had been in love with Tim since the age of 14 and still was.

Ten years later, in 1997, helping the school over a T. H. White feature in *The Stoic*, Demarest urged the editor against an interview with José:

I beg you not to try to get in touch. She feels very proprietary about preserving her version of him and resents anyone else trying to write about him. Gallix[49] tracked her down and she ran him off, she says, with a shot gun, when he started asking about their sexual relationships. She now regrets her conversation with me and wants to be cut completely out of my book ...[50]

---

49 François Gallix was a Sorbonne professor, specialising in twentieth-century English literature. He worked hard to further Tim's reputation. Early on in his researches he had found José very helpful, but his book of White-Potts letters in 1984 upset her. Like all writers over the past fifty years, he had taken Sylvia Townsend Warner as a trusted starting-point.

50 Donald Demarest to Tony Meredith, April 1997

In the fullness of time, Conor Mark Jameson, researching his delightful *Looking for the Goshawk* (2013) and resourcefully assisted by José's nephew Steve, managed an interview with no shot gun in sight. Offered just fifteen minutes, he achieved a longer, fruitful meeting, the tactful acceptance of a proffered cigarette having probably helped clear the air, at least figuratively. Conor was intrigued by the impishness of her stare as she waited to see if remarks she had made would be challenged. In this, he guessed, she had more than a touch of Tim about her. So, too, perhaps, in the slow, refined voice, crystal clear and authoritative. Her devotion to Tim was clearly total. Keen to demolish the suggestion that at Stowe Ridings he was a recluse, living in squalor, she pointed out how much time and expense he put into the cottage's refurbishment and how often he would be going out, either to socialise in a dinner jacket or to find a pub on his bike. Particularly the latter. She stressed, too, the huge, enthusiastic sense of fun with which he could sweep everyone away. Poignantly, on a table beside her recliner chair, lay a copy of *America at Last*, his lecture tour journal, published the year after his death. José in her eighties still had a mind of her own and an enduring affection for Tim.

* * *

It was at Stowe Ridings, next door to Merlyn's cottage, that she died, in 2019 at the age of 93. She was buried in the lovely setting of Stowe Church, not far from her parents. On her memorial stone is carved a quotation for which she had specifically asked:

May God keep my soul and England have my bones.

Few passers-by, of course, would ever understand its complete significance. It was a silent message, impishly made, to those in the know. A charming salute to the novelist whose time at Stowe proved his major inspiration.

13

GEORGE GILLING-LAX

A Grenville Housemaster of outstanding quality
Stowe 1932–41

Grenville in its earliest years had been given a strong sporting stamp by its first two housemasters: Ian Clarke, a rugger Blue of distinction, and Robert Skene, a cricket Blue who had taken a century off Surrey at The Oval. George Greville Gilling-Lax, who took over in 1937, brought qualities of a different kind. As a Cambridge First (in Classics and History), he was a scholar who had much to offer the top forms. But in addition to this he had an uncanny knack of arousing scholarly ambition among the less academically gifted, with whom he took infinite pains. Roxburgh was later to write of him:

> *To all he came into contact with he was able to communicate some of his own appreciation of beauty and love of learning. His power of clear thought and his balanced judgement were more easily admired than imitated, but they too were a constant inspiration.*

He was also special in his deep concern for the underprivileged. This, it seems, was a family trait. At the same time that he was taking over Grenville, his aunt Margaret Gilling-Lax, a much-admired headmistress, was retiring from St Wilfred's, Eastbourne, amid praise for her 'unremitting care and unimpeachable loyalty to the finest ideals of religion, of citizenship, and of humanity'. For George Gilling-Lax, exploring the finest ideals of religion, citizenship and humanity went hand in hand with inculcating the delights of scholarship.

* * *

Both his father and grandfather were well-to-do country vicars. He himself was born in a Surrey rectory in 1909, and his early childhood centred around several vicarages before his father began a remarkable twenty-year crusade at St Paul's Church, Rusthall (a village just outside Tunbridge Wells). George grew up in a stimulating atmosphere of a church devoted to the welfare of the sick, the out-of-work and the poorly-paid. It was work on a major scale. In 1924, for example, St Paul's was actively helping over 150 people in distress. The church had 700 adults on its roll and 300 children. As he grew up, George clearly assimilated his parents' altruistic spirit, finding fulfilment himself in assisting in Sunday schools and other ever-proliferating youth projects.

He also did well academically, winning a scholarship to Marlborough College, where his time coincided with the inspirational headship of Cyril Norwood. George ended up as a school prefect and Head of his House, his five successful years resulting in a long list of prizes, including ones for Music, Latin verse composition and playing the organ. In 1928 he won another scholarship, this time to King's College, Cambridge, and after graduation in 1931 it was thought he would aim at a Fellowship. Instead, at the age of twenty-three, after a year of social work, helping at St Paul's, he arrived at Stowe.

It is not known what personal contact there was, if any, that brought him to north Bucks. It could have been his lifelong friend, John 'Jack' Saunders, a young English master who had preceded him to Stowe from King's College, Cambridge.

* * *

His earliest responsibility set the tone of his nine Stowe years. As form master of Lower Five B he was in charge of the most academically gifted first-year pupils, including all the Entrance Scholars. Not only did he ensure they enjoyed the best possible of starts in 1932-33 but he followed their subsequent Stowe careers with interest, making himself always available for advice or support whenever needed.

He was similarly active early on in progressive extra-curricular pursuits. He founded, for example, no less than three clubs. The Antiquarians catered for those who had lately reached the Upper School but were not yet of age for membership of intellectual societies like the Twelve Club. The Heretics, with a specific mission of calling into question the orthodoxies of the day, became an alternative to the exclusive Twelve Club. George's most significant creation, however, was the Reveillé Club, an initiative to wake the school up to an understanding of, and concern for, those at the other end of the social scale.

It began very simply with fairly modest aims – 'securing, occasional addresses on religious subjects from laymen or clergymen outside the School, and of promoting the study of practical Christianity'. Anyone could join. Leslie Huggins and Alasdair Macdonald were President and Vice-President. A year on, as George's resume in *The Stoic* of December 1933 suggests, the Reveillé Club, eighty-strong, was beginning to blossom:

> *It exists for two purposes. The first is the study of social and industrial questions, with the aid of speakers who have had the practical experience of the problems and the various attempts of solving them. Several good speakers have promised to come next term, and it is hoped that meetings will be well attended.*
>
> *Secondly, we are trying to get into touch with the life of the surrounding villages and to give such help as we can. We have started a scout troop at Thornborough, and helped to start a small boys' club at Leckhampstead. We have established a connection with the Buckingham Boys' club and played them at soccer and table tennis. Members of the school visit Dadford Club about once a week; we are playing the village at soccer at the end of this term, and an entertainment is being organised to raise funds for the club. Finally, individual members have been visiting old people and helping with the local scout troops. It is hoped that their activities will further be extended as the needs of the villages become known.*
>
> *Finally, reference must be made to the expedition which about a dozen of us made to London at the beginning of term, where we saw various educational activities of the L.C.C. both for children and for the unemployed, and gained an insight into the life of a poor district of London.*

The next term his report included a visit to a guest evening of Toc H, the Christian movement 'seeking to ease the burden of others through acts of service'. There was also a film about slum-clearance, preceded by a talk by a director of the Welwyn Garden City project.

As if all this was not enough, George soon became active in Stowe's flourishing League of Nations Club, and was 'Wilf' Archer's deputy in the Scouts, running the second troop as well as the one he'd started at Thornborough.

* * *

Somewhat unusually, George had acquired at Cambridge, like John Saunders before him, a strong interest in country dancing. The pair brought this to Stowe, with understandably mixed results, but the expertise they had acquired from the University branch of the British Folk Dance Society was soon going down really well in local villages. In only George's second term the *Buckingham Advertiser* was telling of the delight at Lillingstone Lovell that 'Mr G.G. Gilling-Lax had kindly consented to conduct the folk dancing classes in the village'. Thanks to the Gilling-Lax-Saunders partnership, Morris dancing soon became a local craze.

A typical event took place in Maytime 1934 when the Lillingstone Folk Dancing troop, immaculately coached by George, 'were dancing their merry measures' not just on the home front but before the good denizens of Akeley, Chackmore, Maids Moreton and Leckhampstead:

In all the villages little groups of residents stood at their cottage gates or around the dancing ground and watched the revelries. Picturesque places were selected in every case. The vernal green of the chestnut trees and the gay flowers in the cottage gardens helped the dancers proclaim the birth of the Month of May.

The dancers were taken round by motor bus. Collections were for the Waifs and Strays Society. Music was by portable gramophone.

* * *

A few months after that Maytime bonanza, George became underhousemaster to Ivor Cross in Chatham. The pair had much in common in their enthusiasm for Modern History, Civics, the League of Nations and new moral leadership in the world. George's arrival in Chatham had swiftly been followed by that of Barbara Cross, Ivor's wonderfully supportive young wife. Over fifty years later, she was to write affectionately of George's fine qualities and how, after the Cross family left

Stowe for Wales, he had kept in touch and even insisted on visiting them when on wartime leave.

George was obvious housemaster material. On his appointment in 1937 it must have been something of a shock for George to move from the purpose-built facilities of Chatham, Spartan though they were, into those of jumbled and equally Spartan Grenville. The Houses in the mansion were still like rabbit warrens.

It may also have been disappointing to learn at his first housemasters' meeting of a parental complaint about Stowe's seeming rejection of 'quiet time' for prayers before 'lights out'. It soon became apparent from the discussion that this was the case with most Houses. Ivor Cross's Chatham still observed the rule, and so, too, Ian Clarke's Walpole, where 'boys knelt down as a matter of House tradition'. George stated that he had found quiet time abandoned in Grenville, and so had reinstated it. As yet, however, Grenvillians seemed keener on their knees in scrums than in prayers. He would persevere. His approach to housemastering was to remain, for its four years' duration, idealistic.

* * *

House plays in the Thirties tended to be occasional excitements. Grenville's success with one such venture in 1938 was accordingly one of the notable events of George's short Grenville tenure. Bill McElwee's review in *The Stoic* stressed the problems of directing plays in the gym. He began with several caveats:

It is a common fault of the worser village dramatic societies that they inevitably seek to produce the impossible. They will put on the latest Ralph Lynn farce without Ralph Lynn, or stage, in a draughty hall, with the most elementary scenery and effects, some grandiose London success like Chu Chin Chow. The choice of A Damsel in Distress by Grenville House seemed to be a similar and obvious blunder. Modern farce, unless supremely well acted, is supremely unfunny. It must move quickly and every word must be audible, and it has seemed in the past very difficult to achieve either on the Gym stage. Finally, Grenville had chosen a play with at least five difficult women's parts in it; and schoolboy female impersonations are apt to be funny for all the wrong reasons.

On all these points Grenville confounded the wiseacres and triumphantly proved that hard work and imagination can overcome all these dangers and difficulties. They gave us a play which was brilliantly staged and continuously funny, in which there was really no weak acting at all, and during which all the old incidental ills of Gym production – swaying scenery, thumping footsteps on hollow boards and the like – had miraculously been cured.

George was almost certainly actively involved in *A Damsel in Distress*, Ian Hay's dramatization of P.G. Wodehouse's novel, for John Saunders had already got him involved in amateur theatricals in Buckingham. In 1934, for example, he, Saunders, Robert Skene and Anthony Ireland starred in A.A. Milne's *The Man in the Bowler Hat* ('an exciting episode of the present age') and he and Skene also led Ian Hay's comedietta *Find the Lady*.

* * *

On going into Grenville, George had handed leadership of the Second Stowe Scout Troop to John Saunders, but he gave intermittent assistance, not least in holiday camps. Indeed, in 1936 he began the first of what would be annual trips abroad in the Easter holidays by taking a party of Stowe scouts to Austria, hiking most days but also sightseeing in Vienna. George's summer camp of 1936 in Somerset included a two days' hike over Exmoor for the party of forty, in which George's troop spent the night on top of Porlock Hill in a gale that nearly carried them all off.

The Reveillé Club by this time had gradually been assimilated into the whole fabric of school life. The Grenvillians, for example, naturally found themselves swept along by George's concern for the less fortunate. House groups would spend leisure and holiday time in places like the Isle of Dogs, seeing poverty and deprivation first-hand and learning about practical measures needed for their alleviation. In 1937 George took a small group of Stoics to visit the mining town of Dinnington near Sheffield. 'The object was to work the allotments of old and disabled colliers and to learn something of life in a mining town'. They stayed with miners' families. One participant later wrote:

Every Stoic that drove out of the town on a wet April morning was a different Stoic from the one that had arrived a week before. Not only had they all gained first-hand knowledge of a less fortunate life than their own, but they were nearer to appreciating and sympathising with the point of view of men who work in the hardest and most dangerous industry in the world.

In 1938 there was a week-long camp in a mining community in Wales. They stayed at Merthyr, surrounded by the unemployed.

* * *

George, as a classicist and historian, was fascinated by Stowe's past. Encouraged by Anthony Radice's recently published booklet, *Some Notes on the Early History of Stowe*, he began to delve deeply. Eventually a lengthy Gilling-Lax book in typescript resulted, modestly titled *Notes on Stowe*. It was ready for publication, but the war intervened. When Alasdair Macdonald brought out his handsome Stowe history of 1951, George received a warm salute:

> *In writing the first half of the book I must acknowledge with deep gratitude the help given me by Notes on Stowe of my late friend and colleague, George Gilling-Lax. This book should really have been written by him.*

* * *

The coming of war had encouraged Air Sections to be formed within public school cadet forces, and in 1939-40 George served in Stowe's A.T.C. In 1941, when he was thirty-two and the recent recipient of 'reserved' status by the War Office, he felt impelled to enlist for active service with the RAF Volunteer Reserve. 'I have been privileged to enjoy the beauty and freedom of Stowe,' he wrote to Roxburgh, 'and it is incumbent on me to repay the debt and help to preserve these things for others.'

Initially he opted to join the ranks, and after training as a navigator proved a popular if somewhat unconventional sergeant. 'Greying hair topped a long, scholarly face,' noted a friend, 'and he stooped slightly in a rather dignified manner. His voice was quiet and carefully and evenly modulated…' After honing his navigational skills in daytime flying, in late 1942 he volunteered to embrace the greater intricacies of night-time navigation. This meant operating the latest version of the Airborne Interception radar system that had just been installed in the new, two-man De Havilland Mosquitoes.

He was duly posted to 85 Squadron at RAF Hunsdon in Hertfordshire, where the new equipment awaited him. Fast and versatile though the Mosquito was, the hazards of night-fighting in 'the wooden wonder' were enormous. 'He seems to have chosen that job because it was the nastiest he could find,' wrote Roxburgh to a friend, 'and the one for which he was least suited by nature. But I have no doubt that he will do it well.'

He was teamed up with Flight Lieutenant Peter Lintott. Although ten years his junior, Lintott was an experienced pilot who had seen service under Douglas Bader in Spitfires. The twin-engined Mosquito was already an agile and effective aircraft, but by the Spring of 1943 the squadron was hard pressed in meeting a renewed night offensive by the Luftwaffe's Junkers and Dornier bombers. Night-fighter crews had a life expectancy of just a few weeks.

George would seem to have accepted the hazards with equanimity. On leave in early April 1943 he paid a visit to Cambridge for a Classical Association meeting, allowing him to meet up with old friends from King's. 'Those who saw him,' wrote one, 'will not forget his quiet happiness of spirit.'

On 23 April 1943, he participated with Peter Lintott in his first night-time 'kill'. They had taken off shortly before midnight to patrol the Foulness area. Half-an-hour later, a ground controller had alerted George to a 'bandit', fourteen miles away. They duly raced towards their target, eventually spotting the exhaust flames of a bomber. By flying above and behind, they confirmed the identification – a Junkers, silhouetted just above a layer of cloud. Having swiftly dropped below the bomber, Peter Lintott pulled up the Mosquito's nose and opened fire with his cannon, hitting the fuselage which immediately caught fire. He fired again. The Junkers' starboard engine flashed in flames, the whole aircraft suddenly flipping onto its back and diving vertically into cloud. Seconds later, a bright red glow lit up the night sky. The shattered aircraft, it was later learnt, had come down on Bromley, its wreckage destroying two large houses. The Mosquito, meanwhile, resumed its patrol, returning to Hunsdon towards 3.00 a.m.

Shortly afterwards the Squadron was moved to West Malling, five miles west of Maidstone. A photo survives of George enjoying a drink on the steps of 'the Manor House', the officers' mess close to the airfield, for he had recently accepted a commission and become a Pilot Officer.

On the night of 15 May Peter and George flew off to intercept thirteen Focke Wulfs, raiding from France. Over the Thames Estuary, they sighted a fighter-bomber silhouetted against the western horizon and closed to 180 yards before firing from astern. Flashes and sparks flew off the Focke Wulf, as it turned away. A second burst of fire missed. A third brought more flashes and sparks through which the Mosquito had to fly. As it did so, the enemy plane suddenly disappeared below the nose of the Mosquito, bound for the sea, where it exploded. A pool of oil and fuel burnt brightly below.

During April 1943 Hitler's latest bomber, a Junkers with boosted engine performance, had joined the Luftwaffe attacks. At the end of May, when Peter and George were patrolling above Lewes at a height of 29,000 feet, they met one of them. It was 2.00 in the morning. Their first attack successfully set its starboard engine on fire. A second burst of fire damaged the port engine and the crew began bailing out. The stricken plane started to go down and then blew up spectacularly. Its remains showered down around the village of Isfield, where the German crew, who had all successfully parachuted to safety, were taken prisoner.

In early July the weather broke. On July 9 1943, in driving rain and scudding clouds, Peter and George were one of a pair of Mosquitoes scrambled to intercept a wave of Luftwaffe raiders coming up the Medway under cover of the bad weather. Twenty minutes after taking off, the sounds of air combat could be heard from West Malling airfield, together with the sounds of anti-aircraft fire. The unmistakable noise of cannon fire from a Mosquito was heard together with the rising scream of a descending aircraft cut short by the sound of a crash. Neither Mosquito returned. Concern on the airfield was considerable. A phone call from a base on the other side of the Thames Estuary brought news that George and Peter's companions had landed safely. After a short while an RAF base across the Medway Valley reported that a Dornier, chased for several minutes by a Mosquito, had been attacked by it and crashed nearby. The Mosquito had vanished. Eventually the tragic news came that George and Peter had been found, dead in the cockpit of their wrecked plane at the village of Boxley near Maidstone. The Mosquito, it transpired, had been damaged by debris from the disintegrating bomber, for it had partially broken up before it hit the ground. The Dornier's four-man crew had perished two miles away.

* * *

Two weeks later Peter and George were posthumously awarded the DFCs for which they had recently been gazetted. George was buried at St Paul's Church, Rusthall, from which his father had just retired. He was an only son. His parents were later to be buried with him. Humphrey Playford led the party of Stowe mourners that included musician Bill Snowdon and the Stowe chaplain throughout George's time, Tim Brook. John Saunders was away with the army on active service, but George's other King's College contemporary, mathematician Raymond Walker, was present.

Such were George's qualities, that, had he only survived the horrors of 1939-45, he might well have become a headmaster, and even, perhaps, one of the great ones of the post-war era. J.F. wrote very movingly in *The Stoic*:

> *His warm heart and gay spirit, his humour and his courage made of him a friend whom it was a delight to know and whom it will be impossible to forget... By all he did and all he was he made himself a part of Stowe, and his name will long be remembered here with admiration, gratitude and affection.*

* * *

George left his extensive collection of books to the school library. He also made generous provision in his will towards a restoration project of one of the Stowe temples and the establishment of two annual Gilling-Lax music prizes.

The choice of music for these regularly awarded prizes reflected one of his greatest loves, for he himself had been a devoted player of the double bass. He had often participated in the school's music-making with Major Haworth beside him on a similar instrument, not least in the pioneering operatic ventures of his friends John Saunders and Leslie Huggins. Outside the school, too, George had happily wielded his double bass. Shortly before war came, he had been playing in a Buckingham Music Society production in the Town Hall of Edward German's *Merrie England*.

* * *

Eighty years on from the tragedy of George's death, his wartime haunts are much altered. RAF West Malling, from where he flew his final mission, is today Kings Hill, a development of 2,000 homes. George would surely have approved.

In 2002 a memorial to those who were stationed at the wartime airbase was unveiled at Kings Hill, and there are one or two other sightings of the past for the sharp-eyed. The Officers' Mess survives as the listed Gibson Building, serving as a Council Chamber. A number of H-block accommodation units are still in use as offices, and remnants of wartime camouflage can even be discerned. The control tower, though largely complete in the form of 1943, is a coffee shop. This considerable change in function would surely have fired George's imagination. What a good essay topic it would have given him for Lower Five B.

14

ROBIN & DOREEN WATT

The couple who inspired the new Art School
Stowe 1934–1948

The partnership of Robertson and Doreen Watt, better known as 'Robin' and 'Dodie', was very special. Married eight years before their Stowe arrival, they were both trained artists, though it was only Robin who applied to Stowe in early September 1934 to replace the departing Herbert Neville. It would soon become apparent, however, that the personable Dodie also had much to offer the Art School, and she was to make a remarkable breach in the staunch male chauvinist bastion that was Stowe in the 1930s by becoming the first woman teacher.

J.F.'s notes after the interview of September 1934 were all about Robin:

Attractive looking, manly fellow, who is apparently a champion rifle shot and a respectable rugger player as well as an artist.

He would like to help with the O.T.C.

He says he is keen on art in all forms and would particularly like to develop the craft side, including etching.

He had a pleasant wife (both noticeably but not offensively Canadian) and they would both like Neville's house.

At present Watt is only teaching private pupils and painting portraits. He is therefore free to come here and would do so for £350 a year, if there were prospects of a rise. He would be a perfectly safe appointment, but I hardly know how much he would appeal to the really artistic type of boy. The rest would certainly like him.

Not wholly satisfied about Robin's abilities, Roxburgh wrote again to one of his referees, Patrick Millard, the young Head of the St John's Wood Art School:

I have seen Mr Watt and his wife and liked them both. There is no doubt that Mr Watt would be an acquisition to any school and I have only one doubt about him in my mind. That is concerned about the quality of his artistic work. I have no means of judging that or his general artistic sensibility...

Millard responded positively, enclosing several photographs of Watt's paintings.

They give some idea of the high quality of his work. He combines very sound draughtsmanship with a keen artistic sense which makes his work quite outstanding... He possesses high artistic sensibility...

J.F. swiftly offered Watt the job. The pay would be '£250 a year, with a married allowance of £100'. After two years, an annual rise of £15 would begin. Extracurricular activities would be entirely up to him:

For any help you can give in other directions – O.T.C, games, shooting etc – I shall be most grateful, but it will be for you to decide how much time you are able and willing to spend on such matters.

Robin Watt accepted with alacrity. 'I will do my best to justify the expense!'

* * *

Dodie was born Doreen Annie Horton Yates in Seattle, USA, in December 1901, daughter of Nellie Yates, a devoted mother who would stay with Doreen even after her marriage. At some point early on, the family moved to Victoria, capital of British Columbia, a perfect town for a budding artist, nestling romantically between the tranquil waters of the Salish Sea and the mighty rainforests of Vancouver Island.

History does not relate whether it was there that Dodie first met Henry 'Robin'

Watt, but it seems likely. Robin was born in Victoria in September 1896, the son of a doctor and a famous feminist, Madge Robertson Watt, who was to introduce the Canadian concept of Women's Institutes to Britain. It was not long, indeed, before the widowed Madge took her two children with her to England, so Robin's schooldays started in British Columbia and ended at Brighton College, just as the First World War began.

At eighteen Robin was accepted at Sandhurst. In due course he served as an officer with the Green Howard Regiment and was wounded in battle four times. (He would later relate that it was during one of his recoveries in hospital that he decided to study art.) He was mentioned in dispatches twice, awarded the Military Cross with bar, and also the Croix de Guerre. He served for a period as aide-de-camp to Canadian corps commander Sir Arthur Currie and was finally demobbed in 1920.

Dodie's early life is less well chronicled. She and her widowed mother likewise sailed to England after a lengthy period in Victoria. During the last stages of the war, the pair were living in Glasgow, with Dodie attending Park School, an independent girls' establishment, suggesting that money was not short at that time. By 1919 they were living in London's Finsbury Park, from where Dodie, at eighteen, attended the Slade School of Fine Art, albeit for just one year.

It is sometimes suggested that the pair met at the Slade. In fact, their times there never coincided. The twenty-four-year-old Robin, having just been demobbed, first arrived there in September 1920, two months after Dodie had left. His three Slade years were not very successful. His results in 1922 (2nd class in History of Art and 3rd class in Fine Art Anatomy) were disappointing. In 1923 he failed the Diploma in Fine Arts, doing badly in no less than four of its sections, but this did not dampen his ambitions. By 1924, taking his inspiration from Augustus John, Britain's leading portrait painter of the period, he was a member of the Chelsea Arts Club, impressing with realistic portraits and still lifes in oil, watercolour and charcoal. By 1925 he was busy painting and teaching private pupils in London as well as setting up an art school in British Columbia. There had been times, too, in this period, when he undertook further study at Paris' Académie Colorossi and the British School of Art in Rome. His work was already being exhibited, notably in the Paris Spring Salon, where his painting of his distinguished mother won particular praise.

Dodie's doings at this time are unknown, but as she and her mother were living in Paris by 1924 she may well have been studying at the Académie Colorossi with Robin. That autumn, however, she and her mother were back in Britain, staying at the Romney Club in Earls Court while Dodie, for one brief term, studied drawing and printing at the Slade. Robin may possibly have had other ideas for her. He was thirty and she twenty-four when they married in Chelsea in 1926.

The pair swiftly returned to Canada, initially working in Montreal, with Dodie's mother on hand to look after the cooking and domestic side of things. Robin's fine painting of Dodie as 'The Golden Girl', which recently resurfaced in Canada, dates from this period. By the early 1930s they had returned to Victoria, where Robin found a market for his portraits and Dodie her paintings of Victoria's old quarters, but commissions during the great depression grew less plentiful and in 1934 they sailed back to England. Dodie's mother, of course, came too.

* * *

Robin had not intended to be a schoolmaster, but the Stowe job and the Watts' financial situation combined to change his mind. The opportunity to take over the Nevilles' old-world accommodation at the New Inn may also have played its part.

From the start it was clear the pair were a team, with Dodie's input helping create an unprecedented interest around the school in art. Before the end of the first term, J.F. was negotiating with Robin about remuneration for all the extra requests for extra tuition outside timetabled lessons:

> *One guinea per term for every 20 pupils? This would make it worth your while to ask Mrs Watt to help you with the work, and I should be very glad if she would agree to come and act as your official assistant during such out-of-school periods as you might arrange.*

For the moment, then, Dodie was only classified as an 'out of school' teacher, though she was already much more than that. She later recalled:

> *Our single ambition early on was to make art absolutely integral to Stowe's daily life. We were to be at the heart of things, not on the periphery!*

There was a sense of style about the Watts, complementing their enthusiasm. The destinations they chose for extra-mural sketching, for example, engendered excitement. Their first Art Club trip was to two grand houses in south Lincolnshire.

They were entertained for lunch at stately Stoke Rochford, the home of millionaire Christopher Hatton Turnor, a former pupil of Lutyens. From there they proceeded to Belton, the seat of Lord Brownlow, where they admired carvings, inside and out, by Grinling Gibbons. 'The house seemed to be full of Lely's portraits,' they noted approvingly. They also admired 'a duplicate Mona Lisa, a Van Dyck horse and some Rembrandts'. They returned to Stoke Rochford for tea and a tour of Hatton Turnor's considerable art collection.

The Art School was opened in the Spring of 1935 in time for the Watts' second term. Alasdair Macdonald, in his school history of 1951, found the art deco building 'somewhat incongruous' amid Stowe's classicism, but he admired its practicality:

No classical design could have provided it with its central feature, a studio more than fifty feet long lit by a window running the whole length of its north wall. In addition, there were two rooms at the east end of the building for such ancillary arts as linocutting, book-binding and modelling, while at the other end a complementary pair of rooms provided a study for the Art Master and a large exhibition studio with special north lighting...

In the early years, Dodie, in addition to all her help in the Art School, had to work on and off in local schools as a part-time drawing mistress, to help make ends meet. Robin, for the same reason, obtained permission to run each August at Stowe a 'Landscape Painting Summer School'.

It took five years before it was finally recognized by J.F. that 'Mrs Watt teaches for as many hours as her husband'. She was awarded £75 a year to complement her husband's £475, the inequality of the arrangement, of course, reflecting the times, as did the lists of the Common Room in the Brown Books and Blue Books, which were never to include Doreen Watt.

* * *

The tradition of art exhibitions on Speech Days naturally continued under the Watts. In the first one in the newly opened building, water colours took second place to oils and linocuts, 'the latter being an especially excellent display due to the initiative of Mrs Watt', several of whose own linocuts were exhibited. Common Room contributions included several portraits by Robin in oils. Tim White, too, 'had some good oils and a lovely large-scale linocut of Pook's Hill' as well as poster colour paintings and designs.

Speech Day, however, was no longer particularly special, in that exhibitions followed each other the year round. Work from the summer holidays of 1935, for example, was one theme, swiftly replaced in the autumn by 'Stowe Art, Past and Present'. In the former, 'as well as the usual exhibitors we were pleased in having the work of Mr and Mrs McElwee and Mr White'. In the latter, illustrious Old Stoics like Laurence Whistler were featured, and, most appropriately, the linocut room was dedicated to the work of the late Douglas Watson ('mainly architectural and charcoal drawings and plaster casts'), in whose memory the Art School had been funded.

Another new initiative was the creation of an enthusiasts' Art Club, that would remain a central feature of the Watt years. It soon had over forty members and a room of its own, complete with sofas and magazines, many of the latter actively encouraging an interest in modern trends like Cubism and Surrealism. Discussion of artists like Picasso, Léger and Braque was often a feature of the Saturday afternoon 'teas and talks' that soon became a feature. The first, in November 1935, had proved a popular innovation:

Forty members accepted invitations and Mr Rudé, our former Vice-President, came with two friends, one of whom, Mr Roger Roughton, gave a most interesting and knowledgeable talk on modern art in general and contemporary British artists and sculptors in particular. The success of the tea-party was almost entirely due to Mrs Watt's organization and energy.

Another means of stirring up a vigorous atmosphere was via three-weekly sketch competitions, usually on one-word themes.

Having turned one of the ground-floor classrooms of the Art School into a highly popular marionette theatre, Dodie herself was the very active President of the Stowe Puppet Club, with Leslie Huggins providing key musical support. Robin, the McElwees, John Saunders and Tim White were the Vice-presidents. The first production, most remarkably, was Eugene O'Neill's *The Emperor Jones*, a contemporary tragedy dealing with big themes in a mixture of expressionism and realism. Having begun by demonstrating that a marionette theatre could be a deeply serious affair, Dodie showed she was not averse to lighter presentations. *Alice Through the Looking Glass*, with the marionettes based on Tenniel's black-and-white illustrations, was a particular success. *Puppet Parade of 1937* featured a burlesque about Napoleon's retreat from Moscow and a colourful ballet, involving Mrs Beeton and a troupe of kitchen utensils.

Marionettes, costumes, scenery, props and lighting were all created with great professionalism, with Dodie herself leading the way, setting the highest of standards and tactfully overseeing the members' best efforts. The seriousness of the undertaking was highlighted by an inspirational visit in 1936 from the famous German puppeteer, Harro Siegel, who lectured to several hundred Stoics in the gym before giving a marionette performance on his own magnificent puppet theatre with the small company touring with him.

* * *

In 1939, shortly before war was declared, Robin, Dodie and Dodie's mother moved from New Inn Farm to the much more spacious surroundings of The Glebe House, Lillingstone Lovell. A lovely Queen Anne home of seven bedrooms, standing in over three acres of grounds beside St Mary's Church, the former rectory provided the Watts with the kind of gracious country living to which they had long aspired. It gave them a certain status in the village, and Dodie was soon being asked to distribute prizes at whist drives and other fund-raising entertainments, something she would do with smiling aplomb. On the Sunday that war was declared, the villagers all listened to the King's Speech on a radio brought across to Lillingstone Dayrell Church by Dodie.

Since 1914-18 Robin had very much remained a soldier. 'Though art was the greatest thing in his life,' commented *The Stoic*, 'he never turned his back on the Army. He was an energetic and inspiring officer in the Corps and the Home Guard.' There was no question, however, of his being involved in active service. 'This officer,' wrote J.F. to the War Office, 'who was four times wounded in the last war, is now 43 and subject to bronchitis and mild asthma in the winter months. He was absent from school duty for a long period in 1938. He is unable for medical reasons to bicycle.'

Nonetheless, as Captain Watt he was soon responding to the calls of Local Defence Volunteers and the Home Guard. In April 1942, with anxieties about an imminent German invasion particularly strong, he was one of the speakers who addressed a packed meeting in Buckingham. 'We are doing everything we possibly can to make the town a perfect hornets' nest for the enemy in the case of an invasion!' he cried. The Home Guard was 'no longer a bow and arrow organization'! But much would be required of the civil population. There must be resolution in the event of things like damaged water and electricity supplies. 'No rumour-mongering either!'

Dodie was doing her bit, too, as commander of the Maids Moreton section of the Women's Home Guard, one of the first in the country. She had no difficulty in organising good shooting practices, first aid, messenger services, signalling and scouting.

* * *

Robin and Dodie ensured that throughout the war, despite all the privations and disturbances, the Art School remained a central feature of the school. They were often to be seen not only tidying up but cleaning and scrubbing. Everything was to go on as normal. When visiting speakers proved hard to come by, they themselves stepped in. Dodie, for example, filled in for the Vitruvians with a long-remembered talk on Interior Decoration.

The Watts' relationship with J.F. grew ever stronger through the war years. J.F. rarely used Christian names with masters, yet with both Robin and Dodie he felt enough at ease to ignore the formality of the times. Dodie even persuaded J.F. to participate with her on a Brains Trust panel one evening in Buckingham Town Hall. To the question 'If you could be a famous person of the opposite sex, who would you choose to be?' J.F. managed to outdo Dodie. While she chose Michelangelo, he opted for Cleopatra.

The rapport between all three was well illustrated in October 1945, when the highly eccentric Lord Berners came to give a talk to Stowe's short-lived Nonesuch Club. This was a big coup. A friend of Salvador Dali and other avant-garde artists, Berners was something of an exotic cult figure in the arts world, well respected as a composer since being commissioned in the Twenties by Diaghilev's *Ballets Russes*. Just before the war he had provided score, set and costumes for Frederick Ashton's avant-garde *Wedding Bouquet* at Covent Garden, and he was about to collaborate there with Ashton and Cecil Beaton on *Les Sirènes*. The visit was doubly complicated in that Berners would be bringing with him the young partner to whom he was long devoted, Robert Heber Percy, an Old Stoic, nicknamed in high society 'the Mad Boy'. The visit from such a pair in the staid 1940s was fraught with potential disaster, but J.F. gallantly saw it as a shared adventure, writing calmly to Dodie a few days beforehand:

I have now arranged to put up Robert Heber Percy on Monday night and told him that you and Robin will be kind enough to put up Lord Berners. We can give them both supper in the Mess before the Nonesuch meeting and I will see that Robert gets something to eat the next morning. They will arrive before dark on Monday. Robert seems doubtful as to what Lord Berners will have to say and appears to think it won't amount to much!

How Robin and Dodie fared in their entertainment of Lord Berners at Lillingstone Lovell is not recorded, but Glebe House would certainly have provided a setting in which he would have felt comfortable. With a resident cook and several maids to back up Dodie's mother, the Watts had every encouragement to live a social life. When the young English master, Richard Gilbert, went off to become a Squadron-Leader, his wife lived with them at Glebe House, and through this contact an RAF band provided the music several times at morale-boosting fêtes that took place in their grounds for good causes. Dodie was expert at organizing children's fancy dress parades, setting up amusing sideshows and mouth-watering produce stalls. Meanwhile the pair would participate with enthusiasm at fêtes put on in Lillingstone Dayrell by Captain Robarts and the Edrich family[51]. Robin often won prizes on the rifle ranges, Dodie on the hoop-la.

* * *

Following the coming of peace in May 1945, there was no question of slipping standards in the Watts' final few Stowe years. When they returned to Canada in 1948, they were to hand over to the excellent Michael Mounsey one of Roxburgh's big ongoing successes.

Throughout their time at Stowe they had been universally liked. The nearest thing to a criticism came from Brian Stephan's description of Robin as 'somewhat taciturn and even outwardly saturnine', when stressing that he and Dodie ('the jolly, ebullient extrovert') were a highly contrasting pair. Brian did, however, praise Robin's 'dry, amusing wit'. Tributes flowed in *The Stoic*. Robin was praised for 'his quiet manner and gentle, slightly cynical, sense of humour, in which there was no

---

51 Home Farm, Lillingstone Dayrell was run by William Edrich, whose son, Bill, had already made a name for himself in Test cricket just before the war. Bill and his cricketing brothers, when war leave allowed, always attended the local fetes.

trace of bitterness'. Dodie, meanwhile, 'possessed a sanity and a wisdom which made her a most treasured and sought-after adviser on all sorts of problems both technical and personal.' Together they were a wonderful pair:

> *Mr and Mrs Watt had that direct approach to things, that blessed freedom from shyness, and that wide knowledge of the world, which all great teachers possess, qualities which are not so easily found in combination.*

Everyone was aghast at their impending departure. 'They were absolute charmers,' remembered Liz Zettl, a great friend. 'They were not really like masters at all – there was never any sense of 'them and us' with Robin and Dodie.' For years Liz was to cherish a Watt painting of Ewald: 'Robin did the main portrait, wonderful as ever. Dear Dodie was given the neck, collar and jacket, to finish it off!'

* * *

Having no children of their own, the pair had been keen to re-forge family links in Canada. There was also the hope that the different climate would improve Robin's health. To a point, it did. He was fifty-two when, on 19 October 1948 they left England, and he was to paint right up to his death sixteen years later.

His new studio in an old carriage house on Drummond Street, Montreal, received regular visitors including many prominent Canadian figures of the 1950s. The national recognition he won as a portrait artist was exemplified by a commission from Earl Wavell, Colonel of The Black Watch, on his 1949 visit to the country. An exhibition in the Montreal Museum of Fine Arts in 1951 had helped set him up. So, too, portraits acquired by the National Gallery of Canada, illustrating 'his confident draughtsmanship and bold, economic style'. Robin, as ever, would receive all the credit, though Dodie, as usual, would still be easing his way. The wife of one client recalled, 'Robin and Dodie worked together, Dodie chatting with the sitter while Robin concentrated on his work.' Though portraits and still lifes remained his most productive outlets, in the later years he branched into abstract work too.

Robin died after a short illness on 11 September 1964, aged 68, at Cowansville, on the outskirts of Montreal. There he and Dodie had felt at home as members of the Cowansville Art Centre, working towards the creation of the superb Bruck Museum art collection.

There was a full obituary in *The Stoic*:

He made art into a way of life. The gentle water-colourist was flung into the excitements of oil-painting; the philistine was persuaded that he had an eye; paintings by boys were hung in classrooms; studies were adorned with murals and pictures on glass; the puppet stage was built and decorated, and plays were written for it; stage sets, Christmas cards, printed fabrics, programme covers and posters emerged in a steady stream; and the Art School became the best-loved clubroom in Stowe.

Dodie, who lived a further twenty years, ran an art gallery in Montreal for a time, and was also involved with teaching art to prisoners. By the 1970s she was back in London, but returned to the Montreal area, spending her last years with Robin's younger brother, Sholto, a successful journalist. She died aged eighty-two in Rawdon, just sixty kilometres north of Montreal, a beautiful tourist resort of mountains and lakes.

When Robin and Dodie left Stowe in 1948, J.F. wrote short personal references for their future use. Robin's was full of praise, but Dodie's was even warmer and publicly acknowledged that the Art School had been run by the pair of them from the beginning:

Mrs H. Robertson Watt has been in joint control with her husband of the art department here since 1934. She has done brilliant work both as an artist and as a teacher, but, what is almost more important, she has been an inspiration to the whole community. I know of no one better able to instill a love of beauty into the mind of youth or to teach appreciation of the methods and achievements of great artists. In addition, we owe her a debt of gratitude for the practical help she has given in the production of plays, the creation and working of a puppet theatre and a dozen other enterprises requiring power of organization as well as a craftsman's skill. It is not too much to say that the whole life of the school will be impoverished by her departure.

* * *

Unlike most Stowe Legends, Dodie and Robin Watt would not be entirely forgotten. On the School's fiftieth anniversary in 1973, a Stoic from the 1930s, Christopher

Cash, contributed an article in *A Stowe Miscellany*, emphasizing 'the charm of their personalities'. It oozed affection:

So many people will have their own memories of the Watts: scarlet cigarette packets, that engaging sheepdog, Robin's well-chosen dark shirts, thoughtfully related to a plain tie, Dodie's laughter. But it is, above all, for years of encouragement and friendship that Dodie and Robin have our love and gratitude.

In 1999, out of the blue, the school received fourteen of Dodie's pencil studies (head and shoulders) of Art School regulars, seemingly all from Dodie's last eight Stowe years, gifted by a relative. As no names were attached, they were all reproduced in the 2000 issue of *The Stoic* in the hope that, even though well over fifty years had elapsed, identifications might still just be possible. Quite a number were, and six of Dodie's fine sketches were to appear with their subjects' entries in the *Stowe Register* of 2001.

The superb Rick Mather renovation of the Art School in 2009-10 was another time when there was a strong salute to Robin and Dodie. And even as late as 2019, an Old Stoic, John Richardson, was paying a warm tribute in a volume of autobiography:

I will always be grateful to them for introducing me to such avant-garde art magazines as XXe Siècle, Verve and Minotaure, which enabled me from the ages of thirteen to fifteen to understand and keep up with what the Masters of Paris were doing... Dodie Watt had taken some of us up to London to check out two shows of Picasso's work. It left me dazzled...

Richardson, indeed, became a personal friend of Picasso's and wrote a definitive four-volume Picasso biography. The dazzle from modern art, that the Watts helped inculcate, was never to leave him.

15

JAMES TODD

Mathematician, Winemaker & Headmaster-in-waiting
Stowe 1934-48

James Maclean Todd was a scholar dogged by restlessness to achieve high personal ambitions. But not everyone, including Roxburgh, felt these high ambitions totally warranted. To J.F. Jimmy Todd simply seemed a useful team man.

He had grown up sweeping all before him, gaining no less than sixteen prizes at Oxford High School, where he had been Head Boy. Having won a scholarship in Mathematics to Queen's College, Oxford, he combined a 1st in Maths with a 2nd in Classics and then abandoned promising postgraduate studies in Theology to teach Maths for a year at his old school. But this was followed by strangely similar one-year stints at Radley, Bryanston and Bromsgrove. In 1934 Stowe became his fifth school in five years.

There was no obvious avenue for professional advancement. 'Wilf' Archer had just been made Maths Tutor and Raymond Walker would be his eventual successor. Both had Cambridge double firsts. Meanwhile Patrick Hunter was already firmly in place as Classics Tutor – he would hold the post until 1962 – and if the Chaplain needed an assistant, there was always Humphrey Playford. Jimmy Todd, for the moment, would have to bide his time.

Clearly a confident public speaker, he made an early mark in the Debating Club as Bill McElwee's Vice-President. Perhaps it helped that the two men were temperamentally far apart. Whereas the flamboyant Bill delighted in propounding the whimsical and outrageous, the earnest and high-minded Jimmy took a more conservative outlook, speaking against motions like 'This House prefers a wolf in sheep's clothing to a sheep in sheep's clothing' and 'This House would abolish the Public School'. When it was debated whether 'This House prefers dissolute brilliance to sober mediocrity', Jimmy Todd naturally argued for 'sober mediocrity' and McElwee 'dissolute brilliance'.

Other early Todd forays included excellent papers on 'Gnosticism' (for Gilling-Lax's Antiquarians) and 'Greek Mathematics' (for Hunter's Classical Society), and he swept the board when the Middle School English Club invited several masters to assume the persona of somebody famous, even outdoing the histrionics of Eddie Capel Cure.

In 1937 came his first obvious setback. His lengthy piece in *The Stoic* reviewing *Macbeth*, the third of Bill McElwee's Queen's Temple bonanzas with his historians, suggested that there was more comedy than the bard had intended and that he himself had had a somewhat indifferent evening. The historians, chatting down at Vancouver Lodge with the McElwees, would certainly not have been best pleased, and it may not have been a coincidence that shortly afterwards the nickname of 'Jethro Miracle Todd' started going the rounds.

Next year Jimmy put some lectures he'd been giving the Upper School to good use, converting them into a 400-page book, *The Ancient World*, in which, most tellingly, he grafted onto the Greeks and Romans a full history of the Jews and Christianity. Published at the time of Chamberlain's meeting with Hitler in Munich, *The Ancient World* pointed readers towards 'a more precise sense of direction and of spiritual values than the world shows at present' and made for an original and compelling read.

Though Roxburgh had contributed three photos and Hunter one, Jimmy's earnest and excellent effort would seem to have made little impact in north Bucks. *The Stoic* simply reprinted, without comment, a laudatory review from the *New Statesman* (that presumably he himself had submitted). Jimmy's disclaimer in the Preface that many of the expressed opinions were not in the original lectures would seem to suggest that J.F. was looking anxiously over his shoulder.

* * *

Seven years into his Stowe career, in 1941, Jimmy became Ivor Cross's underhouse-master. The move into one of the legendary Chatham flats (only approachable via the outdoor iron staircase[52]) did, however, help him make his presence felt, albeit unintentionally. One Old Stoic recalled:

> *Todd was fond of making elderberry wine, which he stored around his bed. During the night these would explode with a loud report all over the House and his ceiling was pitted with the depressions of these accidents.*

Meanwhile Jimmy's Maths teaching was under attack from 'Wilfred' Archer, who complained to J.F. that he had lost all confidence in him. Tackled on the subject by Roxburgh in July 1942, Jimmy was outraged:

> *This lack of confidence is the last straw and lessens my confidence in Wilfred. I could say lots of things I mustn't now, but I must just say that in the last Higher Cert results for which I have any marks, my percentages were easily beyond both Wilfred's and Raymond's. And then these boys go on to scholarships and they get the credit. I could say a lot of scathing things about the Maths side…*

Perhaps Archer, who lived in the other Chatham flat, had been awakened too often by exploding Todd wine. An attempt by J.F. to play down Jimmy's alleged inadequacies received a scathing response. Many boys, wrote Archer, told him that J.M.T. bored them.[53] He was too vague and didn't correct enough work. 'I think the thing has become a scandal and must be ended.'

In the end, an uneasy peace ensued, with Jimmy's ambitions remaining as strong as ever. When, in early 1943, it was learnt that Ivor Cross was leaving Chatham, he was soon knocking on Roxburgh's door. J.F.'s note of the meeting suggests quite an outburst:

> *… He used the phrase 'In reality I am Chatham House'… He claims to be the power behind the throne in Chatham, to have dealt with conspicuous success with many difficult cases which never required to be brought to I.M.C. or to*

---

52 At least there *was* the iron staircase. In 1925 Patrick Hunter, one of the flats' first residents, had to use a ladder.

53 He had an enthusiasm for diversions, sometimes of a philosophic nature. One Old Stoic remembered a double Maths lesson entirely taken up by his reading a Walter Scott ghost story.

me and to be the universal confidante of the House. He thinks he has better understanding of boys than most men brought up in boarding schools and feels that his great qualities are not recognised here.

When J.F. let on that Alasdair Macdonald, currently Acting Housemaster of Cobham, would probably be offered Chatham, Jimmy declared, if that were to be the case, Cobham should his. At the end of the difficult meeting, J.F. noted:

My own feeling about J.M.T. is that he vastly exaggerates trifling affairs and when a boy gets into scrapes is too much inclined to make a personal emotional matter out of the incident. His management of two difficult boys who were farming here in August 1941 was definitely bad, and he got ridiculously worked up and spent hours collecting evidence that did not exist about something that did not matter.

Two days later J.F. was confirmed in his views after speaking to Ivor Cross:

I.M.C.'s view is that he is quite hopeless from the housemastering point of view. He does routine work laboriously and well, and the boys in the House have a kind of tolerant affection for him, but 'nobody takes him seriously'.

A little later, when Ivor Cross departed, Jimmy's farewell gift to him was a copy of the five-year-old *Ancient World*, inscribed: 'To Mr and Mrs Cross, with best wishes and much gratitude from the author, J.M. Todd'. Ivor Cross, though a historian himself, clearly hadn't purchased a copy five years ago. The formal phrasing of the inscription suggests the gift of 'gratitude' might possibly have been a gentle reminder of this disappointing lapse.

* * *

That December. Jimmy began a search for a headship that was to go on for five years, largely because of J.F's cautionary references. He told Bancroft's School, Jimmy's first port-of-call:

I regard Mr Todd as particularly well qualified on the intellectual and organizational sides for the Headmastership of a day school.[54] *In the matter of discipline, control of staff and the capacity for managing a large institution with wisdom, dignity and a sense of proportion, I regard him as adequately qualified…*

As for his classroom methods, they were 'somewhat free and easy'.

Some other applications similarly ended in disappointment, and a scholarly new book, a blank verse translation of Aeschylus' *Agamemnon*, could find no publisher. It was a bad time for the ambitious Jimmy. With McElwee away on wartime service, Jimmy was at least now President of the Debating Society, but even there, when he took to the floor to oppose 'This House approves of Nonsense', he was roundly defeated. 'The President was erudite,' noted *The Stoic* meaningfully. 'He spoke of High Mathematics, Classics, Nazi philosophy and Scottish Lowland folk jingles.'

* * *

In the summer of 1943, however, fate smiled on him. Holidaying in Scotland, he met and fell for a young Scottish lady, eleven years his junior. Twenty-six-year-old Janet Gillespie Holmes, a classics lecturer at Holloway College, came from a prosperous family based a few miles outside Glasgow. She had a 1st from Glasgow University and another 1st from Oxford. By the New Year of 1944 the pair were thinking of marriage.

Renting a school house would be vital, but the only one offered was in Tingewick. 'I am afraid Tingewick has its defects,' Jimmy told J.F., 'as my fiancée may not like the idea that we should live so far from Stowe in these days when transport is so difficult.' She was, anyway, by this time lecturing at Aberdeen University and, though they married in Glasgow in the summer of 1944, initially they had to live apart. Jimmy was still the assistant in Chatham, now enjoying the amiable Alasdair Macdonald regime.[55]

The enforced estrangement continued for over three years, with Janet moving

---

54 Bancroft's had a small but absolutely central boarding provision.
55 'I could not have had a more helpful lieutenant than Jimmy Todd,' wrote Macdonald for the *Chatham Register* in 1985. 'He was a master hand at getting boys through examinations, while his home-made wine parties at the ends of the summer terms were memorable and greatly appreciated by his battle-scarred sets.'

from Aberdeen to Glasgow University. In the meantime, Jimmy was applying for headships all over the country and J.F. writing innumerable variations on the same cautionary theme: 'He is a brilliant fellow and a delightful person in his own way,' he told one school. 'He would do certain parts of a headmaster's job quite admirably.' But, alas, he was not sure that he had the experience to enable him to do all parts equally well. He told another:

> *James Todd himself is a very able and very charming fellow. He is a painstaking and capable organizer and the boys like him very much. Whether he has the tough nervous system, the imperviousness to worry and the capacity for dealing with parents in quantity which every headmaster needs, it will be for you and your governors to decide…*

Peace in Europe was followed by the surrender of Japan, and still poor Jimmy was reaching no interviews. J.F. was on automatic pilot. 'I wish I could make up my mind as to whether Todd is the right man for a headmastership or not.' 'I sometimes think that he is too good for such a job and that it would be a pity for his fine gifts to be used for such dull tasks as occupy most of a headmaster's time.' Schools continued to turn poor Jimmy down.

In 1947, no doubt a little desperate, Jimmy temporarily lowered his sights to a bachelor House:

> *Dear Mr Roxburgh,*
>
> *In view of Haworth's departure from Chandos I think I should remind you that I let you know some time ago that Janet and I were definitely prepared to continue in our present state of being apart during term-time and together only in the holidays, so that as regards work at Stowe I could be reckoned as a bachelor.*

There was, however, disappointment: 'With Haworth's full – indeed, enthusiastic – approval,' responded J.F., 'I have offered the post to Stephan.'

Jimmy pressed on, his spirits remarkably high. Asked by *The Stoic* to review a junior production of *Lady Precious Stream*, there was no repeat of the grumpy handling of the Scottish play. Indeed, he even wrote part of his review in cheery, mock-Japanese.

Eventually, in 1948, the acquisition of a car allowed the Todds to accept a school house in Tingewick, and, ironically, at this time of least personal need, Jimmy's persistence finally had its reward. Reaching the last twelve for the headship of the Newcastle-under-Lyme High School for Boys had suddenly surprised him. J.F., too, for he had been his usual cautionary self:

I like Todd greatly, and I also like his wife who would be a great help to him in his headmastership. My only doubt about Todd's suitability is whether the fine edge of his mind might be blunted by the heavy humdrum toil of a Headmaster's life. If one puts a racehorse to the plough, the results are bad for both the horse and the ploughing.

However, the governors of this long-established Public School that had just given up its boarding provision decided to take a look at the racehorse. Tall and lean, he cut just the right kind of commanding figure. Indeed, with his abundant, well-groomed hair just slightly greying on the sides, Jimmy looked quite distinguished. His strong Christian faith was important. So, too, his scholarly ways. Indeed, with Janet beside him, enchanting everyone with her Scottish brogue, Jimmy Todd seemed just what the school governors were looking for. His disadvantage of being neither a Housemaster nor Head of Department had finally not mattered. The racehorse was put to the plough.

Stowe seemed shocked. *The Stoic*, which in the same issue had spent a good page and a half in saluting Robin Watt's years of service, gave Jimmy's similar fourteen years a single sentence, shared by two very junior masters. In the Societies' Notes he received a passing mention from the Toxophilites (for a paper on 'The scientific study of the Bible') and the Choral Society (who'd miss an 'indefatigable supporter'), and that was that. Stowe was stunned to virtual silence as the forty-one-year-old Jimmy set out for higher things.

* * *

He was to enjoy fifteen highly successful years at Newcastle-Under-Lyme, totally confounding all J.F.'s reservations. Basking in a self-belief that Janet had helped confirm, he contacted J.F. in September 1948 after just a few weeks in the job. 'I hope the term at Stowe has begun propitiously,' he commented cheerily. 'It seemed odd to think of the Masters Meeting on Tuesday taking place, and not being there myself! I think that we are going to like Newcastle very much.' Later that term, however, there was less bonhomie. Jimmy had been contacted by Stowe's Bursar for recent damage to school property and was not best pleased:

It is quite preposterous that we should be charged for dilapidations to Vine Cottage. Throughout our tenancy we took excellent care of it and before we left we had it spring-cleaned by our daily woman. We ought in fact to have been paid for the extensive cleaning we had before we arrived there. When my wife pointed out to the Bursar the dirtiness and untidiness of the place, he merely replied, 'Well, of course, the fact is that the Boyds have been very naughty and nothing can be done about it.'

In the end a disgruntled Jimmy Todd paid two thirds of the requested sum and J.F. himself, to help make the peace, the remainder. There their correspondence ended, apart from Jimmy's note of apology in the summer of 1949 that he would be unable to make the Common Room party and presentation on J.F.'s retirement.

Newcastle-under-Lyme was now all that mattered. At the end of his first term, the school magazine's editor endorsed him spiritedly:

We feel that, with the help of his wife, the school will go from strength to strength and its future be brilliantly assured. Knowing both of them now, we give them a welcome of unreserved warmth, and wish them a very happy life amongst us.

The school *did* go from strength to strength and the Todds *were* very happy in their Staffordshire life. For Janet, the move had meant the end of her career as a classics lecturer, but there proved big compensations. For Jimmy, there was the relish of leading a whole community towards a stronger Christian faith. His new Newcastle compendium of hymns was to include his good friend Leslie Huggins' setting of 'Say Not The Struggle Naught Availeth'. Founders' Day was soon to end with everyone singing the Huggins' version of 'O thou not made with hands'.

In their spare time the Todds began working on a book of translations of classical Greek and Latin texts, a panorama of some 1,300 years. Sometimes they opted for famous translations, sometimes lesser known. And when they could find no translation that pleased them, they would include their own accomplished versions.

After seven years of quiet endeavour, *Voices From The Past* was published in 1955. It was a superb book and deservedly well reviewed. As one of *The Observer's* choices for Book of the Year, it was soon taken up by the Readers Union and later published in paperback in two volumes.

Eight years on, in 1963, as Jimmy's headmastership was nearing its end, there was a second collaboration, *Peoples of the Past*, a rewriting of *The Ancient World*. Janet had done a great deal of cutting and some felicitous re-phrasing. Scholarly objectivity had replaced messianic zeal.

Though Jimmy retired from his headship in December 1963, his successful career did not end there. At fifty-six he had a high-powered job awaiting him as Oxford Secretary to the Oxford and Cambridge School's Examination Board. This meant a return to his birthplace, a final perfect move. Meanwhile, most fortuitously, Janet had come into a fortune. The Todds were soon very happily settled at Headington.

Jimmy eventually retired in 1973. Janet, who had gone into local politics, remained active, working on the city council and eventually becoming Lord Mayor of Oxford. An Old Stoic of the 1940s, Peter Shepherd, who by chance had re-established contact with his old Chatham underhousemaster, reported in 1985:

> *Jimmy is well and thriving in Oxford. He spent a whole day showing my wife and me round Oxford, and we had lunch with 'Fluff' Llowarch[56] who was C.O. of the O.T.C and also my Science Tutor...*

Jimmy died three years later, aged 81. He lies buried in Wolvercote Cemetery.

After his death Janet continued in politics. 'I love canvassing,' she told the *Oxford Mail* in 1989. 'I like meeting people and discovering their problems and, incidentally, hoping to get their vote. I don't always succeed but I am very seldom rebuffed.' As late as 2000, she was still standing in the local elections. When she died in 2006 at the age of 88, her funeral at the church of All Saints, where she and Jimmy had long worshipped, was packed with friends and admirers.

Marriage with Janet had clearly been the turning-point in Jimmy's life. It enabled him, in the end, to fulfil the career ambitions he had pursued with such pertinacity. The great J.F. had clearly felt them ill-judged, but Jimmy had proved him wrong. That thought would surely have made up for his strangely silent Stowe departure.

---

56 Head of Science, 1938-54

16

EWALD ZETTL

Much-loved Modern Linguist & husband of Liz
Stowe 1935-66

Forty miles up the Danube from Vienna lies the historic Austrian town of Krems. It was there, in that most lovely of settings, that Ewald Zettl grew up, his family having moved from Germany soon after his birth in 1905. Ewald's father was a rising star in the Austrian diplomatic corps and his family owned a large estate, which, it was thought, Ewald would help run in the fullness of time. It was not to be. Though Ewald's father found a job as a teacher after the First World War, the family estate was lost and times were hard.

Ewald was lucky, however, in attending the Krems *Humanistisches Gymnasium*, a fine school in which he flourished and acquired a deep love of German and English literature. He followed up a successful degree course in English at Innsbruck University with further university courses in Vienna and Munich, plus Scandinavian studies in Copenhagen. At twenty-two Ewald was impressively well qualified. With his film star good looks and sunny disposition, he was also universally liked. The whole world seemed to be opening up before him, but it was Sheffield that next claimed him.

In 1927-28 he spent a year there at the University, working as an assistant in German, proving a big hit and also making an impact at the city's fledgling Repertory Theatre. Afterwards, he headed back to Austria to become even more impressively qualified. Having first acquired an Austrian State Teachers' Diploma, he used a year attached to the English Department of Innsbruck University to write a dissertation on the English Repertory Theatre Movement to gain a Doctorate.

Ewald loved Innsbruck. He was able to indulge his passion for the open-air life, becoming a fully-qualified ski instructor and the University's champion skier. Whenever he could, he was out mountaineering, rock-climbing or skating. He also won medals for long-distance cycling events and, in the vacations, as if not busy already, was often out testing motorbikes to destruction for one of the big German firms. His studies, however, always prevailed, and his fascination for controversies surrounding the mediaeval epic poem 'Chronicle of England' led to a scholarship at Berlin's superb new research centre (the *Osterreichisch-Deutsche Wissenschafthilfe*), cocooned from the city's many troubles.

* * *

Soon it was decision-time. Teaching in Krems offered Ewald some job security, but Austria seethed with political unrest. As a German citizen, moreover, he was about to be co-opted into the army. Accordingly, in 1930 he returned to Sheffield University, where, for five years, he would be an Assistant Lecturer in German.

He quickly felt at home. To his delight the Repertory Theatre was still flourishing. He was also able to capitalize on his mediaeval studies. After helpful contact with the Early English Text Society at Oxford and the writing of several obscure articles, the fruition of all his scholarly endeavours came with the publication of *An Anonymous Short English Metrical Chronicle*, a book that long remained an important port-of-call for scholars of mediaeval English poetry.

* * *

In 1935, the year of the book's publication, Stowe came into his life. By a happy coincidence Sheffield University's Vice-Chancellor, Arthur Pickard-Cambridge, was also Chairman of the school's governors. That March, Pickard-Cambridge suggested to J.F. that Stowe might employ Ewald:

He only wants to leave here because there is no opening for him in any higher paid post, and we shall be very sorry indeed to lose him. He is a gentleman through and through, speaks English very well, and is one of the most attractive members of the university staff. If he could get a good mastership he would become naturalized in this country. He has proved himself a very good teacher...

J.F. responded positively, and Ewald's weighty C.V. led to an immediate interview, which proved a formality. 'We ought to take Zettl – there is no one within miles of him,' wrote J.F. to Fritz Clifford (Tutor of Modern Languages) and Patrick Hunter. He would be teaching the top German sets and middle school French. His C.V., meanwhile, got better and better, for Pickard-Cambridge marked his departure with an honorary Sheffield degree, and, in the summer holidays, to brush up his French, Ewald undertook a course at the *College Medical d'Annel* near Paris.

Ewald found the Common Room delightfully friendly, and was soon on the best of terms with Patrick Hunter, recently appointed to the new post of Senior Tutor. Early on, *The Stoic* tells of the pair taking members of the Vitruvian and Antiquarian Societies to the Rollright Stones and the fine Tudor house of Compton Wynyates. Another of their shared interests was athletics. Ewald soon persuaded Hunter to add field events to the Stowe Sports Days and proved himself an adept coach of both javelin and discus.

Ewald's first term was also notable for his success in coaching for Oxbridge. 'Congratulations on the scholarship Spencer got,' wrote Roxburgh to him at Krems at Christmas. 'I hope you will forget all about schoolmastering and enjoy the snow.' The next year, he was appointed Tutor of Side Two, taking responsibility for about twenty sixth-formers studying modern languages. Edward Hart Dyke and Eddie Capel Cure (who had combined on several French and Spanish textbooks) worked cheerfully under him, enthusiastically supporting Ewald's often quite esoteric play-readings with the Modern Languages Society. Ewald's arrival encouraged scholarship. He was soon giving a lecture on mediaeval and classical manuscripts, 'aptly illustrated on the epidiascope'. 'Dr Zettl,' noted *The Stoic*, 'soon showed us that he knew more about our own language than most of us...'

* * *

In late 1936 his personal circumstances dramatically altered. He had spent the summer, as usual, with his family in Austria, increasingly unsettled since the Nazi assassination of Chancellor Dollfuss. This time, however, he had come back to England with a bride, a fluent English speaker called Grete, whose parents ran a factory outside Krems. Ewald accordingly moved out of his Stowe bachelor accommodation and rented Bourton Mill on the edge of Buckingham.

The Stoic of December 1936 tells of Ewald and his new wife participating in a play-reading (Lessing's *Minna von Barnhelm*), but it was very much a one-off. Grete was not interested in Ewald's work and never settled in England. By the summer of 1937, when a daughter was born, she was saying that England was not for her. Her homeland was Austria. With war imminent and wild talk of German spies abounding, Ewald had to endure the unpleasantness of a sudden police search of Bourton Mill.

Six months before the outbreak of war Grete finally walked out on Ewald, taking their daughter with her. 'I wonder if you would allow me to live at the school next term,' wrote Ewald to Roxburgh towards the end of the Spring Term 1939, introducing the break-up gently. 'My mother-in-law is very ill and my wife is going out to her next week and will, if conditions allow, stay on for the summer holidays.' In the event, she never came back.

Ewald moved into the central Field House, shared with mathematician Robert Davis and an ebullient Australian scientist, Hector Boyd. A lifelong friendship also soon started with the zany mathematician 'Wilf' (or 'Freddie') Archer, known for his hop, skip and jump way of walking, an intriguing car (Alonso) and a trusty dog (Bojam). The warm atmosphere of the newly-built Field Houses would help sustain Ewald as he slowly came to terms with the loss of Grete and his daughter.

Ewald thrived in his adopted country. He had early on acquired the affectionate Stowe nickname of 'Herr Doctor' and it stuck, even as war drew ever nearer. Though by 1938 he was a naturalized Englishman, his soft accent still showed his Austro-German roots.

One of his main extracurricular concerns was the running of the Stowe Film Society, whose stimulating remit was exclusively for foreign films. His early programmes included the Russian silent classic *Storm Over Asia* and up-to-date talkics from France (*La Belle Equipe*) and Germany (*Der Herrscher*). The latter was particularly controversial with the airing of the Nazi concept of a Fuehrer above the law, and a postscript from Goebbels, denying anti-capitalist intentions. Stoics were having their horizons widened.

Ewald was back among friends in Sheffield when war finally broke out on 3 September 1939, and he enrolled at once as an assistant A.R.P. Warden. War meant, of course, that he might not now see or hear of his daughter for several years. Likewise, he would no longer be able to visit his parents, currently in Vienna. 'They will probably be as safe there as anywhere in this mad world,' he wrote to J.F., 'but I shall try to get them out, at least to some neutral country.' It was wishful thinking.

* * *

Amid all of Ewald's distress at the outbreak of war, there was one saving grace. He had been put into a small Common Room group taking responsibility for the blackout of the South Front, his partners for which would be the cheery Eddie Capel Cure and Robert Davis together with a bright-eyed young lady who worked for the Bursar (Major Russell), Elizabeth ('Liz') Duncan. For Ewald and Liz, it was love at first sight. Or very nearly. Liz, it seems, had earlier spotted (and admired) Ewald 'across a crowded room' at the two big Buckingham social events, the Police and Hospital Balls.

Liz was the daughter of a London stockbroker of Laleham-on-Thames, a village close to Staines. She was twenty-one that September – a birthday she always remembered for J.F.'s kindness:

> *Happening to come into my office, J.F. took in the plethora of cards and telegrams and elegantly enquired, 'Allow me to presume a birthday, Miss Duncan?' I confessed it was. Two hours later he came back bearing a bottle of port with the words 'Congratulations on your birthday' written on a red luggage label. He apologised profusely for his inability to find a proper card.*

There were frustrations engendered by Ewald's failed but ongoing marriage. The effervescent Liz, moreover, felt impelled to leave the Stowe bursary and telephone exchange for work that helped the war effort more directly, at Oxford and High Wycombe. J.F. wrote to her when she left:

> *I am genuinely grateful for all the help you have given us here during these last, not too easy, years, and for the way that you have looked after us all from your conning tower in the North Hall! I am always grateful when I find someone who is genuinely and disinterestedly fond of Stowe – and for your devotion to the place I owe you a further debt...*

Liz kept in touch, not only with Ewald but J.F too. In May 1944, on the School's 21st birthday, he wrote again:

Excuse a card. I have shoals of birthday greetings to acknowledge. Yours was very much appreciated and I am really glad to think that you remembered us. I've had telegrams from Africa and Italy and a comic one from David Niven.

Ewald was a welcome visitor at 'High Elms', Laleham, whenever Liz was staying with her parents. But with war raging on and Grete's whereabouts unknown, there could be no divorce or remarriage.

In March 1944 Ewald broke the news of a possible career development. Sheffield University were looking for someone to take over the German Department. They had made it clear that, if Ewald were to apply, he would be the favoured candidate. Liz kept quiet on the subject, desperately hoping that he would not apply, but feeling it would be wrong to influence him. Ewald was terribly torn. Such an opportunity might not come again, but acceptance would take him much further from Liz. Wartime Common Room friendships were also not lightly discounted. He and Patrick Hunter, for example, were regularly taking parties of Stoics to work at 'harvest farms' in the summer holidays to boost the war effort. He had been Best Man at Hunter's wedding in Devon only three months before. In perplexity, Ewald wrote to J.F., expressing his dilemma. On the one side, there was prestige and a higher salary. On the other, his gratitude to Stowe, which had stood by him in 1939, and his own satisfied ambitions. 'I fully realize,' he told Roxburgh, 'that with my present appointment I have reached the top of my little ladder at Stowe; and I am content.' J.F. gently reassured Ewald how much he was appreciated. It was what Ewald had wanted to hear and he turned down the Sheffield offer. 'I'm so happy here,' he told Liz simply. 'Stowe is really where I want to stay.'

* * *

War in Europe ended in May 1945. By this time Liz was back at Stowe, working for a brief time as a 'land girl' in the orchard (the site of today's running track), before returning as telephonist. Ewald, meanwhile, was able to begin to make contact again with his family at Krems, though still unable to visit them. They had suffered terribly. Their home had been bombed and, having lost everything, they were currently being put up in a dilapidated farm. They did, however, manage to help him contact Grete.

In the Spring of 1947, Ewald's divorce finally came through and in May that year he and Liz were quietly married. The reception was at 'High Elms', the honeymoon, Eastbourne. Ewald's tutees greeted their return with a grand jamboree, and Ewald and Liz responded by hiring a bus for them all to enjoy an even grander jamboree at the Green Man. For their first Stowe term together, the pair lived at Bourton Mill, but Ewald would never speak of his earlier time there. In a chest of drawers, carefully wrapped up, there was an Austrian zither, a lovely old instrument, which he had regularly played when married before the war. He no longer made music with it. It symbolised a part of his life too painful to revisit.

Austria itself, however, was to prove one of their shared delights. They were there first in the summer of 1947, when the country was still subdivided under Russian, American and British control. Money was tight and travel abroad largely unthinkable, but Ewald and Liz found employment as travel chaperones for the children of English personnel in the British sector, at the start and end of the school holidays. Their base was war-scarred Vienna in the British zone (as graphically captured in Carol Reed's *The Third Man*), and Ewald's parents in the Russian zone obtained permission to rent an apartment there, enabling a reunion. Ewald also managed contact with his ten-year old daughter.

Back in Buckingham, Liz swiftly invited J.F. to dinner at Bourton Mill. There was a warm reply: 'I should love to dine with you and Ewald before term begins – and also before petrol ends! As to dress, I shall come in a dinner jacket and soft collar unless otherwise instructed.' 'Please don't bother to change,' responded Liz cheerily. 'I'm head cook and bottle-washer and couldn't possibly cope with a long skirt!'

The war had aged J.F. considerably. The warmth of the Zettls was a much-appreciated restorative. He wrote afterwards:

My dear Elizabeth,

I can't tell you what a refreshment and delight it was to me to spend such an evening as I did yesterday at the Mill House. The friendly welcome you and Ewald gave me, the lovely things you showed me and the wondrous food you offered me will long remain in my memory. You two certainly have the art of home-making – and since you combine it with the art of hospitality your friends are very fortunate. I do hope that the work on the Dadford cottage will go ahead without a hitch. I shall visit the workmen next week…

The Dadford cottage in question, into which the Zettls were to move that November, had only been recently acquired by the school. J.F. had suggested they might perhaps find a name for it, and Ewald responded at once:

Local antiquarians have it that it was built to house the grooms of Vancouver Lodge. Inverted snobbery much prefers 'Grooms Cottage' to 'Allotment View' or 'Ye Olde Yew Tree' but is inclined to leave out the apostrophe of the genitive. Would you object to Grooms Cottage?

Grooms Cottage it became, and in early 1948 J.F. was one of the first guests. It proved another much-needed fillip:

What a dinner you gave me last night – and what a welcome! I am much more grateful to you and Ewald for your kindness than it is at all easy to express in words. Such friendliness means a lot to a rather lonely person like me. (It is possible, you know, to be very lonely although always talking to people and seeing people and writing to people!) Thank you, my dear friends, most warmly and sincerely...

Château Zettl is about as charming a home as one could find. I envy you both your taste and skill!

* * *

A year later, Stowe was under new management, and J.F.'s successor, Eric Reynolds, was struggling in Roxburgh's wake. Liz was later to recall:

The old masters were so hostile to him! Ewald was one of the very few who were nice to him! We liked him very much. He tried so hard, but his sensitivity was misunderstood as weakness. And then, of course, there was the awful climbing accident. We were on holiday in Vienna when we happened to read of it. Somehow everything about the poor man seemed ill-starred.

In November 1952, Ewald was the guest of honour at the Old Stoic Dinner. It was one of Reynolds' first big functions since suffering the psychologically damaging facial injuries, and his long absence had strengthened talk in Old Boys' circles of indiscipline and unrest. Tasked with making a speech in such a tense situation, Ewald used the occasion to remind his listeners that the Stoics in the glorious golden age of Roxburgh, far from being paragons of virtue, had created a distinctly spirited approach to communal living.

The headmaster has just told you all that has happened at Stowe during the past year – all, that is, that he wants you to know. But what about all those happenings that are usually not recorded officially but nevertheless add colour to Stowe's daily routine? The thought struck me that I might record those for you, to complete the picture.

I sent out specially briefed members of my Side to penetrate the various House Iron Curtains, promising kind end-of-term reports for really juicy information. I kept wide awake at Common Room meetings. I tried to listen at the door of the Matrons' Mess. I intruded upon study parties – all in search of material for you.

But – and I am sure you will be rather shocked to hear it – I greatly regret to say that little seems to have happened that you would not expect to find included in the most carefully edited official report:

George has remained undecorated – neglected.

No garments, neither male nor female, have flown from the pavilion flagstaffs.

The British Worthies still have their second set of noses

Open-air smoking parties are dying out – a lost art, almost. For, in the name of Landscape Gardening most of the well-known and inviting clumps of bushes and undergrowth have been removed. And Landscape experts like the Headmaster, Mr Capel Cure and Mr Mounsey are met with in the most unlikely places and at the most unlikely times.

No midnight scavenger hunts reported.

Cobham Pond lies beautifully clean, bordered by lavender and quite neglected except for the odd copy of Revision Exercises in French.[57]

The delights of your generations seem to have gone quite out of fashion…

The 1950s were good years for Ewald. He enjoyed developing his role as the school's first Careers Master, utilizing his extensive contacts with Old Stoics to advantage. He was still having fun running the Internal Combustion Engine section of the corps. And Grooms Cottage was just down the road from the newly-opened Silverstone, where Liz found employment in a variety of important office roles. She recalled:

---

57   A textbook written by Capel Cure and Hart Dyke, first published in 1933.

Ewald used to drive me up there and then return to teach. Later, he'd turn up again, usually having brought two or three boys with him. Tommy Sopwith was one of the first. On Sundays he had to attend Chapel, of course, but after that he'd race back to the circuit, usually with quite a full car.

The space in Grooms Cottage was also put to good use, not least when Ewald's daughter Marlies lived with them while she pursued an Oxford secretarial course. 'I shall ever be grateful to both of you,' Marlies was later to write to Liz, 'for taking me in for those two years and giving my life some emotional stability after a rather unsettled childhood in Austria.' Ewald's father, an ailing elderly widower, was likewise to be cared for by them for five years at Grooms Cottage.

By the late 1950s, Stowe was being run by Donald Crichton-Miller, enthusiastically enforcing 'a more rigorous regime', and easy-going and long-serving masters found themselves under uncomfortable pressure. Ewald was first told that Side 2 had been abolished, and, later, that it would be run by a threesome: the admirable Joe Bain, Ewald himself and Hamish Rutherford, 'a constant thorn in Ewald's side', according to Liz. He was soon passing on Careers happily enough to Roger Rawcliffe, but hated the summary abolition of his Film Society, which had so long provided foreign films of merit.

When Bob Drayson took over from Crichton-Miller in January 1964, Ewald, somewhat miraculously, was still in a job. Three years earlier, to prepare for retirement, he and Liz had acquired a terraced cottage in Buckingham, 34 High Street. It was in a completely derelict state but they steadily restored it, finally moving in there in 1965. Ewald retired from Stowe in the summer of 1966 after some lengthy hospitalisations and one major operation.

* * *

Liz herself kept busy in Ewald's fourteen years of retirement, most notably at the Silverstone booking office. Every summer they motored on the continent, often on month-long odysseys of three thousand miles. Ewald, who had nursed ambitions to enter the Monte Carlo Rally, still relished adventurous driving. Krems, Innsbruck, Vienna and Kitzbuehel were among old haunts revisited in their doughty Renault 4 and there were many new ones including the Grand Prix courses of Monaco, Spa and the Nürburgring.

It all came to an end for him in April 1980 at the age of 74. 'Flu had brought hospitalisation, and a severe stroke followed on his first night back home. Patrick Hunter wrote anxiously, 'If he can still understand, Liz, give him my love and tell him how well and how happily I remember his many great kindnesses'. Ewald had survived many serious illnesses in the past, but this time there was to be no late rally.

Tributes abounded. Eric Reynolds remembered their friendship as 'one of the happiest relations I enjoyed during my years at Stowe', citing in particular the cheerful exchanges they would daily enjoy outside the Pineapple Block. Bob Drayson, in turn, recalled how difficult his own first year had been: 'They were troublous times, and I relied so much on good men like Ewald and Alasdair Macdonald.'

Many former tutees contacted Liz. 'For us,' wrote Peter Rossiter, 'he will always be synonymous with Stowe. I owe him a debt which can never be repaid.' 'Without him,' remembered Anthony Barton, 'my life at Stowe would have been a very different and unrewarding experience.'

Perhaps the most telling tribute of all came from Nathaniel Parsons:

He and I briefly came across one another in his O-level German classes. I learned almost no German – it was the dunces' class, I remember. Instead I sat entranced by the gentleness of my teacher who seemed to be offering us the ability to learn, rather than browbeating us into chalking up yet one more exam ribbon of doubtful value.

To be teaching 'the dunces' class' at the end of a career that began with a weighty C.V. and a highbrow book on mediaeval English poetry might seem something of a regression. Yet the many expressions of deep regard in 1980 seem a complete validation of Ewald's decision to forsake the stimulation of university work for a school he loved. It was testimony, too, to the way that Liz had guided him to personal happiness and contentment.

Liz herself, with a succession of lovely dogs, became a legendary figure in later years, staying on until 2022 in the Buckingham house that she and Ewald had restored, always deeply interested in Stowe's progress, with a fund of anecdotes about its history. She died peacefully in March 2023, having reached the school's centenary year and the wonderful age of 105.

17

PETER WIENER

The controversial founder of Side 9
Stowe 1944-48

Replacing masters who had enlisted in the fight against Hitler could not have been easy. Thirty-year-old Peter Fritz Wiener, with his cosmopolitan background, must have seemed an ideal Modern Languages replacement. The multilingual young man came from a distinguished Jewish family which had fled from Germany after Hitler's rise to power. In addition to teaching at Rugby, he had written an anti-Nazi best seller, been employed for secret missions abroad and had any number of friends in high places. In 1944, to the tired, war-weary Roxburgh, he surely seemed a Godsend, just the kind of vibrant personality to bring some colour to the depleted Common Room, even capable, perhaps, of bringing back a touch of Stowe-in-the-Twenties with all its youthful vitality.

Alas for these nostalgic hopes, it was the controversial nature of Peter Fritz's colourful short stay that would become legendary.

* * *

Facts about his early life are scarce. He was born in Berlin but had an education that took him to eight different countries. He and his family fled Germany in 1934, when he was twenty, relocating in London. At some time he had studied at the Sorbonne, though his claim that the documentation of his Ph.D and LL.D had been seized by the Gestapo after the fall of Paris in June 1940 is clouded by the fact that by then he had been teaching at Rugby for a year, and, on the fall of France in June 1940, like most Germans in England, he was locked up for a while in an internment camp.

He was not to stay on the Isle of Man for long. Refugees, having proved their *bona fides*, tended to be released in due course, but Peter Fritz's return to Rugby after only three months probably outdid them all. Once back, he wrote some strangely ingratiating letters to *The Times*, stressing 'how remarkably well we were always treated by the British officers throughout the internment.' One comment, in particular, seemed particularly odd:

> *The first question all my friends asked when I was released was, 'Were there any fifth columnists among you?' I have seen and spoken to about 1,200 internees during almost three months, and I can truthfully assure you that I have not come across one single person whom I would suspect in this direction.*

Was that really his friends' first question? And did he really chat up as many as 1,200 different people long enough to gather whether they were Fifth Columnists or not? If he did, perhaps he did so as a Secret Service 'mole', thereby earning speedy release?

He was soon making another public show of pro-British feelings with *German With Tears*, published in 1942. This remarkable book had been overseen by the influential diplomat Lord Vansittart, a former private secretary to two Prime Ministers and an outspoken opponent of German appeasement in the 1930s. It expressed Vansittart's belief that since Germany, through indoctrination by a warped education system, had a deep-rooted militarism that went back much further than the Nazis, Britain's post-victory handling of the country needed to be really tough to uproot it. 'Mr Wiener's book,' wrote Vansittart, 'has the true ring of keenness and sincerity... There will be no peace on earth till all this German teaching has been swept into limbo.' With the help of powerful backers, *German With Tears* was translated into several languages, with copies winging their way to many influential political figures. Eleanor Roosevelt noted in her diary that it was 'a must read'.

It was all heady stuff for a young refugee who was a very junior master at Rugby. And he swiftly found a publisher for *German For The Scientist* (based largely on lectures that, before Rugby, he had given at London University). It would enhance his scholarly standing as it ran to several editions.

* * *

In 1943, somewhat mysteriously, the War Office came calling. He later wrote:

I was suddenly called upon to do some work for the War Office, and naturally left Rugby. While serving with the Royal Fusiliers I contracted an illness, and after months in hospital I was invalided out…

The mention of the Royal Fusiliers suggests work that was operational rather than sedentary, for recruits training for S.O.E. operations abroad were always given a morale-boosting 'parent regiment'. His German background would have made him ideal material for the Special Operations Executive. So, too, his contacts. Lord Vansittart had been involved in its formation and was for many years the unofficial head of MI6. It seems as if a long illness cut short whatever dangerous mission he was carrying out. Alternatively, perhaps he was seriously wounded in the course of it?

* * *

Having recovered from illness or wounds, Peter Fritz came to Stowe in the late summer of 1944, instead of going back to Rugby. He wrote of this move somewhat grandly:

The opportunity of being able to compare one of the oldest schools – Rugby – with one of the most modern appealed to me greatly, and, with the approval of both the Chairman of the Governing Body of Rugby School (Dr William Temple) and its Headmaster (Mr P H. B. Lyon), I moved to Stowe.

It is hard to see why he needed 'approval' from the Chairman of Governors (in whose favour Peter Fritz seems to infer he was basking). One of Rugby's housemasters, Eric Reynolds (later Roxburgh's successor), was to write witheringly of Peter Wiener's 'unscrupulousness and disloyalty' there. He thought him 'dangerous', someone who caused trouble wherever he went. Peter Fritz's glossy account of his Rugby departure hardly marries with this highly critical assessment.

Roxburgh's interview notes for Peter Fritz, however, contained no hints of anxiety:

Extremely highly strung, and I should think intellectually quite brilliant. Smokes cigarettes to keep himself calm and prefers a 32 to a 26 period week! Probably works extremely fast. Naturally wants more of the top work than we can give him… No games, corps or anything of the kind. Believes religion should be base of education, but says much hypocrisy and intellectual dishonesty among Rugby masters… Wants to be allowed to teach more or less what he wants and how… Large room needed. Grafton [flat] would do, as has many books.

J.F. was surely dazzled. The self-confident Peter Fritz had waxed lyrical about his many contributions to the *Times Educational Supplement* and a book he claimed to be writing on the Public Schools. In addition, he had gifted J.F. a selection of his newspaper writings and a copy of *German With Tears*. (J.F. was to find the articles 'clear, strong and vigorous, showing a practical and forceful mind' and the book 'deeply moving'.) Always susceptible to name-dropping, J.F. would have been highly impressed when Peter Fritz suggested that maybe his friend 'the Prince de Bourbon' could 'come down to Stowe for a weekend'. Peter Fritz, it seems, had been appointed by J.F. on the spot.

His arrival was heralded in the summer holidays by a dramatic piece of self-advertisement – a letter in *The Spectator*, addressed from Stowe (as if he were there already), attacking a recently voiced suggestion of a generous stance towards Germany in the event of victory. 'Germany needs a taste of her own medicine,' he wrote, declaring that this was what he would be telling his pupils shortly, when he resumed teaching 'after a prolonged absence on active service'. The letter surely raised some eyebrows in the Common Room. J.F., however, wrote to him at once: 'How delighted I was to see the name of Stowe connected with your name and the expression of so much good sense!'

* * *

On arrival, Peter Fritz was no doubt quick to make heavy hints about his exploits with the Secret Service, and in due course they became legendary. Harriet Hall, in her biography of her parents, the McElwees, wrote of his 'immensely exciting war, probably as part of the Special Operations Executive'. He had undertaken, she thought, 'a series of hair-raising exploits with the French Resistance'. Roxburgh himself would confidently write that it had all been of 'a hazardous and secret nature'.

As a hero, then, and a person of consequence, Peter Fritz would hardly have been best pleased at being put in charge of lowly 5D and to find himself far down the Modern Languages Department pecking order. His major effort, accordingly, soon diverted to Modern Studies, where he could teach whatever he wanted and demonstrate his passion for current affairs with a plethora of invitations to visiting speakers and extra-mural expeditions. Roxburgh was delighted.

He must, accordingly, have been shocked when Peter Fritz announced, in his very first term, that he had applied for a job at Winchester. J.F.'s reference reflected the disappointment:

I am rather sorry that he is going after another temporary job, partly because he is a valuable fellow whom I don't want to lose and partly because he ought to stay in a place which he professes to like... I like Wiener immensely and find him most stimulating and refreshing. He has already done good work here by livening up our war-time staff and galvanizing the boys...

In the end, the new arrival had a change of heart. The staff were to be enlivened and the boys galvanized after all. In late 1944 he was also enlivening *The Spectator* ('Peers as Prime Ministers') and galvanizing *The Sunday Times* ('Interpreting Nietzsche'), his considerable confidence further fuelled, no doubt, by the publication of his third book in three years.

Martin Luther: Hitler's Spiritual Ancestor was a highly provocative effort, echoing the beliefs of its chief sponsors, Lord Vansittart and Dean Inge, that Luther's writings were being used by the Nazis to justify the demonizing of the Jews. Roxburgh told its author:

I read your book last night and congratulate you most sincerely on it. It is a masterly piece of advocacy and overwhelmingly cogent... Your book will certainly be attacked, but it will be well able to stand its ground and I feel sure that it can do nothing but good...

However, the Chairman of Governors, Sir Arthur Pickard-Cambridge, was worried enough by the World Evangelical Alliance's reaction that it was 'an evil and venomous attack upon one of the outstanding figures of the Protestant Reformation' to raise the whole matter with Roxburgh. J.F. replied tersely that the W.E.A. was an organisation of fanatics:

I certainly have no intention of being apologetic about Wiener... Wiener is strictly speaking a 'duration' master but he is so useful that I hope to be able to keep him permanently. I shall certainly try to do so if any more attacks are made on him by the Protestant underworld...

Pickard-Cambridge climbed down, though his own view on Wiener and his book remained unaltered:

He is quite uncritical and incompetent as a historian, with little or no sense of the relative value of different sources, and so much of it is taken from one or two other writers that one would class it with the works in which 'The scissors are mightier than the pen'.

The Common Room would have agreed. Its dislike of the Wiener flamboyance was reflected in a review of *Martin Luther* in *The Stoic* from the ironic pen of the wartime English Tutor, Roy Meldrum. He concluded:

The effect of dislocated quotations combined with an urgent theory is one familiar to the works of those who seek to prove that Bacon wrote Shakespeare.

In modern times the book has made a dramatic comeback in cyberspace, reprinted on both Catholic and atheist websites, echoing Roxburgh's enthusiastic response. Luther's writing on the Jews is still a topic of debate.

* * *

In the Christmas holiday of 1944 Peter Fritz bombarded Roxburgh with letters. In one he listed the various speakers he had fixed up for the next term, including the editor of the *New Statesman* and a *Times* journalist whose support of the 1944 Education Act had proved crucial. He had arranged for all his talks to occur in lesson time. 'I really do believe,' he wrote confidently, 'that it is necessary that boys are kept in touch with the outside world, listen to and discuss topical events with some of the best-known writers and thinkers.' Indeed, he went on, it was 'an educational necessity'. Roxburgh gave grateful assent.

Another letter, of striking familiarity, was written shortly after Nazi V2 rockets had been dropping from the London skies:

Being kept awake last night by Hitler's speech (which sounded to me like announcing a very long war) and two very close rockets (which frightened me more than any blitz), I made, amongst other, the New Year's resolution to try in 1945 to be a quiet, peaceful, well-balanced schoolmaster who will give no trouble to Head Master and/or colleagues by phantastic schemes, pomposity and continental excitability. Please remind me of it occasionally!

* * *

The war in Europe was over when Peter Fritz's second year began with an auspicious promotion as Tutor of Side 8a. In this newly-created role he would be acting as assistant to Leslie Reid's Side 8, and it was not long before he had become Tutor of another newly-created group, Side 9, centred around 'General Modern Studies', allowing him to take over most of Reid's tutees.

Current affairs visits in and out of Stowe continued to proliferate. Famous visitors multiplied. Field Marshal Montgomery, Harold Nicolson, Lord Brabazon, A.J.P. Taylor and Malcolm Sargent all fell within his net at this period. Meanwhile, in London in the holidays, as he relayed to J.F. in April 1946, he continued to cultivate distinguished Old Stoics:

I shall not trouble you now by conveying to you the various messages which Old Stoics – whom I always seem to meet somehow or other – have asked me to give you. Except that I met Leonard Cheshire and that his new career strikes me as quite phantastic. He wants to Christianize England, Europe and the World by starting some kind of worthy farming community on a disused aerodrome, being backed by the Sunday Graphic!

In December 1946 his long article in the *Sunday Times* on 'Teaching Current Affairs' allowed him to tell the whole country what a splendid schoolmaster he was. It ended with a couple of showy quotations:

I have never yet discussed politics with a boy who gives the impression of agreeing with Disraeli's dictum: 'Almost everything that is great has been done by youth'. All of them rather seemed to be imbued with the spirit in which William Pitt replied to Walpole: 'The atrocious crime of being a young man, which the

*honourable gentleman has, with such spirit and decency, charged upon me, I
shall neither attempt to palliate nor deny; but content myself with wishing that
I may be one of those whose follies cease with their youth, and not of those who
continue ignorant in spite of age and experience.'*

In late 1946 came the biggest Wiener coup of all – his own article in *Picture Post*
about a visit to the USA. The first person singular was much in evidence, but Wiener
had been mixing with the Roosevelts and his cup was full:

*Earlier in the year Mrs Kermit Roosevelt – who has done so much for Anglo-
American friendship – paid her first post-war visit to England. At a quiet dinner
party, I told her how anxious I was not only to lecture about America and the
Americans but to show the reality of things to my students. She invited as many
boys as I was prepared to take to her house and offered to organise as complete
a tour as was possible...*

His main ambition, he wrote, was to find out how young Americans lived, what
their schools and universities were like, and what they were thinking. In doing this, of
course, another ambition was fulfilled: to make his way into American high society.
Picture Post showed him with his five pupils at Mrs Franklin D. Roosevelt's house at
Hyde Park.

He naturally penned a long account for *The Stoic*. At Princeton, he proudly let
slip, they had 'a very private interview with Professor Einstein'.

In 1947 his English naturalisation papers finally came through after four years of
attempts. Now that he was an Englishman, he began using a new name outside Stowe,
Peter Frederick Winter. He was still Peter Wiener, however, when he had two letters
published in the *Daily Telegraph* that year, one of which attacked the Old Stoic MP
Tufton Beamish. 'Of course the letter is simply a piece of self-advertisement,' wrote
Pickard-Cambridge somewhat testily to Roxburgh, 'but if anything can spoil our
recruitment of new boys, this will. My personal feeling is that we have had enough of
Wiener.' J.F.'s reply suggests that he was at last seeing a new side to his protégé:

*The man is a curse and a nuisance, but hitherto the advantages of having him
here have outweighed the disadvantages... His work as Current Affairs master
here is really valuable and there is not the slightest fear that his influence is*

pro-Russian... But he is one of these irrepressible men who, when they hear an opinion expressed, must always contradict it... He has now had his warning.

Three months later, however, Peter Fritz was at it again, unable to resist joining a *Times* debate about the Civil Service Examinations, which somehow enabled him to pontificate about an alarming drop in teaching standards in schools:

... The best people within the profession are leaving it or trying to do so, and there is little apparent personality and intelligence among the post-war recruits to the profession...

Both Common Room and Governors were outraged. Roxburgh, upset that the demand that Stowe receive no mention in any future letters had been disregarded, asked him to explain himself. Peter Fritz refused, and J.F. asked for his resignation.

The Wiener response was a critical letter of thirty-five pages, commencing with a history lesson:

Stowe started as a young school in the early twenties. It had a young headmaster, young masters, and was imbued by the desire, frequently encountered in the twenties, to make the pre-1914 values come to life again. Alas, in its splendid isolation in the English countryside it has stood still without noticing that the world has changed, that a total revolution has been going on and is going on, that the values of the twenties are dead and never will come back. Today it is indeed a tragic sight to see how this youngest of all by age is one of the oldest, most dated, and most reactionary in spirit. A Chairman of the Governing Body, aged 75, a head master of over 60, a staff of an abnormally high average age, seven out of eight housemasters who have not seen any war-service – is it surprising that this School tries to produce values with which I find myself more and more in opposition?

And so it went on and on. The letter, declared Peter Fritz, would be published, and with it, Roxburgh's response, which he looked forward to receiving. It was not forthcoming.

* * *

J.F. did, however, allow him to serve out his notice with one final term, and, at the beginning of it, even held out a large olive branch. Peter Fritz accordingly felt able to write to J.F. as one friend to another:

You most kindly told me a few moments after I returned to Stowe this term that you hoped our personal relationship would continue – a relationship, I assure you, which meant more to me in many ways during the last four years than you may have realised. This separation between private feelings and official views is exactly what I had hoped would happen. I shall quarrel with you, and I shall go on quarrelling with you, on some fundamental educational, political and ethical questions. But this quarrel will be one with the head master of Stowe. I trust I shall always be allowed to call the private human being a personal friend of mine, a friend whom I like, a friend from whom I learnt, and a friend to whom I owe a great deal.

Roxburgh responded:

I value the feelings you express and warmly reciprocate them... What a deplorable situation it is. I cannot tell you how much I regret it.

Peter Fritz, emboldened, enquired whether he might see Roxburgh one evening:

There are a number of rather important Side Nine cases I should like to discuss with you. There will not be many more evenings when you and I talk together. I have drunk so much of your Port in the past, that I should be more than delighted if you would either come to my rooms or would allow me to bring you some Chartreuse (very good) or Port (utility).

They duly met, though J.F. insisted the drinks were on him.

* * *

Peter Fritz, in the event, did not quite see out his last term. There was another unfortunate incident. He was hosting late-night drinking sessions for selected pupils, enjoying much uninhibited gossip, and eventually one participant was caught emerging from his room, very much the worse for wear, and at once expelled.[58] Peter Fritz was likewise shown the door.

* * *

The last had been heard of the 35-page letter and the long-promised book on the Public Schools was never published. Several months later, however, Roxburgh received from America a Peter Fritz letter, probably of an adroitly ingratiating nature, for J.F.'s reply was remarkably positive:

> I never had an opportunity of thanking you for the many things you did for us, and which nobody else could or would have done. I am thinking of the trips to America and Scandinavia, the American broadcast, Monty's visit, the French Ambassador's lecture and other results of your inexhaustible energy – not to mention the creation of our Current Affairs Department and your care of Side 9. In all these matters you put the school and myself deeply in your debt and I have long wanted to tell you how fully I realise this. I hope that if ever fate brings us together again in a personal way I shall be able to say 'thank you' by word of mouth…

There was clearly genuine warmth in the relationship. This was much more than a mere exercise in the papering over of cracks. A year later, in 1949, Peter Fritz replied from Boston, where he was now teaching, to wish Roxburgh well in his impending retirement:

> I was delighted to get your friendly and generous letter… May I in return assure you that all my personal recollections of you are most happy and that I shall always be grateful for what you did for the School. You may not have approved of it, but you certainly served it well.

There the relationship seems to have ended. In 1950 Peter Fritz was in Australia. It was probably just as well, for that was the year of Patience McElwee's novel *Pride*

---

58   Harriet Hall's researches for *Bill & Patience* unearthed this saga among several anecdotes deploring Wiener's antics.

of Place, set in a public school with Peter Fritz, only very thinly disguised, as her insidious villain.

In 1952 he momentarily reappeared, via a letter in the *Manchester Guardian,* attacking American schools. He was also sighted briefly somewhere in Dakota. And then no more. Perhaps, for all the years remaining, his alternative persona, Peter Frederick Winter, finally and more cautiously, took over.

18

G. WILSON KNIGHT

The Shakespearean scholar moved by the Genius Loci
Stowe 1941-46

G. Wilson Knight came to Stowe as a wartime Common Room stop-gap. It was a remarkable coup for the school, for he was already a highly influential English literary critic. In 1930 he had caused a sensation with *The Wheel of Fire*, which opened up a whole new approach to Shakespearian studies via the exploration of imagery. By his Stowe arrival, moreover, in September 1941, several other books had consolidated his reputation. It was a reputation that still lives on today.

The coup was all the more remarkable in that the forty-four-year-old did not arrive as Head of English, teaching top forms. Instead, for his first term he was form master of Lower Four, teaching Maths and Geography as well as English. It was all a reflection of his currently being in some disarray after an ill-judged attempt to make his mark on the London stage. Stowe was to give him a helpful period of professional retrenchment before further distinguished university work opened up after the war. He was to show his gratitude by writing *The Dynasty of Stowe*.

* * *

Born in 1897, the son of a London-based insurance company manager, George Wilson Knight showed few early signs of his later scholarly distinction. Five unremarkable years at Dulwich College led to work as an insurance clerk and service in the First

World War as a Royal Engineers' corporal and dispatch-rider. Two further years in an insurance office followed before his mother, Caroline, reacting decisively to her marriage breakdown and husband's bankruptcy, determined that her two children, Jackson and Wilson, should become schoolmasters. After brief work in Prep Schools, Wilson, the younger, was persuaded to take a two-year degree course at Oxford.

Armed with a Second in English, in 1925 he settled in Cheltenham as Head of English at Dean Close. Urged by his mother to do some writing, he had three novels rejected, but then found his métier in literary criticism. In 1929 *Myth and Miracle* was published, an essay on Shakespeare's Mystic Symbolism in which he took on the literary establishment, expressing 'a long-standing dissatisfaction with the usual commentaries'. It was time, he asserted, to explore the mystical dimension that always lay at the heart of great poetry, 'the spirit that burns through it and is eternal'. A year later came *The Wheel of Fire,* with a supportive introduction from T.S. Eliot, and he never looked back. In 1931 he left Dean Close for Trinity College, Toronto.

Caroline Knight had triumphed. She had expected only perfection from both her boys, who were to be 'Knights in name and knights in deed'. Through the 1930s, with Caroline never far away, they flourished. Her elder son, the classicist Jackson Knight, had also secured a university job, down in Exeter. At Toronto, as a Professor of English, Wilson Knight was able to put his Shakespearian theories into practice as an actor-director, taking all the leading parts on stage: Macbeth, Brutus, Romeo, Hamlet, Othello, Lear, Timon, Leontes and Caliban. In 1935 he brought a company briefly to London to show England how *Hamlet* should be played. He told the press:

There will be no tricks in my production of Hamlet. I strongly disapprove of the Russian methods of production at the Stratford Festival Theatre where the tricks of the production dominate the lovely lines of the author.

His Hamlet, unfortunately, arrived straight after John Gielgud's and his characterization was as dour as he had suggested in *The Wheel of Fire*. Quite how much money the Knight family lost on the performances at the Rudolf Steiner Hall is not known. Some good actors had been specially engaged, like the excellent Claudius, Clem McCallin (a RADA-trained Old Stoic). The Wilson Knight fortunes, however, were to take an upturn the very next year when his *Principles of Shakespearian Production,* offering the world some highly positive insights into his Toronto productions, went into the first of several editions.

* * *

On the outbreak of the Second World War Wilson moved bravely back across the Atlantic. He had always believed that literature could fill spiritual needs. Now he took the idea further, seeing poetry as no less than a platform for the survival of democracy in the war with fascism.

First, in September 1940, he outlined 'Shakespeare's message for England at war' in *This Sceptred Isle*, a small paperback. Secondly, in 1941, having created the text for a series of dramatic recitals (titled *This Sceptred Isle*) glorifying Shakespeare and England, he cashed in all his savings to support a bold venture as an actor-manager in London. *This Sceptred Isle* was first presented at the Little Theatre, Tavistock Square, Bloomsbury, during the worst of the London Blitz and ended in July with a week's run at the Westminster. It was essentially a one-man show, but he persuaded the distinguished actor Henry Ainley to come out of retirement to read typewritten commentaries between his own Shakespearian speeches. Reviews proved mixed. 'I will certainly give the Professor full marks for both his bravery and his patriotism,' commented *The Sphere*, 'but neither proved enough in the circumstances, which sometimes veered from the ludicrous to the embarrassing.' 'Professor Wilson Knight is a Shakespearian scholar of repute,' noted the *Liverpool Daily Post*, 'but one cannot commend him for turning the theatre into a classroom.'

Audiences were enthusiastic but sparse, and money soon ran out. The exhausted Wilson Knight suddenly found himself in the heavily bombed London without funds or prospects. His brave, eccentric bid to fling the glories of English literature into the fight against Hitler had proved unsustainable. It was then that a friend happened to mention Stowe.

* * *

J.F. was intrigued at Wilson Knight's application, having been impressed by the scope of his recent poetic study, *The Burning Oracle*, 'Frankly I do not think that the temporary job that is vacant here is quite in your line,' he responded cautiously. 'There is a saying about a steam hammer and a nut!' The security of Stowe, however, was what Knight needed.

He duly joined several other bachelors in one of the Field Houses. Wartime meant no hot water and no heating, but as he walked to and from the South Front on his first day he found his spirit deeply moved by his mysterious surroundings, a mixture of 'old-world remembrance' and 'half-fledged newness.'

J.F. was soon meeting the whole Knight entourage. Caroline had been installed by her two sons in Buckingham's White Hart. Every week, whatever the weather, Wilson would cycle to see her, and she was soon holding court with the many Stowe parents who stayed there. J.F. took tea with her with some regularity, too. At the White Hart he also met Jackson Knight, when he was visiting Caroline.

The Stowe Common Room swiftly learned that G. Wilson Knight was just a nom de plume, only really existing in English literature circles. From his early days he had rejected 'George' and chosen 'Richard'. To family and friends, he was 'Dick' and that was the name the Common Room was soon using. With the different names came different personae. 'G. Wilson Knight', holding forth on poetry and drama, spoke distinctively, with a proud, confident passion brooking no opposition. Away from the lecture room, however, 'Dick Knight' could be the mildest of men, wearing his success as a scholar very lightly indeed.

After only one term with Lower Four, Dick was excused the duties of a form-master. There were no sixth-form tutees attached to the English Side being run in wartime by Roy Meldrum, so Dick, spared such commitments, remained first and foremost a writer, scrupulously methodical in maintaining a regular schedule. In his first term, he was busy revising a book on Milton. *Chariot of Wrath*, 'the message of John Milton to democracy at war', was to come out at the end of his second Stowe term. 'I am very much looking forward, to the appearance of your Milton,' wrote J.F. 'I have been reading Macaulay's essay on him with combined amusement and amazement.' The book's premise was that Nazi Germany could only be overcome by a country of greater cultural strength, and its publication struck the mood of the moment. Wilson Knight's Milton, said the *Times Literary Supplement*, was 'a living champion, a national oracle, whose voice his countrymen of today will do well to remember.' 'I do not know whether the success of your book is going to make you rich,' commented J.F. to him, 'but it should certainly make you proud.'

J.F. enjoyed Dick's idiosyncrasies, happily accepting that he was 'not a conventional schoolmaster'. ('He does not, for example, play games.') He also confessed privately that he sometimes found his views on English literature 'somewhat strange'. Nonetheless, friendship and mutual respect would steadily grow.

The Stoic gives some evidence of Dick's involvement in the cultural life of the school. Early on he was speaking from the floor on the Debating Society motion

'It is preferable to be a book-worm than a games-grub', warning the House against 'the dangers of intellectual totalitarianism'. He likewise supported the motion 'Truthfulness remains vital in wartime'. He was soon active, too, in the Twelve Club:

> *Mr G. Wilson Knight gave a profoundly interesting talk entitled 'Poetry is the language of eternity'. It was fanciful but at the same time logical and simple without being superficial.*

He also reviewed for *The Stoic* a Cobham-Grenville House play, Sutton Vane's once popular fantasy *Outward Bound*, directed by Alasdair Macdonald and (the wartime librarian) Iona Radice.[59] It was a thoughtful and sensitive review. He was particularly impressed by George Melly's 'firm piece of character-work, always effective in accent and manner, and capable of genuine pathos at the end'.

Drama had an articulate champion in the newly-arrived A.A. 'Peter' Dams. Dick encouraged Dams in his enthusiasm, and in the Spring of 1942 the pair collaborated on a production of John Masefield's *Good Friday* in the Chapel, with Dick playing the challenging role of The Madman. Little evidence remains of how it went. He, however, was to remember it with pride: 'The speaking and acting of the Madman's central speech, I look back upon as the most rewarding of my stage experiences.' He and Dams, a former Cambridge University hockey Blue, were not natural soulmates. As a director Dams was all for dashing forwards and sometimes found the meticulous Dick frustrating. 'For Knight nothing was insignificant!' he declared. 'In this respect, he seemed to me somewhat lacking in a sense of proportion and, perhaps, of humour.' He was also somewhat patronizing about Dick's approach to acting (that paid homage to the strongly mannered Beerbohm Tree), commenting on 'the sibyllic eyes, his flowing hair and the rapt expression'.

* * *

Dick was living in his own world for much of the time, as he attempted to capture the essence of Stowe. Overwhelmed each day by the architecture and atmosphere, he was single-mindedly committing to pen and paper his observations:

---

59 Iona, who had begun a stage career, filled many a Stowe wartime gap. She was the daughter of J.F.'s great friend, Sheila Radice.

Once in early winter I passed the North Front about sundown, with a leaden sky and light fading beyond the cricket pavilion. The equestrian statue of King George was silhouetted black as the bony fingers of the gaunt wintry trees against the blood-red streaks of the setting Sun, the leaves of his metal garland standing out all dark and thorny. The curving sweep of the house was swiftly becoming a dark mass, above which a palely haloed Moon stood perched in the sky, and an aeroplane with a green light at one wing's tip droned, as a homing cockchafer, overhead. Shortly after, the whole scene would have been moon-drenched. Such buildings as this, even more than natural objects, come by moonlight into a strange enchanted life of their own. The different layers of construction and the various shades, white or greys or browns, are now all softened to one moon-wash of light and shade, with a solemn and studied engraving of pearl lustre in relief against blackness due to the straight lines and shadowed recesses. At such a time the horns of the colonnade on either side converging on the North Portico make a setting as for some ghostly pageant; it all seems to be waiting, while the equestrian statue is tipped with pale luminance and the wide horizontal sweep of the mansion, all newly sculptured by the Moon, as in some new dimension abstracted from the world of colour, waits immobile and eternal.

Sometimes, as in July 1942, when, for the second time in the war, an errant Nazi plane dropped a cluster of bombs on Stowe, the writing became overtly autobiographical:

One day, a day or two before the end of term, when examinations were just finishing, we were wakened about six o'clock in the morning by two pairs of sharp twin bursts. It turned out to have been a German plane dropping four bombs some half-mile from the School. Towards the end of the morning I was pinning my last examination results to the North Hall board and wondering if I had got them right, when a Lower School boy asked me if I had seen the craters, and offered to show them to me. There was an hour till lunch and we went off.

'It sent some of the splinters frightfully far,' he said, as we went down the North Front steps. 'One of the men found a splinter by George.'

We walk past the statue and under the trees by the scoring board... We pass on under the trees and by the bicycle sheds and get on to the Roman Road, once, presumably, part of the highway between Bicester and Towcester. It's only a country lane now. We walk up the Sequoia Avenue towards the Bourbon, and meet a stream of boys returning, some with bits of bombshell. We leave the road and break into the farmland, seeing the Obelisk, memorial to Wolfe, standing up rather lonely in the fields, no longer part of the grounds. Behind, you get a glimpse of Cobham in his Roman toga, pushing up from the Stowe woods on his monument; further along is the rather ugly, barrel-like Bourbon Tower...

In the fields the mud is heavy and we get all clogged. There is a shed and a farm elevator, both badly mauled, and a great crater churning up the earth; and a little way off another; and, in an adjacent field of corn, two more, spoiling the crop. Boys are scattered about searching for relics and mementos.

* * *

Around this time Dick was offered a job 'for the duration', with plenty of English teaching in the Upper School. His finances were still precarious and he confessed to J.F. that the deduction of £100 a year for his rooms from the salary of £450 left him unable to pay his way:

My books, though beginning to get a lot of attention, can scarcely be said to make money as yet – proof corrections, tax and preliminary typing only leave a small sum every year. I have hope of my new Milton doing fairly well, with a more popular sale since it is topical.

J.F.'s reaction to this was immediate. A salary of £540 without deductions was provided. 'I hope that this will enable you to stay for a time,' commented J.F., tactfully asking him to keep the pay rise confidential.

Dick celebrated this new deal with a production of *Macbeth* in the Winter Term of 1942, presented in the gym under the aegis of Dams' newly-formed 'Stowe Dramatic Club'. For his Macbeth Dick had chosen Colin Moffat Campbell, soon to be a wartime MC with the Scots Guards, and, in the fullness of time, Sir Colin, the 8th Baronet of Aberuchil. Lady Macbeth was played by the fifteen-year-old George Melly, who had already shown much histrionic talent. Melly was a Wilson Knight devotee. 'It was a tremendous inspiration,' he would recall, 'to be in the company of someone whose mind was full of excitement for poetry, history and literature.'

We shall never know, for sure, the true nature of the Wilson Knight *Macbeth*, for, unfortunately, the *Stoic* review was written by a sixth-former (Tony Quinton) who was inordinately pleased with himself and, at the same time, loftily amused by Dick Knight. He was later to write that a Wilson Knight lesson was like 'a master-class by Macready', the early Victorian actor-manager:

> *He was a splendid and kindly man, but too remote in his empyrean of romantic speculation for us to enter into much closer relations with him than we might have had with the Aurora Borealis or some other glorious natural phenomenon.*

Quinton's 'review' comes over as an entertainment to amuse and impress. Whether the production was at times unintentionally funny we shall never know. The review only achieved one result. A Shakespearian expert would offer no more Shakespeare on a Stowe stage.

In 1943, however, he did venture forth alongside Peter Dams, directing *Androcles and the Lion* for the Stowe Dramatic Club, and the audience loved it. One of the leading actors was Lyndon Brook, who shortly afterwards was thanked in Dick Knight's next book, *The Olive and the Sword*, for 'valuable assistance in the preparation of the text and the checking of references'. A development of patriotic wartime ideas already expressed in *This Sceptred Isle*, *The Olive and the Sword* challengingly suggested that the German menace was best confronted by those who understood Britain's destiny, which was to be found expressed in the country's great poetic heritage, with Shakespeare as the supreme prophet. It was an invigorating read.

* * *

Struggling in two winters with pneumonia, Dick found it easier to fight Hitler with words than in deeds, but he turned out for the Home Guard's Intelligence Department – 'We did one or two schemes at night, on the backs of motor bikes in the country' – and was a regular Stowe fire-watcher:

> *This meant going round all the buildings to see if there was any chink of light showing. It took about an hour, unless the outbuildings and the temples were in snowdrifts, as often in winter. It was quite a business then, because of the complete darkness – you had to know it well to do it well.*

In 1944 Dick was still presiding over The Symposium and giving the odd talk to the Twelve Club of which he was a Vice-President. These included a 'colourful and erudite' one on Persia, founded on his First World War experiences. By 1945, however, he seems largely to have been immersing himself in writing about the conquest of the Incas. There was a need, too, as the war drew to a close, to look around at job prospects, something which J.F. facilitated with strong endorsements:

> *Personally, Mr Wilson Knight has won the regard and affection of us all and I myself feel I am losing not only a colleague but a friend.*
>
> *He has become a great friend of ours. If we could possibly have found room for him on the staff we should have besought him to stay here indefinitely. But we have from eighteen to twenty men returning from the Forces and we cannot keep any of the 'duration' masters.*

Dick soon accepted the University of Leeds offer of a job from Easter 1946. There was still time to play the Inquisitor in Dams' production of *St Joan* (the Congreve Club's second production under its new name). Perhaps in December 1945 his mind was already on Leeds. According to Alasdair Macdonald, it was only a modest swansong: 'Mr Wilson Knight looked and acted the part of the Inquisitor convincingly, but used his voice a little monotonously in his long speeches...'

* * *

Dick's return to university life was enlivened by the extra Leeds brief of looking after its Union Theatre Group and inaugurating a course in World Drama. Sixteen rewarding and successful years were to follow, the last six in the role of Professor of English Literature.

Not long after their frail but still dominant mother died in 1950, Dick and his brother bought a house in Exeter, immediately renamed 'Caroline House'. It was there that Dick settled after his retirement in 1962. Spiritualism had become the brothers' abiding leisure interest, Dick becoming Vice-President of the Spiritualist Association of Great Britain. His (unpublished) biography of his mother was called *Caroline: Life and After-Life*.

Jackson was to die in 1964, but Dick enjoyed a fruitful retirement: more writing (including a biography of his brother), lecturing and, most especially, acting all over the country, and even across the Atlantic, with Timon of Athens still the central character in his impressive one-man show. In playing this role, the actor-lecturer would strip to his bare chest, often to the considerable surprise of the audience. He had always done this, long ago acquiring the nickname 'Tarzan of Athens', and saw no reason in his old age to alter this practice.[60] His Shakespearian performances were usually inspirational. Students were amazed to meet someone whose ability to quote Shakespeare extended to whole plays.

Most mornings in his later years were spent in correspondence with his many academic contacts, old and young. He had become, said his friend, the writer Adelaide Ross, 'One of the rare people who carry into wise old age the ardour and curiosity of youth, so that they seem ageless'. When he died in Exeter 1985, aged eighty-seven, he had thirty-nine publications to his name.

* * *

One of them was *The Dynasty of Stowe*. In March 1944 Dick had submitted the proofs to J.F., to cut as he wished, but Roxburgh saw little need. The book, he told Dick, had given him great pleasure – 'even greater than I felt at the first reading'. It was published in 1945 and reprinted in 1946.

An odd conflation of history, geography, autobiography, whimsy, patriotism and educational crystal-ball-gazing, *The Dynasty of Stowe* very soon became out of date. It did, however, contain some passages of Stowe description so outstanding in command of language and powers of observation they have never been bettered. The coming of a Stowe autumn was typical:

> *As the weeks pass, the tints change, as though delicately fingered by the brush of some unseen artist; every day creates new harmonies of tone. From Chatham you look down on the black waters of the lake just visible within the panorama of soft colours in every stage of transition, the dark unchanging firs mixing with misty browns, pale greens tinting to yellow, and dark coppery reds. But all is a single canvas. The contours of every slope, once moulded with a self-effacing artistry and now further softened and graduated by age, collaborate with the season. The*

---

60 A flawed 'biographical study' from a little-known American academic was unhelpfully called *Tarzan of Athens*.

beech trees are the most beautiful, but the variety of shades is the chief beauty. The different levels and prospects give you an endless succession of views. You see the Rotondo at evening, through a framework of copper leafage, a pale lemon sunset cut by the straight bars of its stone pillars, like the ghostly ship in Coleridge's poem, its lines in the October mist melting into the dun shades of darkening trunk and sky till all is one wraithly piece of autumnal creation, a golden-grey and mist-enwreathed marvel. Its canopy covers no statue, it is a shell only; but no statue could increase its charm.

Perhaps the crumbling stone of these old shrines would seem less appropriate in the sudden flush of summer's rebirth; but now, when a sharp earthy smell of sodden leaves reminds you of the turning year, when the floors of the Chestnut Avenue are paved with brown and gold – the colours of Stowe always with the brown cedar, gilt decorations and gold emblazonry of the Chapel and bright buff of the main building – you feel into the meaning of autumnal existence, the ripeness of nation or building, dynasty or tree; the cycle of life and death, mysteries of the past and of the future; the mystery of Stowe, now a school, a palatial death more richly living than ever in its history.

The most startling thing in the book, with striking modern day resonances, was Dick's constant reiteration of Stowe as a place of growing national importance. Several passages (not least the one inspired by the Chapel) declared that Stowe was so suffused with beauty and history that its essence, 'the spirit of Stowe', could offer something very special to the country as it looked, post-war, for inspiration and new directions:

Today, when our Church tradition is enervate and our national faith non-existent, what positive drive can there be? What better, perhaps, than to wait; wait for some answer, for the new thing.

And where better to wait for such an answer than among these classic temples and woodland slopes? It may be that our twentieth-century education teaches little worth the boys' remembering, but this spot at least is something for them to remember; something to take with them into the greater world. They are offered no urgent gospel. But Stowe itself says to them, like the Ghost in Hamlet, 'Remember me'; and in so far as they do this, they do something greater than they know, for there are spirits about the place...

They can spread, then, something of Stowe's secret; the high air and exhilaration; the grounds that invite, no, force, freedom; the ordered lines of buildings; the power – and the peace. They can make these flower from community to community, from nation to nation, across the globe.

This vison of a special future that had already taken root was heady stuff. A.A. Milne, a former Stowe parent, in reviewing *Dynasty* for *The Observer*, homed in on it. The beauty of Stowe, he wrote, had spoken to Wilson Knight 'with all the voices of its historic past'. The spirit of Stowe, 'which once, in the eighteenth century, had been the very spirit of England, seemed to him to be watching over, and fashioning, the new England which was growing up there...'

* * *

This was something for Roxburgh to muse upon in the last years of his headship and at Great Brickhill, when, like all those in retirement, he may well have questioned the value of his working life. All the struggles would clearly have seemed worthwhile to him, if, as Dick Wilson Knight had prophesied, 'the spirit of Stowe', challenging dull conformity and deadening dogma, would be providing a steady stream of wide-thinking change makers for the future.

There was one further, thoroughly deserved reassurance for Roxburgh, too, in the book's affectionate dedication. Any gloomy days at Garden Cottage, Great Brickhill, would surely have been immediately brightened by just a single glance at

For
J.F.R.
who has made Stowe to flourish
in our time

BIBLIOGRAPHY

Ambrose, Linda, *A Great Rural Sisterhood: Madge Robertson Watt* (University of Toronto Press, 2015)

Annan, Noel, *Roxburgh of Stowe* (Longmans,1965)

Aston, James, *They Winter Abroad* (Chatto & Windus, 1932)

Aston, James, *First Lesson* (Chatto & Windus, 1932)

Bevington, Michael, *Stowe: The Gardens and the Park* (Stowe, 1994)

Bevington, Michael, *Stowe House* (Paul Holberton, 2002)

Blacklaw W.S., *More Than A School To Us*, (J. Cocker & Co., 1997)

Brodribb, Gerald: *Hastings and Men of Letters* (Hastings Preservation Society, 1971)

Browne, Philip Austin: *Brahms: The Symphonies* (OUP, 1933)

Croom-Johnson, Sir Reginald, *The Origin of Stowe School* (W.S. Cowell,1953)

Demarest, Donald, *The Once and Future Merlin* (Unpublished ms, 1987-96)

Earle, Ernest (ed.), *The Epicurean 1-12* (Stowe, 1932)

Gallix, Francois (ed.), *T.H.White: Letters to a Friend* (Alan Sutton, 1984)

Gallix, Francois, *T.H. White, An Annotated Bibliography* (Garland, 1986)

Gresham, Douglas, *Lenten Lands* (Collins, 1989)

Habershon, E.F., *Research*, (The Churches' Fellowship for Psychical and Spiritual Studies, 1965)

Hall, Harriet, *Bill & Patience* (The Book Guild, 2000)

Heckstall-Smith, *Doubtful Schoolmaster* (Peter Davies, 1962)

Jameson, Conor Mark, *Looking for the Goshawk* (Bloomsbury, 2013)

Knight, G. Wilson, *The Wheel of Fire* (OUP, 1930)

Knight, G. Wilson, *Principles of Shakespearian Production* (Faber & Faber, 1936)

Knight, G. Wilson, *This Sceptred Isle* (Blackwell, 1940)

Knight, G. Wilson, *Chariot of Wrath*, (Faber & Faber, 1942)

Knight, G. Wilson, *The Dynasty of Stowe* (Fortune Press, 1945)

Knight, G. Wilson, *The Olive and the Sword* (OUP, 1944)

Lloyd, Nathaniel [JFR a subscriber], *A History of the English House* (The Architectural Press, 1931)

Macdonald, Alasdair, *Stowe: House and School* (W.S. Cowell, 1951)

Macdonald, Alasdair, *Stowe School* (Dalton Watson 1977)

Macdonald, Helen, *H is for Hawk* (Cape, 2014)

McElwee, Patience, *Pride of Place* (Faber & Faber, 1950)

MacLaughlin, Martin, *Newest Europe* (Longman, 1931)

Manners, Terry, *The Man who became Sherlock Holmes* (Virgin, 2001)

Maxwell, Gavin, *The House of Elrig* (Longmans Green, 1965)

Meredith, Anthony (ed.), *Chatham House 1925-85* (Stowe, 1985)

Meredith, Anthony (ed.), *T.H. White At Stowe* (The Stoic, 1996)

Morris, Nick (ed.): *Stowe House, Saving an Architectural Masterpiece* (Scala, 2018)

Neville, Hastings M., *A Corner in the North: Yesterday and Today with Border Folk* (Reid, 1909)

Newell, Philip & Sankey, Bernard, *Gresham's in Wartime* (Gresham's, 1987)

Pearce, Tim, *Then & Now* (The Cheltonian Society, 1991)

Playford, Humphrey & Brittain, Frederick, *The Jesus College Cambridge Boat Club, 1827-1962* (Heffer 1962)

Playford, Humphrey & Fremantle, the Hon. J.W.H, *Notes on First Class Rowing* (Fab & Tyler, 1921)

Potter, Roger (ed.), *A Stowe Miscellany* (Stowe, 1973)

Radice, Anthony, *Some Notes on the early history of Stowe* (Stowe, 1932)

Radice, Sheila, *Not All Sleep* (Arnold, 1938)

Rawnsley, C.F. & Wright, Robert, *Night Fighter* (Crécy, 1998)

Rees, Brian, *Stowe, 1923-1989* (Stamp Publishing, 2008)

Richardson, John, *John Richardson at Home* (Rizzoli, 2019)

Ross, Adelaide, *Reverie* (Robert Hale 1981)

Roxburgh, J.F., *The Poetic Procession* (Blackwell, 1921)

Roxburgh, J.F., *Eleutheros* (Kegan Paul, 1930)

Saltmarshe, Christopher et al.(ed.): *Cambridge Poetry, 1929* (Hogarth Press, 1929)

Scott, Ronald Macnair, & White, T.H., *Dead Mr Nixon* (Cassell, 1931)

Stanksy, Peter & Abrahams, William, *Journey to the Frontier* (University of Chicago, 1984)

Stephan, Brian, *Stowe - Hearsay and Memory* (Stowe, 1998)

Todd, James, *The Ancient World* (Hodder and Stoughton, 1938)

Todd, James & Janet, *Voices from the Past* (Hutchinson,1955)

Todd, James & Janet, *Peoples of the Past* (Arrow, 1963)

Van Domelen, John E., *Tarzan of Athens* (Redcliffe Press, 1987)

Ward, Richard Heron, *Progress to the Lake* (Nicholson & Watson, 1934)

Ward, Richard Heron, *A Gallery of Mirrors* (Gollancz, 1956)

Ward, Richard Heron, *Names & Natures* (Gollancz, 1968)

Warner, Sylvia Townsend, *T.H. White* (Cape & Chatto & Windus, 1968)

Whistler, Laurence, *Children of Hertha* (Holywell Press, 1929)

White, T.H., *Darkness at Pemberley* (Gollancz, 1932)

White, T.H., *Farewell Victoria* (Collins, 1933)

White, T.H., *Earth Stopped* (Collins, 1934)

White, T.H., *Gone to Ground* (Collins, 1935)

White, T.H. *England Have My Bones* (Collins, 1936)

White, T.H., The *Sword in the Stone* (Collins, 1938)

White, T.H., *Mistress Masham's Repose* (Cape, 1947)

White, T.H., *The Goshawk* (Cape, 1951)

White, T.H. *The Once and Future King* (Collins, 1958)

Wiener, P.F., *German for the Scientist* (Bell, 1943)

Wiener, P.F., *German With Tears* (Cresset Press, 1942)

Wiener, P.F., *Martin Luther, Hitler's Spiritual Ancestor* (Hutchinson 1943)

Williams-Ellis, C. & A., *The Pleasures of Architecture* (Cape, 1924)

Williams-Ellis, Clough, *England and the Octopus* (Geoffrey Bles, 1928)

Williams-Ellis, Clough, *Architect Errant* (Constable, 1971)

Willson, D. Wynne, *Early Closing* (Constable, 1921)

Zettl, Ewald, *An Anonymous Short English Metrical Chronicle* (Humphrey Milford, 1935)

Aberdeen Grammar School, 57

INDEX

Aberdeen University, 57, 64, 207, 208

Acland, Theodore W. G. 'Charlie', 1, 68, 73, 74, 99

Addison, Joseph, 48, 72

Aeschylus, 34, 207

Ainley, Henry, 237

Alexander, Charles, 67

Andrews, Julie, 176

Annan, Noel, 31, 122, 123, 158, 160, 161, 176

Annan, Thomas, 125, 126

Ansermet, Ernest, 145

Anstey, Peter, 111, 112

Armstrong, Thomas, 40, 42

Archer, A.G. 'Wilfred', 183, 203, 205, 215

Arnold, Francis, 39, 99, 106

Ashton, Frederick, 198

Aston, Augusta, 151

Aston, Judge Harold Faure, 149-151

Atthill, Robin, 130

Auden, W.H., 123

Austen, Jane, 156

Bach, Johann Sebastian, 35, 42, 146

Bacon, Francis, 228

Bader, Douglas 187

Bain, Joe, 221

Baker, Peter Fyfe, 126, 131

Baldwin, Stanley, 95

Balfour, Frederick, 63

Balliol College, Oxford, 38, 133

Bancroft's School, 206

Barbirolli, John, 145

Barratt, Fred, 40

Barton, Anthony, 221

Beamish, Tufton, 230

Bean, William, 63

Beaton, Cecil, 198

Beecham, Thomas, 139

Beethoven, Ludwig von, 145

Bell, Clive, 18,

Bell, Julian, 156

Beresford, Louisa, 44

Berners, Lord, 198, 199

Bertram, Oliver, 47

Betjeman, John, 173

Bevington, Michael, 102

Bilton Grange School, 1-3, 5, 6, 8

Blaize, Jimmy, 162

Blake, William, 50

Bostock, Dr John 'Jack', 113

Boult, Adrian, 36, 143

Boyd, Hector, 210, 215

Boyd-Carpenter, John, 6, 15, 95

Brabazon, Lord, 229

Bradman, Don, 115

Brahms, Johannes, 41, 108, 135, 143, 145

Brain, Dennis, 145

Braque, Georges, 196

Brett, Jeremy: see Jeremy Huggins

Bridges, Robert, 34

Bridie, James, 100

Brightlands School, 122

Brighton College, 193

Bromsgrove School, 203

Bronowski, Jacob, 156

Brook, Lyndon, 242

Brook, the Revd. Tim, 110, 188, 189

Brown, David, 107

Browne, Dr Philip 'Pa', 33-43, 99, 121-123, 126-130, 136, 143

Brownlow, Lord, 195

Bryanston School, 128, 203

Buchan, John, 64

Burton, Richard, 176

Capel Cure, Edward, 17, 24, 64, 75, 99, 107, 108, 113, 204, 214, 216, 220

Carden, Andrew, 52

Carr, Granville, 5, 6, 38

Cash, Christopher, 201, 202

Cassel, Lady Helen, 19

Chamberlain, Neville, 24, 64, 171, 204

Charterhouse School, 79, 81, 128

Cheltenham College, 152, 153, 155, 173

Cheshire, Leonard, 167, 229

Chopin, Frédéric, 143

Christ Church College, Oxford, 57

Clare College, Cambridge, 67, 71

Clarke, Alasdair 'Sandy', 64-66

Clarke, George, 4, 106, 116, 117

Clarke, Ian, 37, 56-66, 88, 99, 137, 180, 184

Clarke, Janet, 64, 65

Clarke, Margaret, 63-65

Clements, the Revd. Henry, 48

Cleopatra, 198

Clifford, Alfred B. 'Fritz', 70, 75, 92, 108, 109, 113, 162, 214

Clive, Nigel, 158

Clifton College, 122

Coke, Desmond, 87

Connaught, Arthur, Duke of, 150

Connor, Mary, 32, 140

Connor, Thomas, 140

Constantine, Learie, 40

Cooke, Alistair, 129

Cornford, John, 123, 166

Cotman, John, 50

Crichton-Miller, Donald, 30, 78, 107, 221

Croft, Andrew, 83

Croft, Cyril, 159, 160

Crome, John, 50

Cross, Barbara, 21-23, 26-31
Cross, Greville, 13, 28-29
Cross, Ivor, 1, 3, 7, 11-32, 37, 38, 50, 57, 64, 111, 133, 138, 183, 184, 204- 206
Cross, Karin, 12, 16, 28-29
Cross, Kenneth, 14, 16
Currie, Sir Arthur, 193

Dali, Salvador, 198
Dams, A.A. 'Peter', 239, 242, 243
Davenport, John, 175
Davis, Robert, 215, 216
Deacon, Chris, 106, 115
Dean Close School, 236
Debussy, Claude, 143
Degas, Edgar, 45
de la Mare, Walter, 123
Demarest, Donald, 162-165, 167-170, 176, 178
Denton, Alexander, 47
Devine, George, 124
Dewing, Edward, 26
Diaghilev, Serge, 198
Dickens, Charles, 158
Dodd, Fielding, 23, 51, 63, 137
Dollfuss, Engelbert, 214
Douglas, Norman, 158
Drayson, Robert, 30, 31, 221, 222
Drinkwater, John, 124
Dulwich College, 235
Dvorak, Antonin, 35
Dyson, George, 133, 142, 143

Earle, the Revd. Ernest 'Pop', 1-10, 37, 44, 54, 78, 99

Earle, Granville, 9
Earle, Ion, 9
Earle, John Greville, 8
Earle, Stephen, 9
Earle, Walter, 1
Eastbourne College, 13, 14, 128
Edrich, Bill, 175, 199
Edrich, Brian, 175, 177
Edrich, William, 199
Edward, HRH Prince of Wales, 136
Einstein, Albert, 230
Elgar, Edward, 145
El Greco, 50
Eliot, T.S., 20, 154, 236
Ellis, David C., 6
Empson, William, 156
Eton College, 35
Euripides, 38
Exeter University, 236

Fairley, Richard, 30, 31
Fernihough, the Revd. Clifford 'Fernie', 147, 173
Fidler, Harry, 49
Fitzgerald, Scott, 158
Flecker, James Elroy, 154, 155
Ford, Henry, 71
Fox, Adam, 42
Franck, César, 145
Freeman, P.B., 106
Frost, Ernie, 141

Garnett, David, 173-175
George VI, HRH King, 115
George, HRH Prince, 74

German, Edward, 145, 189

Gibbons, Grinling, 195

Gielgud, John, 236

Gilbert, Richard, 199

Gilling-Lax, George, 27, 180-90

Gilling-Lax, Margaret, 180

Gilling-Lax, the Revd. Canon Thomas, 181, 188

Glasgow University, 207, 208

Glasson, Lancelot, 51

Gloucester, Henry, Duke of, 173

Goebbels, Joseph, 215

Gonville and Caius College, Cambridge, 13

Granger, W.E.P., 37

Gresham's School, 74, 75

Gustav, King of Sweden, 94

Habershon, the Revd. Edward 'Om', 54, 67-78, 138

Habershon, Mary, 73

Habershon, Norah, 73-78

Haig, Dawyck, 160

Hale, Lionel, 124

Hall, Harriet, 226, 233

Handel, George Frideric, 146

Hankinson, John, 74

Harding, Michael, 145

Hardy, Robert, 151

Hart Dyke, Edward, 53, 92, 214, 220

Haworth, Major Richard, 37, 57, 60, 64, 65, 79-92, 99, 189, 208

Hay, Ian, 185

Haydn, Joseph, 145

Hearne, Jack, 40

Hendren, Patsy, 40

Henn, Thomas, 154, 155

Herkomer, Hubert von, 44-46, 49

Herkomer, Lulu, 45

Hesketh-Prichard, Alfgar, 19, 20

Heckstall-Smith, Hugh, 20, 59, 69, 70, 95, 96, 124, 130, 160

Higham, David, 177

Hitler, Adolf, 74, 75, 97, 101, 129, 171, 188, 204, 223, 227, 229, 237, 242

Hogarth, William, 163

Hole, Robert, 70, 99, 133, 134, 138

Holloway College, 207

Hopkins, Gerard Manley, 158, 164

Horton Hall School, 79

Huggins, Colonel H.W., 146-148

Huggins, Jeremy, 137, 138, 147

Huggins, Dr Leslie 'Hug', 124, 132-48, 182, 189, 196, 210

Hunter, Patrick, 24, 25, 42, 50, 64, 109, 113-116, 122, 123, 203, 205, 214, 217, 222

Hutchinson, Jeremy, 20

Huxley, Aldous, 20, 156, 158

Huyton Hill, School, 91

Hyett, Thomas, 151-152

Inge, Dean, 227

Innsbruck University, 212, 213

Ireland, Anthony, 50, 185

Isham, Gyles, 124

Jameson, Conor Mark, 179

Jesus College, Cambridge, 104

Johnston, Muriel, 26, 27

Keats, John, 155
Keble College, Oxford, 93
Keigwin, R.P., 122
King's College School, 117
King's College, Cambridge, 181, 187, 189
Kingswood House School, 118
Kinvig, Harold, 75, 140
Kipling, Rudyard, 15, 16, 48
Knight, Caroline, 236, 238, 243
Knight, G. Wilson 'Dick', 235-46
Knight, Jackson, 236, 238, 243
Knox, Ronald, 123

Laffan, the Revd. Robin, 155
Lambert, Constant, 139
Lancing College, 11-12, 14, 16, 32
Lapley Grange School, 27-31
Lawrence, D.H., 158, 169, 170
Lawrence, Frieda, 170
Lawrence, T.E., 158
Lawrenceville School, 128
Laycock, Robert, 129
Leeds University, 243
Léger, Fernand, 196
Lehmann, John, 156
Lely, Sir Peter, 195
Leonardo da Vinci, 96
Lerner, Alan Jay, 176
Lessing, Gotthold, 215
Lewis, C. Day, 158
Lewis, C.S., 28
Lintott, Peter, 187, 188
Llowarch, W. 'Fluff', 211

Loewe, Frederick, 176
London University, 224
Loveday, Alan, 145
Lucas, P.B. 'Laddie', 59
Luther, Martin, 227, 228
Lutyens, Edwin, 51
Lynn, Ralph, 184
Lyon, P.H.B., 225

McCallin, Clem, 236
Macaulay, Thomas Babington, 238
Macdonald, Alasdair, 66, 91, 111, 147, 182, 186, 195, 206, 207, 222, 239, 243
MacDonald, Ramsay, 95
MacDowell, Edward, 41
McKean, Lloyd, 159, 162
McElwee, Patience, 19, 162, 196, 233, 234
McElwee, William, 18, 19, 88, 107, 108, 116, 117, 137, 159, 160, 162, 166, 184, 196, 203, 204, 207
MacLaughlin, Martin 'Cluffy', 16, 50, 93-103, 121, 123, 130, 160
Macready, William, 242
Magdalen College School, 21
Magdalen College, Oxford, 33, 34, 36, 42, 47, 121, 122
Malory, Thomas, 155, 167
Marconi, Guglielmo, 96
Marlborough College, 2, 136, 180
Marlowe, Christopher, 154
Mary, HRH Queen, 19, 73, 99, 118
Masefield, John, 123, 239
Mather, Rick, 202
Matthews, Denis, 145

Maxwell, Gavin, 5, 94, 118
Meldrum, Roy, 228, 238
Melly, George, 239, 241
Melvin, James, 52
Michelangelo, 198
Millais, John Everett, 44
Millard, Patrick, 192
Milne, A.A. 125, 185, 246
Milton, John, 125, 126, 238
Moiseiwitsch, Benno, 139
Monaco, Prince of, 141
Montague, C.E., 71
Montgomery, Field-Marshal, 229
Moody, Dwight, 67
Mortimer, John, 20
Mosley, Sir Oswald, 99
Mounsey, Michael, 199, 220
Mountbatten, Louis, 172
Mozart, Wolfgang, 139, 145
Mussolini, Benito, 96

Negus, Ainger, 147
Neville, Hastings, 44
Neville, Herbert 'Bertie', 37, 44-55, 78, 124, 167, 191, 194
Neville, Martin, 49, 54
Neville, Michael, 49, 54
Neville, Margaret, 45-46, 49, 50, 53-55
Neville, Sophie, 54
Neville-Rolfe, Edmund, 107
Newcastle-under-Lyme High School, 209, 210
New College, Oxford, 2, 51
Newstead School, 100, 101
Nicholl, the Revd. J. E. 'Jos', 115, 119

Nicolson, Harold, 229
Nietzsche, Friedrich, 227
Niven, David, 4, 217
Norwich School, 74
Norwood, Cyril, 181

O'Neill, Eugene, 196
Orde, Peter, 158, 159
Orwell, George, 150
Owen, Wilfred, 133
Oxford High School, 203

Packwood Haugh School, 133
Palmer, Felix, 151
Paradies, Pietro, 37
Parish, Fanny, 49, 50
Parsons, Ian, 154
Parsons, Nathaniel, 222
Patterson, the Rt Revd., 119
Percy, Robert Heber, 198, 199
Picasso, Pablo, 196, 202
Pick, George, 6
Pickard-Cambridge, Sir Arthur, 110, 213, 214, 227, 228, 230
Pitt, William (1st Earl of Chatham), 95, 229, 230
Playford, Elizabeth 'Betty', 117-120
Playford, the Revd. Humphrey, 70, 104-20, 145, 188, 203
Pollak, Anna, 146
Pope, Will, 147
Potter, Beatrix, 33
Potts, Leonard, 154, 156, 178
Poulenc, Francis, 143
Prittie, the Hon. Terence, 93, 94, 98

Purcell, Henry, 37
Pye, Edwin 'Ted', 81, 82, 89, 92
Pye, Mildred, 81, 82, 89, 90

Queen's College, Cambridge, 153-156
Queen's College, Oxford, 203
Quennell, Miss, 117
Quinton, Anthony, 241, 242

Rachmaninoff, Sergei, 145
Radice, Anthony, 124, 186
Radice, Iona, 239
Radice, Sheila, 239
Radley College, 35, 134, 162, 203
Ramponi, Guglio, 99
Ratcliffe, C.W.G. 'Ratters', 116
Rauschning, Hermann, 75
Ravel, Maurice, 135
Rawcliffe, Roger, 123, 221
Raynor, Fred, 138, 139, 141-142, 144, 146, 147
Redgrave, Michael, 156
Reed, Carol, 218
Reeves, James, 50, 52, 95, 156
Reid, Leslie, 229
Rembrandt, 195
Renoir, Pierre-Auguste, 45
Repton School, 93
Reynolds, Eric, 76, 92, 114, 115, 146-48, 219, 220, 222, 225
Richards, I.A., 158
Richardson, John, 202
Ridley, M.R., 123
Ridley Hall, Cambridge, 67, 105
Rimsky-Korsakov, Nikolai, 35

Robarts, John, 199
Rollins College, Florida, 99
Rondebosch High School, 111
Roosevelt, Eleanor (Mrs Franklin D.), 224, 230
Roosevelt, Mrs Kermit, 230
Ross, Adelaide, 244
Rossiter, Peter, 222
Roughton, Roger, 196
Rowlandson, Thomas, 163
Roxburgh, John Fergusson, 1, 3, 10-27, 29-31, 33, 42, 46, 48, 54, 58-61, 63-66, 69, 70, 74-77, 79, 81-92, 95, 99-102, 105-107, 109-114, 121-125, 130, 134-137, 139, 140, 142, 144, 145, 147, 148, 152, 157, 158, 161, 167, 171, 172, 174, 176, 177, 180, 186, 187, 191, 192, 194, 195, 197-199, 201, 203-211, 213-219, 223, 225-233, 237, 238, 241-244, 246
Royal Latin School, 35, 172
Rubens, Paul Peter, 163
Rudé, George, 50, 166, 196
Rugby School, 39, 76, 92, 133, 162, 223-225
Ruskin, John, 44, 47
Russell, Major, 216
Rutherford, Hamish, 221
Ruysdael, Salomon van, 102

St. Catherine's College, Cambridge, 154
St. David's School, Reigate, 156
St. Paul's School, 104
St Wilfred's School, Eastbourne, 180
Saunders, John, 50, 92, 137, 147

Sackville, Lady Margaret, 100

Sackville-West, Vita, 100

Sankey, Ira, 67

Sargent, Malcolm, 229

Saunders, John, 124, 145, 146, 181, 183, 185, 189, 196

Savill, Patrick, 35

Schubert, Franz, 143

Schumann, Robert 36, 37

Scott, Christopher Fairfax, 151

Scott, Ronald McNair, 155, 156

Scott, Walter, 205

Segovia, Andrés, 145

Shakespeare, William, 125, 137, 169, 228, 235-237, 241, 242, 244

Sheffield University, 212-214, 217

Shepherd, Peter, 211

Sherborne, Lord, 2

Sickert, Walter, 51

Simmonds, D.M., 38

Simunich, Baron von: see Anthony Ireland

Sitwell, Edith, 123

Slade School of Fine Art, 193, 194

Skene, Robert, 180, 185

Smith, Sir George Adam, 63

Smuts, Jan, 25

Smythe, F.S., 72

Snagge, John, 117

Snowdon, Bill, 135, 188

Solomon, 145

Sopwith, Tommy, 221

Sorbonne University, 11, 94, 223

Spencer, Charles 'Spuggins', 50, 121-32, 137

Spencer, Major James, 130, 131

Spender, Stephen, 158

Stanford, Charles, 35-37

Stephan, Brian, 90, 92, 116, 199, 208

Steynor, Dudley, 4, 35

Stewart, F.I.W. (HM of Shirley House School, which had evacuated to Akeley Wood in WW2), 26

Stewart, Haldane Campbell, 34

Stirling-Maxwell, Sir John, 63

Surtees, R.S., 166

Sutcliffe, Halliwell, 45, 49

Suttle, Stephen, 134

Swanbourne House, 110

Talmadge, Algernon, 46

Tankersville, Countess of, 100

Taylor, A.J.P., 229

Taylor, Stephen, 7

Temple, Grenville Newton, 8

Temple, William (Chairman of Rugby's governors and former Archbishop of Canterbury) 25, 225

Tenniel, John, 196

Theobald, Richard, 118

Thomas, R.S., 29-31

Thurston, Jack, 41

Tillyard, E.M., 158, 161

Timberlake, Robert, 38, 87, 88

Todd, James, 137, 203-11

Todd, Janet, 206-11

Toulouse-Lautrec, Henri de, 45

Tree, Sir Herbert Beerbohm, 239

Trinity College, Toronto, 236

Trollope, Anthony, 42

Turner, the Revd. Christopher, 120, 178

Turner, Bill, 141
Turner, J.M.W., 50
Turnor, Christopher Hatton, 195

Uppingham School, 101

van Dyck, Anthony,195
Vane, Sutton, 239
Vanbrugh, Sir John, 95, 174
Vansittart, Lord, 224, 225, 227
Velasquez, Diego, 50
Vermeer, Johannes, 28
Virgil, 96

Wagner, Richard, 134
Wake, Hereward, 7
Walker, Raymond, 147, 189, 203, 205
Walpole, Robert, 229
Ward, Richard Heron, 70-73, 77
Warner, Sylvia Townsend, 154, 163, 177
Warrack, Guy, 36, 42
Warrack, John, 36
Warren, Herbert, 34
Warrington, Percy, 3, 39, 48, 68, 69, 73, 74, 87
Watson, Douglas, 196
Watson, Sydney, 35, 37, 42, 134
Watt, Doreen 'Dodie', 53, 152, 191-202
Watt, Madge Robertson, 193
Watt, Robertson 'Robin', 53, 162, 191-202, 209
Watt, Sholto, 201
Watts, George Frederic, 195
Waugh, Evelyn, 129, 130, 166
Wavell, Earl, 200

Weldon, George, 145
Wellington College, 2, 82
Westminster School, 162
Wheeler, Bob, 178
Wheeler, Mrs Bob, 178
Wheeler, Cyril 'Chubb', 167, 171-172, 176
Wheeler, Josephine Surete, 171-179, 179
Wheeler, Lilian 'Mammie', 167, 178, 179
Whistler, Laurence, 52, 59, 196
Whistler, Rex, 52
Whitaker, Edward, 51
White, Constance Edith Southcote, 149-153, 156
White, Garrick Hanbury, 149-153, 164
White, T.H. 'Tim', 107, 108, 149-79, 195, 196
Whitman, Walt, 14
Whitwell, Stephen, 159
Wiener, Peter Fritz, 223-34
Wilkes, John, 7
Williams-Wynn, Watkin, 102
Winchester College, 33-36, 142, 227
Windsor-Richards, the Revd. Cyril 'Windy Dick', 146, 147
Wodehouse, 28
Woolf, Virginia, 20
Woolpit School, 118
Wordsworth, William, 92

Yarlet Hall School, 1
Yates, Mrs (Doreen Watt's mother), 192-194, 197

Zettl, Elizabeth, 117, 200, 216-222
Zettl, Ewald, 117, 212-22

Zettl, Grete, 214, 215, 217
Zettl, Marlies, 221